THEMES AND TEXTS
Toward a Poetics of Expressiveness

ALEXANDER ZHOLKOVSKY

Foreword by JONATHAN CULLER

Translated from the Russian by the author
Edited by Kathleen Parthé

Cornell University Press

ITHACA AND LONDON

1984

THIS BOOK HAS BEEN PUBLISHED WITH THE AID OF A GRANT FROM
THE HULL MEMORIAL PUBLICATION FUND OF CORNELL UNIVERSITY.

First published 1984 by Cornell University Press.
Published in the United Kingdom by Cornell University Press Ltd., London.

International Standard Book Number 0-8014-1505-5
Library of Congress Catalog Card Number 83-45152
Printed in the United States of America
*Librarians: Library of Congress cataloging information
appears on the last page of the book.*

*The paper in this book is acid-free and meets the guidelines for permanence and durability of
the Committee on Production Guidelines for Book Longevity of the Council on Library
Resources.*

For my father,
Lev Abramovič Mazel'

Foreword

The revival of the ancient discipline of poetics in our century begins with the Russian Formalists. From about 1915 until roughly 1929, when political repression put an end to the most productive and impressive critical movement Russia had ever known, a group of linguists and literary critics—Roman Jakobson, Viktor Shklovsky, Yury Tynyanov, Boris Eikhenbaum, Boris Tomashevsky, Vladimir Propp, and many others—developed original and compelling analyses of the techniques of literary art, especially the devices that make language literary. When the activities of this school were brought to an end in the Soviet Union, the Formalist legacy passed to the Prague Circle and later to the French Structuralists, who rediscovered the Formalists' writings in the early 1960s. At the same time, in the USSR itself, the Formalists' questions and proposals, which had been forced underground for twenty-five years, were allowed to emerge once again.

In the cultural thaw of the Khrushchev era, Alexander Zholkovsky and his collaborator Yury Shcheglov took the lead in rehabilitating the Formalists and in promoting at the same time the theoretical work of the Formalists' contemporary, Sergej Eisenstein. Discussion of poetics recommenced but in a new context, modified by two powerful influences. On the one hand, the development of semiotics, particularly in the work of Jurij M. Lotman at Tartu, placed reflection on literary devices and artistic forms in the context of a general science of signs. On the other hand, in Moscow, work in linguistics on formal models of language and interest in the semantic problems encountered when exploring machine translation—the technological "cover" under which the most provocative and pioneering work in linguistics and poetics was carried out—led many linguists to address problems of poetic language in the context of information theory and formalized semantic models. As Jakobson's and Propp's fame grew in the West, the structuralist and semiotic work they had influenced became known in the USSR, and a lively community of linguists and critics—Vjač. Vs. Ivanov, V. N. Toporov, B. A. Uspensky, I. A. Mel'čuk, E. M. Meletinsky, and others—debated books and articles from the West. For a brief period, poetics flourished once again in Russia, as the commerce between Moscow and Tartu produced theoretical proposals and detailed analyses of topics in poetics and the semiotics of culture. But in the late 1970s the political situation worsened, and many of this group, including Zholkovsky, emigrated to the West.

Zholkovsky's work in poetics is rooted in this contemporary critical and linguistic tradition. Trained as a linguist, he has worked on, among other things, Somali (traces of which appear here in his discussions of a Somali proverb and a Somali folktale). But he is best known among Slavists for two ambitious collaborative projects. With Igor Mel'čuk, now at the University of Montreal, Zholkovsky developed a model for the description of semantic competence: a theory of lexical functions accounting explicitly for speakers' ability to paraphrase freely and idiomatically a given message. This experience of providing explicit, formal representations of speakers' linguistic knowledge and understanding underlies his work in poetics. Second, between 1962 and 1980 he developed with Yury Shcheglov a poetics of expressiveness, or generative poetics. Analyzing works in several languages and literary modes, they have striven to define in explicit terms the devices by which themes are given expressive force. This book, in which Zholkovsky treats a wide range of texts and topics, from an aphorism of Bertrand Russell's, a Somali proverb, and a lesson in film making by Eisenstein to the "poetic worlds" of Pasternak and Pushkin, offers for the first time in English a sustained presentation of this impressive project. Joining the Formalists' interest in literary devices with the goal of formalization which has played such an important role in the advances of modern linguistics, Zholkovsky attacks central problems of modern poetics. The attempt to represent in the most explicit terms the functioning of literary devices and of an author's invariant motifs enables us to see what we understand and what we do not yet understand about the workings of verbal art.

Since Zholkovsky expounds his project with lucidity and wit, there is no need for me to expatiate upon it here. As readers will see, this work, in revolt against the dominant Slavic tradition of literary appreciation, has affinities with some native American critical traditions, which it could be said to reinvent in a different idiom. His work on invariant motifs, for example, might be seen as a formalization of image criticism, the attempt to describe the imaginative world of an author in terms of recurrent image clusters. Zholkovsky is also committed to the activity of close reading, which has a long and honorable tradition in the United States. I shall simply comment on aspects of his program that might be misunderstood.

First, there is the problem of poetics itself: its nature and role. Today it is frequently assumed that the task of literary theory is to make claims about the nature of literature (drawing perhaps upon insights from philosophy, linguistics, anthropology, psychoanalysis, and so on) which can give rise to new interpretations of literary works, and that this ability to generate plausible new interpretations is the test of literary theory. This assumption produces a fundamental misunderstanding of poetics, which since the days of Aristotle has sought not to produce readings or interpretations but to understand how literary works are constructed to achieve the effects they do. Their effects for experienced readers are the point of departure for poetics, and its analyses seek to understand and to represent systematically how these effects are achieved. Zholkovsky's attempts to spell out the way themes and artistic devices are combined may, of course, have an impact on future interpretations, for descriptions of what we do or know can always affect future behavior, but this is neither the goal of his analyses nor the criterion by which they are to be judged.

How, then, one might ask, is work in poetics to be judged? By its success in accounting for the meanings and effects works have for readers, in showing us explicitly what we implicitly know. Zholkovsky's analyses should be seen not as interpretations but as explorations of a metalanguage, a special vocabulary (technical definitions of which are supplied in the Glossary) for naming the devices by which themes are given artistic force and expressiveness and for analyzing as "motifs" the invariants that make up a poetic world. In thinking of a poem or an image as "Keatsian" or "Wordsworthian," we implicitly employ notions of an author's "poetic universe," and analyses such as Zholkovsky's try to spell out as explicitly as possible what might be involved in such a concept.

Finally, some critics may resist analyses of this kind because they seem to violate a basic principle of literary criticism by distinguishing between form and content (as *device* and *theme*) and thus to suggest that literary form does not carry meaning. It is one of the ironies of literary theory that the theorists who are most interested in literary form and artistic devices are accused of devaluing form by isolating it as form. If analysis is to proceed at all we must distinguish between something which we may say is being presented and a mode of presentation. The most devout believers in the inseparability of form and content cannot avoid making such distinctions; they can only conceal their procedures in a pious rhetoric. In trying to distinguish as rigorously as possible between theme and device, Zholkovsky is certainly violating critical etiquette, but progress comes at the price of tact, as recent theory has abundantly shown, and analyses that break this particular critical taboo may well be more subtle and sensitive to literary effects than those that unthinkingly respect it. One must write in a different style if one is to explore and represent explicitly what is involved in a range of artistic phenomena, from the functioning of a maxim to the unity of a poetic world.

JONATHAN CULLER

Ithaca, New York

Contents

Contents

Preface

This book brings together, for the first time in English, a series of articles in a "poetics of expressiveness" written between 1960 and 1980. They appear here in a roughly chronological order that also reflects the logical design of the model of literary competence they elaborate.

In the Introduction, I outline the theory and establish its relation to the literary-critical tradition.

In Part 1, I expand the Introduction into three chapters, each of which deals with a major aspect of the theory. Chapter 1 shows the indebtedness of the model in its early version to Sergej Eisenstein and concentrates on the format for describing literary structure. In Chapter 2, I introduce the concept of the "ready-made" object and of the model's "dictionary." The theory's approach to the study of entire oeuvres is formulated in Chapter 3. Each of the topics in Part 1 is elaborated in one of the subsequent sections of the book.

Part 2 is devoted to the description of individual texts—a sophisticated folktale, a remarkably artistic proverb, and an example of English humor. In each chapter I examine shorter and shorter texts with greater and greater rigor, ending the part with Chapter 6, which illustrates the theoretical and technical apparatus of the model most fully.

The discussion, introduced in Chapter 3, of authors' poetic worlds is more fully developed in Part 3. Chapter 7 concerns a recurrent motif in the writings of Pasternak; the next is an overview of the poetic world of Pushkin, which sets the stage for Chapter 9, an analysis of the structure of a Pushkin lyric in terms of the poet's invariants. In Chapter 10 I use the concept of invariance in comparing entire poetic systems.

The two chapters in Part 4 deal with the "grammar" and "diction-ary" of the model and engage in minute analyses of literary texture. Chapter 11 is concerned with the discovery and formulation of rules of iconic expression, Chapter 12 with techniques of closure.

To demonstrate the universal applications of the theoretical frame-work, I have drawn on the diverse material of drama (Chapter 1), narrative (Chapters 2 and 4), elementary forms (Chapters 4 and 5), and poetry (the bulk of the volume), in Russian, Somali, English, and French.

The Glossary contains definitions of the major concepts of the theory.

The general framework of "poetics of expressiveness" and many of the ideas and analyses in this book evolved in more than twenty years of close collaboration with Yury Shcheglov. My indebtedness to him is greater than any acknowledgment (short of coauthorship) can indicate.

The book and the effort it reflects originated in the atmosphere of the Moscow linguistic-semiotic "thaw" of the 1960s and 1970s. My most important intellectual debts are to my mentor, Vjač. Vs. Ivanov, and my friend Igor Mel'čuk. For response to and discussion of ideas and portions of the book I am grateful to S. G. Bočarov, F. A. Dreizin, B. M. Gasparov, M. L. Gasparov, S. I. Gindin, Lydia Ginzburg, Ju. I. Levin, G. A. Levinton, M. Ju. Lotman, E. M. Meletinsky, Z. G. Minc, E. S. Novik, N. V. Percov, and many others. I recall with gratitude discussions in the Laboratory of Machine Translation of MGPIIJa, at the VINITI Seminar on Semiotics, at the "Informelectro" Linguistic Seminar, in Tartu, on Metrostroevskaja, and elsewhere. My special thanks go to Ju. D. Apresjan, Efim Ètkind, Sergo Lominadze, Ju. M. Lotman, G. L. Permjakov, V. Ju. Rozencvejg, Ju. A. Šrejder, and V. A. Uspenskij for making possible the public existence and discussion of "poetics of expressiveness," in some form or other, in the USSR. I also thank Evgenij and Elena Pasternak for their kind permission to acquaint myself with unpublished manuscripts by Boris Pasternak and for the helpful discussion of my work on the poet.

I am grateful to Adriano Aprà, Robert Belknap, Ralph Cohen, Teun A. van Dijk, Lubomir Doležel, Umberto Eco, Jan van der Eng, Aage Hansen-Löve, Maria-Renata Mayenowa, Nils Åke Nilsson, L. M. O'Toole, Antonio Prieto, Daniel Rancour-Laferrière, Tilmann Reu-ther, Ann Shukman, and Kiril Taranovsky for initiating the publica-tion or discussion of parts of the work in the West. The idea of the book in its present form belongs to Philip Lewis, and it would not have materialized without the friendly assistance of Jonathan Culler and Bernhard Kendler. My work on it was kindly supported, at various stages and in various forms, by PGEPL, the semifictitious but very helpful "Problem Group in Experimental and Applied Linguistics," and by Cornell University's Society for the Humanities, Department of Russian Literature, Committee on Soviet Studies, Humanities Research Grant Committee, and Hull Memorial Fund.

I thank Patricia Carden, Caryl Emerson, George Gibian, Edward Morris, Jon Stallworthy, and Cornell 1980–81 graduate students in Russian literature for discussions of the content and mode of presentation of parts of the book. I am especially grateful to Cornell University Press's anonymous advisers, whose suggestions concerning the plan of the book helped determine its present shape. Thanks for de-russifying my English in some of the chapters go to Leonard Babby, Robert Channon, Bernard Comrie, Margaret Dailey, Christopher English, Marguerite Mizelle, Johanna Nichols, L. M. O'Toole, and, of course, to the Press's editor John Ackerman and to Kathleen Parthé. The Russian text of the original essays and the English text of the book's chapters have been patiently typed and retyped by, respectively, Nina Mixajlovna Volkova and Diane Williams; to both of them I extend my sympathy and gratitude.

I owe more than I can express to my (step)father, Lev Abramovič Mazel', my wife, Tatiana Korelsky, and my once and future "boss," Viktor Julievič Rozencvejg; without their intellectual and human influence, care, patience, and love, not much could have been achieved.

Thanks are probably due to the Unknown Philologist: his stiff opposition to the ideas that follow was a sign of their uncommonness, stimulated their development and presentation, and thus made this book possible.

Some of the chapters in this book have appeared previously in English. Chapters 1 and 8 are reprinted by permission from *Russian Poetics in Translation* 8 (1981): 40–107. Earlier versions of Chapters 5 and 11 and portions of Chapter 3 appeared in *Poetics* 7 (1978): 309–32, 8 (1979): 405–30, and 6 (1977): 77–106. Chapters 7 and 9 were published in *New Literary History* 9 (1978): 263–314. Chapter 10 appeared in *Diacritics* 10 (Winter 1980):60–74; in its present version it includes a section first published in *Poetics* 6 (1977): 94–97. Quotations from Vladimir Nizhny's *Lessons with Eisenstein,* copyright © 1962 by George Allen & Unwin Ltd., are reprinted by permission of George Allen & Unwin (Publishers) Ltd., and by permission of Hill

Preface

and Wang, a division of Farrar, Straus and Giroux, Inc. Brief excerpts from Boris Pasternak's *Doctor Zhivago*, copyright © 1958 by Pantheon Books, are reprinted by permission of Pantheon Books, a division of Random House, Inc. I am grateful to the editors and publishers who granted permission for the use of these materials. The rest of the book has not appeared in English before.

Unless I have indicated otherwise, I am also responsible for the English version of quotations from Russian, which I either translated myself or edited (e.g., those made by L. M. O'Toole for *New Literary History* and *Russian Poetics in Translation*) in order to make them as literal as possible.

ALEXANDER ZHOLKOVSKY

Ithaca, New York

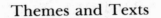

Themes and Texts

Author's Note

In transliterating Russian, I have used the system known as Shaw III (see Shaw 1967: 8), except for certain proper names, which are given in the form in which they have become familiar to English-speaking readers (e.g., Akhmatova, Pushkin).

The Bibliography lists works in the "poetics of expressiveness." In the text these works are referred to by the date of original publication, or, if unpublished, by the date of writing, in brackets. All other works referred to in the text are listed in the Works Cited. In the text these works are identified by author and date in parentheses; where two dates separated by a slash appear for a single work, the first date indicates that of the edition I have used, the second, that of original publication or writing.

I use single quotes for motifs and other thematic entities, except in numbered formulas, which are set off by small type. Quotations in the original language are italicized (except for poems quoted in columns); translated quotations are in double quotes.

Introduction:
A Pre-Poststructuralist Poetics

1. Preposterous?

The essays that follow were conceived as parts of a single theoretical project, developed in collaboration with Yury Shcheglov. It has been referred to by various names: "Soviet generative poetics," "Theme–Text model of literary competence," and "poetics of expressiveness." I will abbreviate it as PE.

In brief, the project proposes to construct a model of literary competence as a system of correspondences between themes and texts. It proceeds from the assumption that a literary text is an expressive embodiment of a nonexpressive theme. "Theme" is defined as the invariant of all the components of a particular text. Description of literary structure takes the form of "derivation" in terms of "expressive devices" (EDs)—universal elementary transformations responsible for the gradual heightening of expressiveness on the way from the theme to the text. Thematic invariance underlying expressive variation is also characteristic of entire sets of texts, for example, the oeuvre of a given author. In PE terms, the "poetic world" of an author is a derivational hierarchy of his "invariant motifs," that is, of the recurrent expressive realizations of his central theme. The present book sets forth, for the first time in English, all the major aspects of this theory.

Twenty years' experience in dealing with the response to PE has convinced its authors that their presumably simple and consistent idea of a scientific poetics is perhaps original after all, and, in any case, that it is far from self-evident. Most of the doubts and dissatisfactions that the project has provoked seem to suggest that PE is at once trivial and impossible. On the trivial side, PE has been accused of taking a very limited—static, immanent—view of the literary text; being "circular"—adding nothing new to the analyzed texts; severing form from content; offering a rigidly deterministic path from a "fixed" theme to the text and thus ignoring the multiplicity of the text's readings and the implicit conventionality of structuralist mentality itself; lacking a discovery procedure; and so forth. On the impossible side, PE is reproached for its forbidding formalism; its abundance of technical terms and abbreviations; its diagrammatic rather than discursive presentation; and so on—all of which is said to make for difficult reading ("Where in these dull accounts is *le plaisir du texte?*"). In addition, it is attacked for attempting to paraphrase art (and in pathetically plain language, too), and, in general, for daring to model poetic creativity. The grudging praise that PE work sometimes elicits is either for individual literary-critical perceptions (which allegedly owe nothing to the method and all to mere intuition) or for the commendable—if futile—exploration of ultrastructuralist avenues of study.

In short, opponents see PE as aiming at too little with means that are too complicated. I have long been familiar with these objections, none of which is really disturbing. But misreadings, as we all know, deserve to be taken seriously. I therefore offer the well-intentioned reader some explanations, inevitably selective and sketchy, after which the book should be able to speak for itself.

2. Modeling the Traditional

2.1. *Explicitness, Constructs, and the Role of Intuition*

In a sense, PE is both old-fashioned and modern, which explains, for example, the trivial/impossible paradox. It is *traditional* in that it focuses on the age-old goal of poetics—the shock of recognition: it tries to capture and formulate the reader's natural reaction to and reasoned judgment of the work of art. If the shock seems to eclipse the recognition, it is because PE is *new* in pushing recognition to the extreme of modeling. The possibilities of traditional criticism are, in fact, far from exhausted, provided one is prepared to draw all the conclusions inherent in it and to shoulder the tasks this entails.

PE takes its inspiration from breakthroughs in the modeling of linguistic behavior, which originated in a deliberate concentration on the formalization of traditional grammars. One lesson to be learned

Introduction

from linguistics is precisely how difficult it is to state explicitly what one already knows intuitively about one's natural semiotic behavior, and at the same time how pleasurable this work can be. *Explicitness* is the most crucial claim of structuralism (even more so than, say, truth): to be falsifiable, a statement has to be accurately formulated in the first place.

This approach, of course, threatens to make literary criticism difficult both to read and to write. But then why should it be any easier—chattier—than the sciences, than linguistics or musicology? As soon as literary science (if one may use this term) accepts the responsibility of accounting for one of the most complex and sophisticated domains of human behavior ("artistic logic"), it will realize that in its present state it should look up to, rather than down on, "dull accounts." As a genre of writing, literary criticism should compete with Einstein, not Shakespeare; in a sense, the plainer the language the better.

Scientific discourse calls for clear distinctions: between the object and the metalanguage used to describe it; between different tasks, objects, and levels of description; and so on. Such rationalistic dissection (murderous as it may seem to the mysterious Slavist soul) in fact helps account for the "text as a whole": each of its aspects is taken care of by the corresponding component of the model, while its wholeness is explicitly reflected in the links between components.

Emphasis on formalization should not obscure the role accorded to the scholar's intuition and heuristic ingenuity. In fact, the modeling approach to the humanities proceeds from the recognition that intuition has a double importance: one models intuitively one's own (or others') intuitive behavior. Accomplished literary intuition is, therefore, taken for granted. Intuitiveness (in the sense of imprecision) is banned only from the final product, which must be an explicit and formal model. But, of course, the rigor of this mold is certain to influence—educate, discipline, guide—the intuition that is to be cast in it. As a result, PE has good chances of seeing more and better than other methodologies in its chosen—narrow but important—field of vision.

2.2. *The "Tradition"*

Since PE's indebtedness to and kinship with structuralist thought are obvious, I will try to identify what is probably less clear—the "tradition" that PE purports to model.

Since Aristotle, one major goal of poetics has been to state *what*

21

works of art convey and how they convey it. Leo Tolstoy's explanation was surprisingly semiotic: "Art is a human activity consisting in this, that one man consciously, by means of certain external signs, hands on to others feelings he has lived through and that the others are infected by these feelings and also experience them" (1929: 123). This is the view of literature which PE sets out to formalize in the light of modern scientific concepts. It is remarkable, though, how many elements of these concepts were always inherent in traditional poetics.

Aristotle's *Poetics* formulated the theme of tragedy as 'pity and fear' and offered a complete calculus of the situations that can, with varying degrees of accuracy, instill these feelings in the spectator. The ideal of "generative calculus" inspired Mixail Lomonosov's 1748 treatise, "A Brief Guide to Eloquence," examining all theoretically possible ways of conveying the theme 'sleepless labor overcomes obstacles' (Lomonosov 1952/1748: 110 ff.); Edgar Allan Poe's 1846 essay, "Philosophy of Composition," a systematic "generation" of "The Raven" (Poe 1965/1846); and Sergej Eisenstein's inquiry during the 1930s and 1940s into the universal principles of expressiveness (Eisenstein 1964–70, 1968, 1975a, b). Some of these generative concepts (e.g., Lomonosov's "conjunction of remote ideas" = Coleridge's "reconciliation of opposites") were formulated even before such concepts as "literariness," "device," and "function" were consciously introduced by the Formalists. Meanwhile, the school of "close reading" (= *explication de texte* = Geršenzon's "slow reading") set the stage for absorbing the linguistic principle of accounting for everything in the corpus—especially as the relevance of linguistic detail to "reading" was realized; compare William Empson's discovery of "ambiguities" (1966/1935) and Lev Ščerba's "linguistic interpretation of poems" (1957/1923). The linguistic perspective also led to an emphasis on metalanguage: perhaps Empson's most lasting contribution is his insistence on laborious formulation of poetic meanings, which he pointedly set off in single quotation marks. The New Critics elaborated further both the concept of the literary text as a thematizable whole and the corresponding methods of description. A new, pragmatic awareness was introduced by Sergej Eisenstein and by Kenneth Burke, both of whom saw literary texts as symbolic *actions* (by the author, upon the reader), rather than as pure messages, and concentrated on the rhetorical (= expressive in PE terminology) aspect of literary form. Yet another dimension was added to traditional poetics by the influence—direct and indirect—of psychoanalytic thought, bent on discovering subliminal layers of literary content and the mechanisms of its expression-suppression in the actual text. (In a sense, modern trends in the humanities owe their deep structures to Freud.)

The framework of PE is an attempt to integrate the traditional concepts briefly outlined above in a consistent model of literary competence. A crucial methodological problem involved in this project concerns the possibility of paraphrasing literature.

2.3. *The Heresy of Paraphrase?*

Paraphrase has been disowned by writers and critics alike. Compare Tolstoy's rebuttal (1978: 437–38) of critics' interpretations of *Anna Karenina* with Cleanth Brooks's "The Heresy of Paraphrase" (1975: 192–214). Both argue the following:

1. The overall message of the text *does not equal the sum total* of the "effects" and "ideas" expressed in it (Tolstoy: "every thought . . . is terribly impoverished when taken out of the connection [*sceplenie*] in which it occurs"; Brooks: "in that case . . . a poem becomes merely a bouquet of intrinsically beautiful items").

2. The content is *structured* (Tolstoy's "labyrinth of connections"; Brooks's "pattern of resolutions and balances").

3. A successful paraphrase, if at all thinkable, would be *no shorter* than the text itself (Tolstoy: "to say in words everything that I intended to express in my novel, I would have to write the same novel I wrote from the beginning"; Brooks: as the "proposition approaches adequacy . . . it increases greatly in length . . . fills itself up with . . . qualifications and . . . begins to fall back upon metaphors of its own").

4. Literary structure is an experience, *an action rather than a proposition* (cf. above Tolstoy's "infecting" with emotions and the "pragmatics" of Burke and Eisenstein; Brooks: "the unity is achieved by a dramatic process, not the logical; it represents an equilibrium of forces, not a formula").

In spite of what amounts to a total indictment of literary criticism, both authors remain constructive. Brooks proposes to describe the work of art as an "experience which . . . triumphs over the apparently conflicting elements by unifying them into a new pattern." For Tolstoy the literary work is an act of communication by means of an "endless labyrinth of connections," "made up not by the idea, but by something else" which it is impossible to "express directly in words"—a labyrinth, however, based on certain "laws" that it is the task of critics to "guide readers through."

Tolstoy's and Brooks's quest for an appropriate metalanguage for poetics all but suggests that a way out of the "paraphrastic heresy" might be to replace conventional discourse with scientific discourse. As paraphrasing gives way to modeling, a clear distinction between the studied text and the scholar's own metatext relieves him of the need to worry about their stylistic incompatibility, comparative length, and so on. Instead of speculating indefinitely on whether processes can be reduced to formulas, the scholar concentrates on evolving adequate metalanguages for the two basic aspects of artistic structure which are "not expressible by words" and are "different from ideas": the enacted experiences (= "themes") and the laws of their patterning (= "expressive devices").

3. PE: Strategies and Issues

What, then, are some of the conceptual gains bought at the price of "dehumanization," and what are some of the problems involved?

3.1. *Theme*

One innovation (or, rather, reformulation of an old notion) is the concept of "theme." To talk sensibly about poetic expression one has to separate what is expressed ("theme") from what expresses it ("text") and from the correspondence between the two ("expressive device"). As a result, "theme" is placed at the start of the derivation, as if it existed apart from and prior to the text. This, however, is but a technical convention necessary for demonstrating precisely how the theme is embodied in the text. Since theme is defined as that invariant entity of which everything in the text is an expressive variation, *"text" is "theme" elaborated by "expressive devices."*

The concept of theme involves yet another break with traditional critical practice: the order of derivation is pointedly different from that of the usual presentation, a characteristic example of which is the simulated "discovery" of the text's secrets (a method that makes for excellent suspense in a critical or classroom analysis). PE rejects this approach as one that substitutes performance for competence (one might call it "performance fallacy"). Instead, it insists on distinguishing statements about competence (i.e., about the text's artistic logic) from any kind of statements about performance: author's (creative), reader's (interpretive), or critic's (heuristic and presentational).

One typical reproach is that PE resuscitates the specter of schoolroom "ideas." In fact, the definition of "theme" is general enough to cover any kind of invariant (or dominant, to use the Prague terminology), be it ideological or, say, syntactic: PE has *Class I themes,* which are messages about the referential sphere ("life"), and *Class II themes*— messages about the code sphere ("literature"). Nor do Class I themes equal traditional "ideas": to qualify as invariants, the latter would have to be both more subtle and more abstract.

In sum, themes are explicitly formulated referential or code-sphere invariants from which the text can be derived on the basis of expressive devices.

3.2. *Expressive Devices* (EDs)

No critic questions the expressive power of poetic texts. PE takes the logical step of isolating this aspect of literary competence and devising a special metalanguage to account for it. If themes are the objects—matter, substance, *"things"*—handled by literary competence, EDs are the *operations* that do the handling.

Ten elementary EDs seem to underlie all more complex expressive structures: CONCRETIZATION, AUGMENTATION, REPETITION, VARIATION, DIVISION, CONTRAST, COORDINATION, COMBINATION, PREPARATION, REDUCTION. As the names themselves suggest, EDs are an attempt to systematize the vocabulary used by critics in describing literary expressiveness, to make it "poor" enough—explicit, unambiguous, operational. But mere perfecting of terminology is not the main issue; more important are two conceptual innovations.

First, EDs are ruthlessly *separated from themes:* the whole point is that themes be nonexpressive and that EDs be "meaningless," that is, theme-preserving.

Second, EDs are *defined formally* as transformation types operating on thematic entities (themes or products of previous transformations). An ED transforms thematic entity X into entity Y (or into the complex entity YZQ . . .), which conveys the same theme as X with greater "force." For example, 'love' can be CONCRETIZED as 'sensual love'; can be AUGMENTED into 'eternal love'; can yield a CONTRAST: 'love and hate'; can be PREPARED by a sequence 'sympathy—liking— love' or 'hostility—love'; and so on.

PE, so to speak, takes literally the idea of "artistic logic" underlying any literary convention—a logic in which vividness, symmetry, variety, contrast, fusion, and so on, constitute proofs. EDs are blueprints for the basic operations of this logic.

Combined with each other into a derivational description of a particular work, EDs form a chain that represents graphically the theme-text correspondence. It is crucial for the model's explanatory power that the chain links be standard (i.e., usable in other derivations), cover every inch of the gap between theme and text, and smuggle in no uncontrolled effects. Developing this slow-motion picture of the theme's embodiment in the text—counting the "tricks" (= EDs) that go into it—is one way of explicating the reader's intuitive, and often immediate, grasp of the theme that has been dissolved in the text. As we are dealing with the competence of an Everyman, it is an asset, not a liability, that perceptions of widely diverse texts are modeled by trivial, universal EDs. The structures are infinite in number and idiosyncratic, but the kinds of "bricks" from which they are fashioned are few and simple.

As a grammar of artistic expression, EDs determine the format of the other major component of PE, the "dictionary of reality" (DR), which models that knowledge of "life" and "literature" which is shared by writers and readers and thus makes possible their literary communication. For each thematic entity, this dictionary must specify the "natural" ways of CONCRETIZATION, AUGMENTATION, and so on, which the expressive process can tap. It is in terms of elementary devices that more complex expressive patterns—tropes, motifs, and "ready-made" objects—are formulated in DR.

Paradoxically, it is the separation of EDs from themes which makes possible a systematic description of their "indissoluble" ties. The general assumption is that any ED applies to any theme, thus accounting for "pure expressiveness" unaltered by considerations of content. (To be sure, in a given derivation the choice and order of EDs are not arbitrary but so contrived as to portray the text's structure.) Cases of *special theme-ED attraction* are reflected in the rules of CONCRETIZATION via EDs, which state, for example, that one way to CONCRETIZE thematic entity X (e.g., 'monotony') is to resort to a certain ED (e.g., REPETITION). Themes that predetermine recourse to a particular ED (such as 'unity,' 'harmony,' 'conflict,' and 'regularity') seem to play a central role in the thematic universe of literary discourse, which can thus be said to see the world *through the prism of expressive devices.*

3.3. *Invariants*

A third major innovation comes in PE's treatment of entire oeuvres, that is, sets of texts by one author. By extrapolating the concepts of theme and derivation to the study of an author's recurrent clusters of images, situations, syntactic and compositional patterns, and so on, PE has evolved a corresponding metalanguage, based on the following concepts: (*a*) "central theme" (Θinv): the most general thematic invariant of an oeuvre; (*b*) "invariant motifs" ($\bar{M}inv$): its recurrent manifestations; (*c*) "poetic world" (PW): the derivation of all the invariant motifs from the central theme; and (*d*) "local theme" (Θloc): that specific part of a text's theme which is not accounted for by the author's invariants.

Once again, "rigid"—standardized, static—constructs help explicate and elaborate important intuitive perceptions. Thus "poetic world" models that permanent thematic-expressive base of a writer's work which gives it unity and identity (= his "individual mythology": his favorite "figure in the carpet"). The format of a complete hierarchical set of motifs ensures a thorough description of the author's imagery in both the referential and the code spheres: *le style* and *l'homme* are portrayed in terms of the same standard patterns derivable from the central theme. The derivation of an individual text expands to incorporate a demonstration of the local theme's translation into the author's language—its transposition, as it were, on the keyboard of his favorite motifs.

3.4. *PE: Other Issues*

I will now try to answer briefly some questions that are typically raised by PE and that may be bothering the readers of this Introduction.

Q. Is not PE circular in that it derives the text from the theme that it gets from that same text?

A. Yes and no. Yes, because models aim at reproducing their objects, not at enriching them. It will be quite a sufficient breakthrough if after two thousand years poetics produces one functioning model. No, precisely because the theme-text derivation is a model—not a repetition—of the intuitive reading. Epistemologically, then, PE is not a circle, but a spiral: what is acquired is explicitly formulated knowledge. In a sense, PE is both humbler and more arrogant than current criticism: not presuming to engage in a dialogue with literature, PE treats it the way biology does guinea pigs, frogs, and *Drosophilae*.

Q. Is PE a general theory of literary competence or a source of interpretations?

A. Neither. It is less than a full-fledged theory because it covers (tentatively) only some of the basic principles underlying literary conventions and does not claim to have reduced even these to a formal grammar. Nor does it generate interpretations; rather it offers a (provisional) notation for those interpretations prompted by intuition. Therefore, it is probably best described as a research project providing for a creative feedback between the elaboration of a theoretical metalanguage and the practical description of literary data.

Q. Doesn't PE impose just one "correct" interpretation on the analyzed text?

A. Not at all. As a theory, PE is interested in providing a metalanguage for any reading: one important methodological contribution consists precisely in the realization that the typical object of modeling in poetics is the semiotic pair "a text—a reading." When it comes to interpretive practice, one naturally opts for more or less rich and/or representative readings—the most widespread, complete, consistent, and so on. The explicitness of PE description is of help in establishing these readings, as well as in guiding the intuition by the derivational format into which it will eventually have to fit.

Q. Doesn't this practice impose a standard order of derivation?

A. The order is standard because it must, by definition, proceed from themes to texts in order to reflect the logic of correspondences between them. As grammar, PE allows for multiple alternative derivations from any theme and of any text; but a particular derivation reflects the actual correspondence linking a given text with its theme. Reversed, a derivation turns into a "subtraction" of EDs from the text, a sequence modeling the passive (= reader's) competence. PE concentrates on the active (= writer's) order of the theme-text correspondence because synthesizing procedures (in modeling in general and in linguistics and poetics in particular) seem to be easier to formalize than those of recognition and discovery.

Q. How, then, does PE account for the different paths followed by the creative process in different authors?

A. It does not, being a model of competence, not of performance. It is a mistake (akin to the intentional fallacy) to confuse the theme-text logic with the actual order of text production. In a performance model, generation may start from a theme (which can later be changed or left intact), from any purely formal element (a provocative rhyme, a verbal or plot *pointe*, etc.), or from a real-life incident (which can remain a part of or be dropped from the final text). The general design of competence models is the same for different authors (relevant differences being accounted for by the way the models are "filled in"), whereas performance designs should vary from author to author. Only if the two types of modeling are first clearly distinguished can they profit from eventual comparison and integration.

Q. What does PE make of the deconstructionist questioning of the conventions that pervade the rhetoric of literary discourse and the logic of structuralist description?

A. Since simpler problems should be solved first, PE postpones this kind of inquiry, finding enough to do within the narrower task of accounting thoroughly for at least one type of convention. Modest as it may seem, this program is indispensable and can keep poetics busy for decades. Each explicit formulation of a theme, an ED, or a link between them and each generalization about such formulations raise many stimulating fundamental problems never before confronted by poetics. In fact, they are simple only with respect to what they might lead to.

In the next section I will outline the main avenues of inquiry actually pursued by PE.

4. Types of PE Study and the Plan of the Book

The general theoretical framework is elaborated in the present Introduction, Chapter 1, and the Glossary of PE terms, as well as in [1967d, 1975a, b, 1978b].

Detailed *derivation of an individual text* from its theme, on the basis of EDs (ideally via its deep design, deep and surface structure), is undertaken in Chapter 1 (Eisenstein's mise-en-scène) and the three essays of Part 2; especially elaborate is the analysis of Bertrand Russell's joke (Chapter 6). See also derivations of Petronius's "The Ephesus Widow" [1970b] and of a La Rochefoucauld maxim [1978a].

Portrayal of the poetic world of an author is represented by Chapter 9 (Pushkin) and a part of Chapter 8 (Pasternak). See also the studies of: Ovid's "Metamorphoses" [1962c, 1980f]; the Sherlock Holmes cycle

[1973b]; the poetry of Akhmatova [1979a] and Okudžava [1979e]; Molière's comedies [1979h(1)]; Leo Tolstoy's children's stories [1979j]; and the prose of Zoščenko [1981c].

Description of an author's invariant motif and of its place in his poetic world is the topic of Chapter 7 (Pasternak's 'window'). See also [1980d, 1981b] (on Pushkin's 'superior peace' and 'idleness') and [1980k, 1982a, c] on a poet's code-sphere invariants (a syntactic construction and a type of adverb in Pasternak). Close to this type of study is the *description of "the poetic world of a personage,"* see [1975c] on the invariant structure of "Benderisms"—the wisecracks of the Ilf and Petrov hero.

Derivational description of a text as a part of its author's poetic world, displaying the gradual saturation of the local theme with a set of invariant motifs, is exemplified by Chapter 9 (on a Pushkin lyric masterpiece). This approach has been elaborated in [1979h(2), 1979i, 1980e, g, 1981d, 1982d], dealing, respectively, with Molière's "Mr. de Pourceagnac," a Mandel'štam poem, poems by Pasternak, the "Mock Penitent" of the Archpoet of Cologne, Victor Hugo's "Sur une barricade," and poems by Akhmatova.

Comparison of entire poetic worlds, pressing the concepts of derivation and invariant motif into the service of contrastive poetics, is the project of Chapter 10; see also [1980c] (a detailed comparison of four texts of two Russian poets).

Characterization of expressive devices, their subtypes, combinations, relations with one another and with the themes they implement, is represented by the last section of the book. Chapter 11 concentrates on one subtype of CONCRETIZATION, and tries, by examining intricate cases of iconicity, to formulate correspondences between expression-plane patterns and the themes they mimic. If all such CONCRETIZATIONS have to be listed in the model's "dictionary," certain other EDs can be stated in the "grammar"—as general transformation types and subtypes. One subtype of ED PREPARATION is considered in Chapter 12, which, by pointing out its function in the Pushkin poem discussed in Chapter 9, rounds off the book with a fusion of general theory and practical description. For a systematic characterization of EDs see [1973a, 1974a, 1977a, 1979k, 1980i, 1981a] and sections in [1976a, b, 1978a, 1980g].

To conclude, poetics of expressiveness seeks to combine two objectives: to describe the deep thematic level of literary structure and, in light of this, to account for all the details of the text. It aims at a precise and sensitive portrayal of literary works in terms of a standard metalanguage.

Results so far obtained are mostly *paradigmatic* in nature: PE can claim relative success in discovering and formulating vertical links between themes and texts. Other problems—such as the syntagmatic links within levels, the very definition of level as a horizontal stage of a derivation, and some related problems, for example, the formalization of the derivational process—remain open. Another possible direction of future efforts is to reformulate the problem of intertextuality in terms of the PE framework.

In sum, PE, not unlike other products of Russian literary scholarship, ends up somewhat "over-contentual" and "under-formalized," stopping short of the harmonious combination of "essence" with "grammar." This long-cherished Russian ideal of Westernization is, however, what PE strives to achieve.

At any rate, in this book I have been concerned with making the theory palatable to humanists, rather than with perfecting its formalism. I have tried to keep "technology" to the minimum necessary for imprinting PE's fundamental message: *that poetics is about the way something is successfully expressed by something else.* In fact, I do not mind if the book proves readable to those who will choose to ignore its message and use it merely as a collection of "individual observations" about literature.

PART ONE

AN OUTLINE OF
THE THEORY

1

Eisenstein's Generative Poetics

1

The construction of generative grammars, that is, the modeling of the speaker's linguistic behavior, is one of the most important principles of modern synchronic linguistics. Moreover, the recent stress on the semantic aspect of language competence points to the creation of models that generate texts from given meanings. Thus, linguistics is coming closer to modeling such banal truths as: "language is a means of communication" and "language is a vehicle for the expression of thoughts." Semiotic poetics, too, can be envisaged as generative, that is, as aiming at modeling artistic creation as "expression through images of thoughts and feelings," "expression through depiction," "thinking in images," and so on.

Sergej Eisenstein seems to have been one of the precursors of this approach. "His [theoretical] writings view art as a means of expressing ideas and 'amplifying emotions,' and thus undertake an exhaustive retracing of how a work of art is constructed in its entirety and how the image of the theme is 'born' from the properties of the objects and materials used in the construction" [1967d: 178]. Eisenstein, it emerges, was an astonishingly modern thinker who attempted to model the behavior of a film creator on his own experience just as the linguist models his own ability to speak or to translate texts from one language to another. Naturally, Eisenstein's was a kind of "gut generativism," like that of a very good and sensitive translator who, to share his experience, writes a manual in which he strives to explain the underlying rules of the art.

This chapter is a revised version of [1970a].

35

As it happens, the linguistic analogy helps to clarify what poetics still requires in order to proceed to the construction of functioning models. A linguist engaged in constructing generative models is normally competent in the language being described; in particular, he can generate any of its utterances (or has a native speaker at his disposal), and its traditional grammar gives him at least some idea of the language's structure.

In poetics, the researcher normally has only a passive command of the "language," that is, he understands to some degree the works of art which are addressed to him, but he can neither produce similar works himself nor rely on really accurate traditional notions in, as it were, "parsing" literary texts.[1] Eisenstein's notes on directing put us in a position comparable to that of the linguist, for they present us with a record of the active use of the language of his art as well as information about texts, structure, the interrelationship of their elements, and often even the basic rules for generating them.

In this discussion I refer to the material in Vladimir Nizhny's book *Lessons with Eisenstein,* which demonstrates how the generation of a film goes through several stages that develop a certain dramatic task into a mise-en-scène, the mise-en-scène into a sequence of shots, and each shot into a set of acted moments filmed from a single point (the "mise-en-shot"). One can see that the entire generative process is determined by a set of consistent principles which should be brought to light and ultimately formalized. I will take the first stage of this process—the construction of the mise-en-scène—and use it to envisage the structure and working of a "program" for generating artistic texts.

I will thus be claiming for my conclusions some degree of generality for *poetics in general,* aware as I am of how restricted and elementary the material is that I am considering and how simplified and technically imperfect my "formalization" is. All the same, even this might make a useful starting point; "the art of generative grammar," after all, began with attempts to explicate such an elementary case of linguistic behavior as the grammatical parsing of a simple sentence of plain prose English.

2

The embryo script that Eisenstein presented to his students to turn into a mise-en-scène can be summarized as follows:

In order to trick and capture Dessalines, the popular leader of Haiti, who is a general in Napoleon's army, the French commander invites him to dine at a house of a priest. When Dessalines learns about the plot from a black serving-woman, he runs along the table toward the window and escapes. He foments a Negro revolt. The author's and the audience's sympathies are with Dessalines against the French.

Nizhny's book describes the process by which this outline is turned into a mise-en-scène, that is, into a concrete sequence of movements, gestures, and speeches by the characters.

In order to present explicitly the product of Eisenstein's "poetic machine," I have brought together all the separate directing decisions taken by Eisenstein and his pupils and have described the resulting mise-en-scène in the Appendix to this chapter. Thus we have available to us information as to: (*a*) the "input text" (the embryo of the script); (*b*) the "output text" (the description of the mise-en-scène); (*c*) the "parsing" of the output text (indications as to the way the components of the mise-en-scène link up and relate to each other); and (*d*) the 'transformational history' of all the elements of the output text. We can attempt, on the basis of this information, to envisage the general rules for transforming an input text into an output text. In order to do this we will first consider how several components of the mise-en-scène are generated:

(1) *The priest . . . embraces D . . . and leads him over to the officers in Zone II . . . They greet him and take up positions around him.* Why does this have to happen in precisely this way?

"But we must get the feeling not of a welcome, but of the first attack on D." "Both one and the other," explains S. M. [Eisenstein]. . . . "This embrace will also in a degree foreshadow the subsequent encirclement. Incidentally, embracing is the typical style of welcome in Latin America. . . . After the priest has treacherously kissed D., . . . he leads D. into the group of officers. According to the content of the actual [inner] story, the priest leads D. into the encirclement, and, according to the line of our externalized story he takes D. towards the officers for them to be presented to him" (Nizhny 1979: 47).

(2) Why is precisely this the role of the priest?

"One protagonist is D., and the other . . . is . . . the entire group of officers. . . . However, . . . there is one figure . . . that . . . links the antagonists—the priest! . . . On the one hand he is a good pastor and hospitable host, . . . and on the other the . . . organizer of the trap. . . . Since, in the story, he lures D. into the room, so, in the mise-en-scène he must draw D. into the ring of officers" (p. 25).

(3) *The serving-woman . . . goes up to D. with a bowl. . . . He . . . holds out his*

hands but doesn't encounter the bowl. . . . [She] leads him aside. . . . This is repeated several times. . . . D. moves away from the Frenchmen. Why does the serving-woman behave in this way?

"The old serving-woman plays a role counterposed to that of the priest . . . [She] represents the Negro masses of the island" (p. 25). "[The] dramatic function [of this section] requires that D. should seem drawn away from encirclement by the information" (p. 35). "With such an image, the requirement of the inner content of the narrative—fulfilled by the old serving-woman—to bring D. out of the encircling ring is fully achieved in action" (p. 55).

(4) Whence the requirement that D. be surrounded (rather than, say, attacked, poisoned, etc.)? Why should the serving-woman represent the people of Haiti here?

"The servant represents the Negro masses of the island. If we bear this in mind, remembering the end the whole episode is leading up to, then out of the story itself arises a structure like two encirclements. At the beginning D. is surrounded by the French and the link between them is the priest. At the end, when the servant links the people to D., the French themselves are as though surrounded by the Negroes, by the colony as a whole. . . . Thus the conflict in the first part of the episode—the conflict of a single individual with a group of officers—grows into a conflict between a group of colonialists and the mass of the people. . . . This episode contains an 'ecstatic'[2] structural movement—the course of events intensifies to an explosion and then passes over into a contrary course but on a broadened scale" (pp. 25–26).

(5) Let us consider the following details relating to various stages in the development of the mise-en-scène:

The adjutant . . . quietly gives the priest and officers a message. . . . He goes up to D. . . . D. gives up his sword. . . . The adjutant carries it, passing between all the officers, toward Door A. . . . An officer says that the sabre has not been taken away for nothing. . . . The serving-woman's facial gestures. D. turns sharply, his face is enraged.

This turns out to be a single line, consciously introduced into the action.

"The spectator must be warned of this . . . before D. . . . The spectator may surmise the presence of danger from the section 'Waiting for D.' To achieve this effect we must give there too the feeling of a plot. But this feeling of danger must be evoked again after D. has entered; more precisely, it must start increasing in the spectator into a sense of alarm. Hence, placed between 'Welcome' and 'Warning,' there must be a section that gives this feeling of increasing danger, that is, that repeats the inner content of the first section, but with greater intensity" (p. 33).

"Should there . . . be a discussion among the conspirators on the seizure of D. right at the beginning? . . . Here we have at one and the same time to make clear their intention and not say a word about it. For this, let the officers, after the brief message from the spy, whisper among themselves: the spectator doesn't yet know about what. But this muttering will create an impression of uneasiness, of not everything being quite right. Then . . . we must . . . give a clearer hint of the conspiracy . . . but not speaking out openly until the old Negro woman tells all" (pp. 37–38).

"Could they really disarm D.?" "Precisely. . . . They take his weapons from him. To justify this, they make use of the etiquette of the situation. After a ceremonial introduction and before a banquet, before sitting down to table, it would be customary to remove weapons. . . . Each time raise your solution to a higher level of the content if the situation requires it. Does the surrender of weapons help to heighten the sense of horror? Do it, then. Here you must bring the spectator to such a state that he wants to cry out: 'Stop! . . . Don't disarm!'" (p. 49).

"But it's not enough just to take his sword from him.[3] This action has to be underlined. . . . It can be underlined by remarks and acting on the part of the officers. . . . But who approaches D. to take his sword?" "The adjutant-spy!" answer the students. . . . "Notice how, [continues Eisenstein] from a series of functions, a new character not originally in the scenario may often be assembled. . . . Where does the adjutant take the sword?" asks Eisenstein. "To Exit C . . . ! The nearest exit . . . !" prompt the students. . . . "On the contrary . . . ! To Exit A . . . ! The furthest exit away. The passage of the sword must display to the interested officers the fact that the weapon has been removed" (pp. 49–51). "Yes, D. would have his back to us, but after the communication is made we should turn his face to the audience again. The transition from his alert but polite demeanour to raging anger . . . will . . . be rendered not as a gradual change, but as an explosive leap, and can be an exceedingly powerful moment in the production" (p. 55).

(6) Why are there so many exits in the set and why is the table placed diagonally?

"It would be more effective to have several doors, so that D. can be gradually convinced . . . of the reality of his peril. . . . Only when it becomes clear to him that all exits are barred and that a normal exit is impossible does the situation . . . itself force him to the necessity of escaping through the window. . . . The window must be the last and only possibility for his escape. . . . And it must be situated so that it does not obtrude . . . into the spectator's consciousness or rouse in him the awareness of a 'gaping'[4] window. Besides, to put the window in the centre would mean that D. would have to run along the table-top in a direction away from the spectator and into the background . . . and the run would not be well seen. Suppose, to lengthen the line of his run you make D. run parallel to the footlights, you have then to put the window in the side wall, which equally would not be good. Obviously, the table has to be aligned diagonally. It is clear that the window should form a continuation of the table, . . . constituting a sort of second level for D.'s action following . . . the manoeuvres . . . on the floor. A window at the end of the table will not at first catch the attention of the spectator, but when D. begins his action on the table it will appear as his surprise, and sole means of exit, the most natural one" (pp. 27–28).

"He first sees the table simply as affording a freer road to Exit A. . . . To the window he has not yet, of course, given a thought" (p. 56). "They do not let D. get to the stairs, and there is nothing left for him to do but plunge through the window" (pp. 57–58).

(7) *'Back!' commands D. The officers retreat.*

"In answer to the movement of the group of officers, . . . D. first cries 'Back!'—or something of the sort." " 'Stop!',," comes the suggestion from the seats. "Not 'stop,' but precisely 'back,'" S. M. objects, "or some equivalent military command. Apart from the fact that D. himself is a soldier, and that words of command are the first that will come into his head, we cannot forget that those in front of him are also military men. They may obey, at once and automatically, words of command" (p. 60).

(8) Why does Door A have a curved flight of steps?

At a certain stage in the working out of the mise-en-scène, the problem arises of making the adjutant-informer enter from Door A and approach the officers standing in Zone I from the table-side. "If the spy appears at Door A, then he either has to go through the group of officers, which would obviously be bad, or to go round them, which would also be bad. . . . It would pay to think over how to make the spy's arrival at that spot both possible and natural. . . . Let's try changing the character of Door A: instead of a door, let's have the platform of a gallery . . . and let a small flight of stairs lead from it along the window. . . . As you see, a director should be in possession of a store of visual material relating to architecture (as well as everything else)" (pp. 39–40).

I have given Eisenstein's motivations for only some of the components of the mise-en-scène, but they are all spelled out in details in the Appendix. Let us now try to pin down some of the general features of the process by which any one detail of the mise-en-scène is derived from the embryo script.

In the first place, it is evident that the generation of a specific fact or object occurs in several steps as the mise-en-scène is gradually evolved in all its concreteness; in the most general sense this process is analogous to the immediate constituent derivation of a sentence from its base structure. Thus the serving-woman's actions emerge as the opposite of the priest's, which in turn are defined by his intermediate position between D. and the Frenchmen, and so on (see exx. (1)–(4) above). The generative process is thus multileveled; the output of each stage serves as the input for the next, and each stage involves similar operations: the serving-woman is opposed to the priest, the encirclement of D. is opposed to the encirclement of the Frenchmen, and so on. Furthermore, we can easily see that the generation of each new element of structure comprises, as it were, two operations: (*a*) the formulation of certain requirements dictated by the previous level of generation; and (*b*) the retrieval[5] of a real object (or person, object, property) which meets these requirements.

First a problem is posed: "we *have to* [my italics here and below] get a sensation simultaneously of a greeting and a first attack" (ex. (1)); "the dramatic function *requires* that D. should seem drawn away from the encirclement" (ex. (3)); "the spectator *must be* warned . . . before D."; this feeling "*must* start increasing into a sense of alarm"; "it *must* repeat the inner content of the first section, but with greater intensity"; "we *must* give a clearer hint of the conspiracy"; "you *must* bring the spectator to such a state that he wants to cry out: 'Stop!'; But *it's not enough* just to take his sword from him. This action *has to be* underlined" (ex. (5)); "D. *has to be* gradually convinced of the reality of his peril" (ex. (6)); "it *would pay to* think over how to make the spy's arrival on the spot both possible and natural" (ex. (8)).

The formulation of the requirements for the object or episode to be chosen is already its generation, but only on an abstract level, on that of what one might call the object's "distinctive features," to use a linguistic term, or of its "functions," in the language of formal poetics.[6] The formulation of a function is followed by the choice, or invention, or "composition," of a concrete fact that is within the script's thematic context and that incorporates the necessary functions. In example (1) this fact is the priest's embrace; in example (3) it is the serving-woman's manipulation of the bowl; in example (5) it is the woman's pantomime, the whispering of the officers, the taking of the sword, the officers' comments, the sword being carried past; in example (6) it is D.'s headlong rushing between the many exits; in example (8), the curved steps by Door A.

This second step—choosing the concrete fact—seems to be the formal analogue of "the work of the artist's creative imagination." Eisenstein's direct observations about how necessary it is to bear in mind various kinds of factual material ("Incidentally, embracing is the typical style of welcome in Latin America" [ex. (1)]; "before sitting down at table it would be customary to remove weapons" [ex. (5)]; "we mustn't forget that military men may obey, at once and automatically, words of command" [ex. (7)]; "a director should be in possession of a store of visual material relating to architecture" [ex. (8)] highlight one general principle of the workings of imagination which is not always so clearly evident: *the components of the text being generated are extracted from memory in accordance with previously formulated requirements, or functions.* This means that one of the most important parts of the "poetic automaton" must be a correspondingly organized "dictionary of reality."

We will now examine more closely the first step in the generation of each fact—the formulation of its functions, that is, the requirements it has to meet. Since the output of one stage serves as the input to the next, it follows that a fact that emerges at one stage as a concrete object drawn from the dictionary of reality, at the next stage itself imposes requirements as to the subsequent selection of concrete objects, that is, it acts as a function itself. Thus, the combination of 'greeting a guest' with the attempt 'to seize him' yields 'encirclement'; to give this ecstatic form involves counterposing with it a second 'encirclement'; 'the role of the priest in the encirclement' is defined at the point of intersection of the Frenchmen and D.; counterposed to 'the priest' is 'the role of the serving-woman'; the 'reception' is elaborated into 'waiting', 'meeting', 'introduction', 'greeting', and so on; the combination of 'encirclement' with 'meeting' D. leads on to 'D. being drawn into the ring of officers'; the combination of 'encirclement' with 'greeting' leads on to 'embrace'; and so on.

Thus, the functions come to be formulated on the basis of objects of the previous (higher, more abstract) level through a number of operations which are common for the various stages of the generative process. We can see this clearly if we compare the transformational histories of various components of the mise-en-scène listed above. I will try to itemize the most regular of these operations, commenting as I go along on their aims and the constraints they impose on the organization of the dictionary of reality.

Several of the operations aim to present the material in greater relief.

AUGMENTATION: "Does the surrender of the weapons help to heighten the sense of horror? Do it, then . . . But it's not enough just to take his sword from him. This action has to be underlined" (ex. (5)); "the run would be very poorly visible . . . to lengthen the line of his run . . ." (ex. (6)).

REPETITION: "it is more effective to have several doors, so that D. can be gradually convinced . . ." (ex. (6)). Usually REPETITION is accompanied by AUGMENTATION, resulting in INCREASE; as far as this example is concerned, pure REPETITION relates only to the doors, while D.'s movements are made to grow in urgency. (REPETITION is similar to AUGMENTATION in that it may itself be regarded as an AUGMENTATION in number.)

INTENSIFIED REPETITION, or INCREASE: "there must be a section that gives this feeling of increasing danger, that is, that repeats the content of the first section, but with greater intensity . . . ; then . . . we must . . . give a clearer hint, but not speaking out openly until the old Negro woman tells all" (ex. (5)); the table "constitutes a sort of second level for D.'s actions following the manoeuvres on the floor," that is, the same actions but on a higher level (ex. (6)); cf., too, the growing force of the drawing of their sabres by the officers (in the description of the mise-en-scène in the Appendix).

CONTRAST: between the serving-woman and the priest; between one encirclement and the other; between polite demeanor and raging anger (ex. (5)); between the Negro's run with the torch into the room from the window and D.'s run toward the window (in the final part of the mise-en-scène).

As far as the dictionary of reality is concerned, AUGMENTATION requires that indication should be given, for each fact, of the aspects by which it may be blown up in scale and the form it may take as a result; similarly, CONTRAST requires that various "antonyms" of each fact should be indicated; for instance, for encirclement: 'A surrounds B' → (a) 'A moves out of the encirclement'; (b) 'A does not allow himself to be surrounded'; (c) 'A himself surrounds B'; and so on. The realization of REPETITION in the dictionary of reality requires the listing of the many variants of the initial fact which can be used for repeating it: for example, a 'door' may be 'a front door', 'a window', 'a back door', and so on (cf. below).

To go on with the operations: ECSTATIC DEVELOPMENT (the transition of some action into an action opposite to it in all respects, but broader in scale—a combination, as it were, of several simultaneous CONTRASTS with INCREASE): the transition from the encirclement of one black by several whites to the encirclement of all these whites by a vast mass of black inhabitants (ex. (4)). The applicability of this operation is clearly determined by the nature of the given events and their ideological tenor (see Eisenstein's comments in ex. (4)).

CONCRETIZATION: of a 'reception'—into 'waiting', 'meeting', 'introductions', 'greetings', 'invitation to the table'; the CONCRETIZATION of a purely ideological element such as the spectator's 'alarm on behalf of D.' works in just the same way. Where the 'alarm' itself originates, Eisenstein does not explain, presumably taking it to be self-evident.

We may assume that it arises at the intersection of 'the spectator's sympathies for D.' (the input data) and 'the fact of his being surrounded'. From the necessity of 'rousing alarm' in the spectator, Eisenstein concludes: "The spectator must be warned before D. Here we have at one and the same time to make clear their intention and not say a word about it . . . this will create a sense of unease" (ex. (5)). This train of thought seems to suggest that this is what the CONCRETIZATION of 'alarm' consists of and that in the dictionary some correspondence is maintained between 'alarm' (in the spectator for the hero) and the indicated degree to which each is informed. Obviously, other ways of concretizing 'alarm' (to use T. S. Eliot's term, other "objective correlatives" of this thematic entity) are also possible and they all ought to be included in the ideal dictionary.

Note that CONCRETIZATION is applied in exactly the same way to event elements and to ideological elements of the structure, its function always being the translation of some initial requirement into a striking graphic form.

One of Eisenstein's most significant insights was to show that just as concrete and precise generative operations are involved for the ideological-emotional elements of structure as for the external line of events (e.g., respectively, 'alarm' and 'encirclement' in the first part of the episode). In the dictionary of reality this insight would have to be reflected in the form of dictionary entries of roughly the type: 'alarm (by A on B's behalf)' → 'A has vague information about the danger facing B; B suspects nothing'. With 'encirclement' we have an "idea" on a lower level, only operating for that section of the mise-en-scène where it represents the "internal" action, as opposed to the external action of 'receiving the guest' (see exx. (1) and (2)); in another context it might itself have turned out to be the external element of plot while the 'reception' would be internal. This shows how well-founded the principle is of a unified approach to ideological and event elements of structure. Both are subject to CONCRETIZATION and hence must be described correspondingly in the dictionary.

But let us return to the operations for generating a poetic text. One of the most important is that of COMBINATION, or CONCORD, whose most general function is to create an object combining the presentation of the required events with the expression of the required idea, while in its technical manifestations it ensures naturalness and congruence of all the elements of the structure.[7]

For illustrations see examples (1)–(4) and also: "But who approaches D. to take his sword?" "The adjutant-spy!" . . . "Notice how,

from a series of functions, a new character . . . may . . . be assembled"
(ex. (5)); the table is first a way of getting to Exit A, then a surprise
way out to the window; the diagonal placing of the table COMBINES a
good view of the run with several conditions (see ex. (6)); the command "Back!" is a CONCORD between D.'s shout and his and the
Frenchmen's military status (ex. (7)); the doorway with a platform and
flight of steps makes possible an approach from Door A and at the
same time from the table-side (ex. (8)).

COMBINATION is one of the central principles in the generation of a
poetic text.[8] It helps impose the required theme on the reader, automatically and unquestioningly, by dressing it up as a complete natural
object. (Note how often Eisenstein uses the words "naturally," "automatically," "most typical," "the situation itself," and so on, when he is
discussing the incarnation of whatever is "needed," "required," "has
to be," etc.—exx. (1, 4, 6, 7, 8).)

COMBINATION may be expressed both in the merging of two objects
into a single object (COMBINATION PROPER: 'the platform with a flight
of steps' ← (a) 'Door A' and (b) the requirement to 'approach the table
from a definite point'; 'encirclement' ← (a) 'attack' and (b) 'receiving a
guest'), and in the addition of new characteristics to an already existing object in order to make it congruent with surrounding objects
(CONCORD: cf. the function assigned to 'the priest' of 'drawing into
the encirclement'; the function of 'taking the weapon' assigned to 'the
adjutant'; 'D's shout' taking the form of 'a command').

How does our imaginary artist set about finding a fact that combines the required functions? Let us suppose that he has to find a
COMBINATION for 'greeting' and 'encirclement'. For this he has, on
the one hand, to scan all possible modes of 'greeting'—'shaking
hands', 'bowing', 'kissing hands', and so on—and on the other hand,
the possible modes of 'encirclement', that is, the situations that contain its distinctive features, as for instance the 'outline of an enclosing
circle'. We get 'a greeting by embrace' with the priest's arms joining
behind D.'s back. The episode of the removal of the sword (ex. (5)) is
achieved in just the same way: the distinctive feature of 'disarming' is
isolated—'removal of weapon'—and then from all the possible ways
of removing a weapon there is selected the one that is congruent with
the situation of 'greeting'—"After a ceremonial introduction and before a banquet, before sitting down to table, it would be customary to
remove weapons." We can imagine searching through the dictionary
in reverse as well: from all the possible modes of 'behavior at a reception' choose the one involving the 'removal of a weapon.' In all these

cases the look-up procedure is made up of two steps: (*a*) each of the initial facts (on the higher level) is realized in many ways as facts of a lower, more concrete, level; (*b*) the logical product of these realizations is selected.

Thus, the requirements imposed on the organization of the dictionary of reality by COMBINATION are the same as for CONCRETIZATION: an abstract fact has to be mapped onto all its more concrete forms. In addition, for those cases where some fact has already been preselected (for instance, 'a door'), and it has to be transformed in some way to achieve CONCORD, we need to have at our disposal all the "synonymous" variants of the fact on the same level of concreteness ('an ordinary door', 'a door with a platform', etc.).

Finally, the fact being sought does not in all cases have to be stored in its ready-made form in the dictionary. Thus at the intersection of 'encirclement', 'greeting', and 'the priest's intermediate position between D. and the Frenchmen', his role of 'drawing D. into the encirclement' is defined; that is, one further, new characteristic is added to those he already has as an object. Clearly, in a case of this sort we do not require a dictionary, but a number of rules and conditions permitting us to assign to him this new characteristic.

The last operation I will mention is that of SUDDEN TURN (which is, in fact, a complex combination of almost all the previous operations—a COMBINATION of two CONTRASTING AUGMENTATIONS): The mise-en-scène shows how the officers gradually surround D. and how "this gradual constriction, this inability to get away, literally flings D. up onto the table" and out the window (Nizhny 1979:32). SUDDEN TURN is usually used at moments of climax (particularly in the short story) where a "natural" and "unexpected" (note Eisenstein's stress on these words in ex. 6 and elsewhere) denouement must be provided.

3

The operations I have listed constitute only one part of the system of expressive devices worked out by Eisenstein. I may not have examined them in the best way possible or proposed any classification or hierarchical ordering for them. Thus, some operations clearly must be counted as obligatory for a particular genre: for instance, SUDDEN TURN is obligatory in the short story. For these and other reasons, the operations I am proposing are primarily of heuristic value.

To represent the generation of the mise-en-scène from the initial script more vividly, I will trace the "transformational history" of some of its elements, indicating which operations are involved. The "derivational process" goes through a number of steps with each step achieving a successive approximation to the final text. Thus not only the definitive mise-en-scène but all the intermediate results and even the initial formulation may be regarded as deep (nonterminal) representations of the actual text.

In the fragment of derivation that follows, the initial script is deliberately simplified. Each approximation is followed by the operation that transforms it into the next, more detailed one which is closer to the final text. In each approximation those elements that are to be operated upon are marked by numbers in angle brackets.

F = the Frenchmen, D = Dessalines.

The initial theme: *F try to seize D* ⟨1⟩. *D runs away and raises an uprising against F* ⟨2⟩. Operation: ECSTATIC DEVELOPMENT from ⟨1⟩ to ⟨2⟩ yields

Approximation I: *A group of white F tries to seize* ⟨2⟩ *D, a black, by a trick* ⟨1⟩. *D gets away and, rousing the whole black population of the island to open revolt, seizes F.* Operation: COMBINATION of ⟨1⟩ and ⟨2⟩ results in

Approximation II: *F surround D at a reception* ⟨1⟩, *D gets away and, rousing a revolt, seizes F* ⟨2⟩. Operation: CONTRAST of ⟨1⟩ and ⟨2⟩ →

Approximation III: *F surround D at a reception* ⟨1⟩, *D gets away* ⟨2⟩ *and, together with the Negroes in revolt encircles F.* Operation: SUDDEN TURN from ⟨1⟩ to ⟨2⟩ →

Approximation IV: *F squeeze D into an encircling ring and in so doing drive him to a sudden exit. D gets away,* etc. Operation: CONCRETIZATION of elements 'reception' and 'seizure-encirclement' →

Approximation V: *. . . the host* ⟨1⟩ *awaits his guests* ⟨2⟩, *greets them* ⟨3⟩, *introduces them to each other* ⟨4⟩, *offers them drinks* ⟨5⟩, *the guests chat* ⟨6⟩ *. . . F organize a conspiracy* ⟨7⟩, *begin to surround D* ⟨8⟩, *disarm him* ⟨9⟩, *tighten the encircling ring* ⟨10⟩. *. . .* Operations: COMBINATION of ⟨1⟩, ⟨2⟩, and ⟨7⟩; ⟨1⟩, ⟨3⟩ and ⟨8⟩; ⟨1⟩, ⟨4⟩ and ⟨8⟩; ⟨1⟩, ⟨5⟩ and ⟨9⟩; and of ⟨6⟩ and ⟨10⟩, yields

Approximation VI: *. . . before D's arrival the host gives F instructions about surrounding D; the host embraces D; the host leads D into the circle of F; the host invites D to take a seat and remove his weapon: F do not let D get near the door by engaging him in conversation. . . .* Operation: CONCORD of the elements 'drive to sudden exit' (see IV) and 'do not let him get near the door' (VI) →

Approximation VII: *. . . F do not let D near the door and in so doing "propel"* ⟨1⟩ *him through the window.* Operation: INTENSIFIED REPETITION of ⟨1⟩ →

Approximation VIII: *. . . in not letting D get near the door* ⟨1⟩, *F "propel" D onto the table; in not letting D jump through the door from the table, F "propel" him through the window. . . .* Operation: REPETITION of ⟨1⟩ yields

Approximation IX: *. . . F do not let D get near door A, then door B, then door C. . . .*

If we write out the "text" generated in these nine steps in full, we get:

F organize a reception in order to unexpectedly seize D. Before he arrives the host of the house gives F instructions about surrounding D. D arrives. The host meets him, embraces him and leads him into the circle of F, thus starting the encirclement. The host invites D to sit down at the table and take off his weapon. At each attempt of D's to go up to doors A, B, and C, his path is blocked by F engaging him in a conversation. D, surrounded, jumps up onto the table in order to get to Door A, he is stopped, then he turns and jumps through the window. He gets away, raises an uprising of Negroes and encircles the F in the house.

This text is still a long way from the final mise-en-scène, but it is probably time to cut off the derivation, which I undertook only by way of illustration.

4

These, then, are the broad outlines of the workings of a mechanism for generating a text and the main operations involved. As we have seen, such traditional notions as script, or fabula ("what happened"), ideology (the author's attitude, the readers' feelings), and composition (devices) have found their place in this scheme of things and have acquired a "working" definition; so too have such things as "knowledge of life" and "creative imagination" (= the dictionary of reality). Thus the script and ideology turn out to be features of the input text, while operations and dictionary belong to the "poetic machine."

In order to make the analogy with the generative model as clear as possible, I have consciously oversimplified my account. I wanted to represent things as if the input consisted of an already formulated theme and material and as if the artistic construction were generated from these. In Eisenstein's lessons things were not quite like that. The fabula and the ideological orientation were not clearly distinct; from the start events were given in far more detail than I have represented them and the attitude toward them was not formulated at all; it was partly presumed to be self-evident and partly "read out," as it were, from the story line. Thus, from example (4) it is evident that the given events correlate with certain more general information that makes one think of a 'conflict between the people and their oppressors'. This realization leads, in turn, to the selection of ECSTATIC DEVELOPMENT as the most suitable means for embodying it.

Thus, we can say that Eisenstein was not engaged in merely *synthesizing* the mise-en-scène on the basis of ready-made input data, but in *translating*, as it were, a certain plot (i.e., also an artistic text, but in a different genre—that of narrative prose), extracting from it as he went along the initial data for synthesis. The problem of the form and nature of the initial input for text generation is one of the most difficult and, incidentally, has not been resolved in linguistics. It can probably be solved (in both linguistics and poetics) through the practical construction of many generative models. We may simply note the usefulness and the essentially generative character of the concept of "fabula," that is, *the artistic story line minus its artistry,* as introduced into poetics by Viktor Shklovsky and other Russian Formalists. The "practical" series was sharply contrasted with the "poetic" as a kind of raw material, not yet processed by art, or, in terms of modeling, as an input text.

Incidentally, as for subtracting expressive devices from the artistic text, the input does not always break down clearly into fabula and ideology, as the latter is, as it were, "dissolved in the events" from the start. It seems quite sensible to assume that this is often exactly how the idea for a work arises. To model this type of creative performance one should add to the poetic machine some mechanism for "distilling" ideology from facts—"creatively interpreting" the dry factual information. In this case only a kind of chronicle of events would be fed in as the input, while the ideology and the artistic construction would be created by the machine. Or one might imagine a mechanism into which would be fed only ideological stances, while, with the help of a special dictionary (not so very different from the one I have been considering) the mechanism itself would select a train of events for embodying the ideological views. Or one could try to model the kind of creative activity whereby an author has a fixed view of the world or a number of favorite ideas and strives to read them into those facts he learns about: at the input there are only events, the ideology is built, ready-made, into the program.[9] Finally, a system is conceivable that would have in its memory store (or would be able to develop) all possible ideologies and by sorting (or even itself constructing) various sequences of events, would attempt to process them using expressive devices until it arrived at an artistic construction that embodies one or another ideology.

Out of all these possible approaches I have chosen the simplest and most natural, corresponding to Eisenstein's view of art as a medium "for the expression of thoughts and the intensification of emotions," whereby "raw" facts are assembled into an artistic construction in accordance with an ideological attitude to those facts.

In spite of the many crude oversimplifications, one can hope that the outlined project for generative poetics may be of some theoretical value. It is clear that poetics, whether or not it aims at modeling, is bound to *analyze* works of art, that is, break them down into their elements. The correct breakdown should be the one that analyzes the work into those constituents from which one might then, according to certain general principles, put it together. It is just to such an approach that the generative principle and the operations and structure of Eisenstein's "poetic machine" seem to point.

Appendix
A Description of the Resulting Mise-en-Scène (see Fig. 1.1)

The time: evening. A hall. The table is covered with a tablecloth and set out with candelabras. There are officers all over the set. In Zone I is a group of officers with, in the center, a priest in a crimson cassock. From Door A an adjutant appears, he halts by the table and quietly gives the priest and officers a message. They whisper among themselves, then together with the priest move across to Zone II; some remain by the left-hand wall. There is an announcement from Door A: "General Dessalines!" A trio of officers of Dessalines' escort enter, and then another trio. The rear trio halts. D. continues forward. The front trio joins up with the officers who have stayed in Zone I. D. reaches the corner of the table and stops; the adjutant follows him and also stops. From Zone II the priest approaches, holds out his hand to be kissed, embraces D. D. does not look him in the eye. The priest leads D. over to the officers in Zone II and introduces them. They greet him. D. does not look them in the eye, they take up positions around him. One of the officers of his escort moves from Zone I nearer to Zone II. One of the officers gives a sign. The adjutant goes up to D. and wants to take his sword. D. does not give it up. The priest says that it is customary, "look, the adjutant will take it for you." D. without looking into their eyes, gives up his saber. The adjutant carries it, passing between all the officers toward Door A. One of the officers of the escort, following the saber with his eyes, goes from Zone II up to the officers in Zone I. He asks why D is behaving so strangely. The other tells him of D.'s vow never to look the colonizing

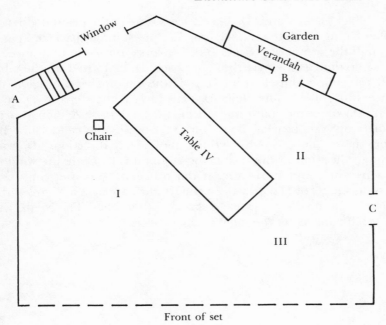

Figure 1.1. The setting of the Dessalines episode

French in the eye. A third says that he has good reason for mistrust, the saber was not taken away for nothing. From Door C a black serving-woman appears, she stops, the priest signals to her, she walks round in front of the group of officers and goes up with a bowl to D., who is talking to the priest and officers. Without looking, he holds out his hands; he doesn't encounter the bowl. The serving-woman leads him aside. This is repeated several times. D. looks at the serving-woman. She again turns aside with the bowl. D. moves away from the Frenchmen, stands with his back to the front of the set. The serving-woman's pantomime. D. turns sharply, his face is enraged. D. walks in a curve toward B.; of the five officers by the table three block D.'s way, D. manoeuvers toward Door C, three officers come to meet him with conversation, the others watch D. sideways. He goes straight to the table, begins a conversation with the priest and officers. One officer from Door C goes up to the two officers by the table and they block D.'s way. D. quickly goes in a straight line toward Door A. Three officers cut across his path. D. jumps up onto the table, seizes a candelabra. The priest at the head of the officers in Zone II advances on

51

him. "Back!" commands D. The officers retreat, the priest doesn't. D. makes a lunge with the candelabra. The priest jumps back and passes through the group of officers. The officers from Zone I advance. At the same time as the priest jumped back, D. had lifted up the table-cloth, shielding himself from Zone II; now he makes a lunge at the officers in Zone I. They halt. D. runs toward the steps by Door A, jumps down onto a chair; the officers by the door seize their swords; soldiers appear, bearing down on D. D. raises the candelabra and bangs it on the table. Everything flies in all directions. D. leaps through the window (a variant: the adjutant is blocking the window. D. seizes him and hurls him at the officers). A pause, confusion. Outside shouts of 'To arms!'. In the window appears a Negro with a torch. In all the doorways are Negroes with torches. The Negro with the torch runs along the table at the officers.

2

Deus ex Machina

... the unraveling of the plot ... must arise out of the plot itself, it must not be brought about by the *Deus ex Machina*.
—Aristotle (1961: 82)

This essay originated as a series of examples illustrating the idea that "a work of art is constructed of fragments of reality as a complex, multistep amplifier operating in and on the reader's mind. . . . The automatism of human imagination is tapped by the artist . . . as a reservoir . . . of energy that permits him to bring our thoughts and emotions to the exact points of an itinerary which is the work's plot" [1962d: 169–70].

According to Aristotle, a story line can develop either naturally, by itself, or with the help of a machine, the latter choice (deus ex machina) being less desirable. It is my thesis that any artistic text is a machine working on the reader: a "machine" not only in the figurative sense, but in the strictly cybernetic sense as well—as a transforming device.

One way to substantiate this thesis is to point out the many plots actuated and resolved by machines made of iron, cogs, wheels, and so on. The device is then laid bare: the role of the "plot machine" is played by a "machine proper"; the essence of the artistic mechanism crystallizes into a tangible, solid construction. As a result, the denouement can both logically follow from the plot (Aristotle) and rely on a machine—provided the latter is well built into the plot.

This chapter is a revised version of [1967b].

1. Physical Machines

In "The Lovely Lady," by D. H. Lawrence (1955: 761–78), a strong-willed and jealous mother keeps her son from marrying his cousin Cecily. One day Cecily, while sunbathing on the roof of a remote manor house, hears a mysterious voice that turns out to be the mother's, transmitted, distorted, and amplified by a water pipe. The mother imagines that she is talking to her elder son, who died when he was quite young after she had refused to let him marry the girl he loved, and she tries to justify herself. In the denouement, Cecily secures the mother's consent by talking to her through the same water pipe, which transmits Cecily's voice as if it were that of the dead son.

In this case the machine—the water pipe as a loudspeaker—is the central mover of the action. Moreover, it is both physically built into the house's masonry and emotionally fitted to the gothic atmosphere of the story—a nice complement to the remote manor, the mysterious and beautiful old woman living off the souls of her sons, the skeletons in the closet, the psychological warfare between the protagonists, and so on.

One of the machine's plot functions in this story is to betray the thoughts of one character to another. This function is embodied in a tangible and powerful amplifier—the water pipe turned megaphone. In other cases the same function can be carried out by less-evident mechanisms: instead of a loudspeaker the plot will use an aperture in a wall; or, the physical wall removed, the plot will have a character overhear a conversation between two people who do not know him and so speak quite openly in his presence. Note, that in this case both functions, that of the wall (something that separates) and that of the aperture (something that connects), are still there, effected as they are by other means of plot mechanics: they do not know him (= 'the wall'), he is there and knows them (= 'the aperture'). In still less physical cases, a character may guess another's hidden thoughts from indirect clues highlighted by other circumstances.

It is thus clear that the physical reification of the artistic mechanism has many grades. In this section I am interested in cases of extreme crystallization. This focus, however, does not imply that a real machine necessarily serves a plot structure better than one assembled out of human relations—it is just a more graphic manifestation of the principle.

Elaborating a film episode about a Haitian revolutionary, Eisenstein (Nizhny 1979: 19–62, and Chap. 1 of the present volume) devised a mise-en-scène in which the circle of enemies surrounding the hero gradually closed in, first forcing him onto a table that led across the stage to the window, then chasing him along the table, and finally propelling him, as it were, out the window and to an unforeseen salvation. In an earlier draft of the mise-en-scène, however, the hero "escapes from encirclement by clinging to a huge mechanical fan that carries him right across the table as far as the window ledge. A complete detailed plan of the fan is there, with its construction. But on almost the last page, in the margin, is scrawled: 'Too far-fetched!'" (Nizhny 1979: 91–92).

Eisenstein finally replaced the "far-fetched" solution (typical of innumerable adventure films) with a more organic one. But what happened? The functions of the mechanical fan were transferred to the mechanism of the dramatic action—the manoeuvers, clashes, and movements of the characters—and, as a result, the hero described exactly the same trajectory as Eisenstein had originally envisaged.

What makes machines so convenient for artistic purposes? A machine is designed with a specific function in mind, has its characteristic "moves," realizes a preprogrammed course of action, connects certain points in the space of human activity. And what it does, it does infallibly, automatically, with an "iron" certainty. That is why the role played by a machine is often predictable. A gun must fire; a horse, car, or train can be ridden; a wheel turns; and so on.

In Jack London's story "Diable, a Dog" (1960: 353–72), a man and a dog are old enemies. One day the man commits a crime, and the people in the camp try, convict, and sentence him to death. The noose has already been put around his neck when the people have to hurry away to deal with an emergency. The dog, however, stays behind and pushes away the hanging block.

Gallows are for hanging. There is a whole class of plots based on similar trigger-effects. Pulling a trigger or pressing a button that releases a powerful mechanism is a pure case of amplification, a typical manifestation of the machine's aesthetic potential.

In the English film *There Was a Crooked Man*, a long comic sequence lays this stock device bare—an orgy of pressing entire keyboards of buttons with a finger, a palm, both hands, feet, which leads to the destruction of a city.

2. Social and Linguistic Machines

If a machine is not cast of real iron, it is often forged out of social conventions (rules, customs, etc.)[1] which can be just as inexorable. A close parallel to the Jack London story is found in the ending of Marcel Carné's film *Thérèse Raquin* (script by C. Spaak), though not in Émile Zola's novel.

A blackmailer warns the heroes that in case of his sudden death the police will receive a letter denouncing their crime. The blackmailer then dies in an accident and his maidservant keeps her promise to mail the letter if he is not back by the appointed hour.

There is a whole chain of social triggers in this plot: the black-mailer's death sets in motion the instruction given to the servant and the contract binding her; the mechanism of the mail service will deliver the letter to the district attorney; he will start the machine of the law; and so on. Structurally, all these machines function in the same way as the gallows. Their parts are welded together so firmly that they automatically relay action in a given direction up to a given point. An object, an action, and so on, once fed to the machine's "input," is quickly and without fail delivered to the "output."

What would counterparts of such machines *in the verbal sphere* be like? Any kind of idiomatic (i.e., set, ready-made) collocations in the broad sense—proverbs, aphorisms, quotations, myths, and other unchangeable texts, linguistic situations in which having said A one cannot help saying B. Here is a plot, once read and always remembered by Yury Olesha:

"An engineer . . . is constructing a 'time machine' capable of going into the future as well as the past. Once, while he is occupied with calculations in his study, his two sons penetrate the workshop, where his contrivance already stands completed. . . . Hearing voices, he rushes into the shop, but, alas, he is too late: the shop is empty. . . . The engineer is in despair. . . . And then begins the construction of a kind of magnet possessing, so to speak, the power of drawing the machine back from the reaches of time. . . . Then it is finished. . . . The engineer turns the levers and steps back in fright: with a crash a Roman in beard and cuirass falls to the ground in front of him. . . . 'Father,' the Roman whispers. . . . 'Is it you? . . . But where is your brother?' . . . And . . . the son says: 'Father, I was Romulus'."

Olesha concludes that "the action of the magnet was that lightning during whose discharge the great Romulus—in his time a fratricide—was taken up to heaven" (Olesha 1979: 237).

In this plot the principle is pushed to the extreme. Almost the entire course of events is "automated," entrusted to machines—from the moment the boys get into the time machine up to the denouement. The first of the two physical machines takes the heroes into the past, placing them exactly at the input of the "mythological machine"—the legend of Romulus and Remus. The second arrives precisely in time (at the moment of Romulus's death) to receive him at the output (Olesha stresses the flawless fitting of the machines) and deliver him back to his father and the readers.

The operation of the mythological machine is very prominent in this plot. Thanks to the fantastic time machines, the characters *become* the heroes of the quoted legend. In less ingenious cases of quotation the author will confine himself to *comparing* his heroes with those of a ready-made text. The comparison itself may be more or less pronounced. One of the more explicit strategies is the so-called "play within a play" (cf. the classic "mousetrap" in *Hamlet* or the "Fiery-furnace play" (*Peščnoe dejstvo*) in Eisenstein's *Ivan the Terrible*).

Quite often a machine achieves a comic effect, for example, when it does something undesirable to a hero who cannot stop it precisely because it is an automaton. For physical machines, see the classic case of Charlie Chaplin dragged into an assembly line (*Modern Times*). As for linguistic machines, the same structural principle seems to underlie some of the comic effects in Zoščenko's style: phraseological collocations automatically, as it were, "carry" the speaker further than necessary, for example, "Is it possible that science makes such a Kursk anomaly in its laws?" ("A scientific phenomenon"). The word "Kursk" is out of place in this sentence; only "anomaly" is meant, but the semiliterate narrator cannot help using the prestigious expression of the times.[2]

3. "Ready-made" Objects: Natural and Other Machines

A legend is a "ready-made," preprogrammed event; proverbs and quotes are "ready-made" statements; a real machine is a "ready-made" movement, action, transformation. They are all amplifiers, buttons one has only to reach. The author embeds them in the plot whenever he wants to "conjoin remote" ideas or objects.[3] A character at a distance learns the secret thought of another; a dog executes a man; and so on. Embodying a thematic program in one whole, graphic, and familiar object that carries it out thoroughly and without fail is an essential characteristic of artistic thinking—"thinking in images". A machine is merely the clearest manifestation of the principle.

Therefore, alongside machines we find various ready-made objects, whose function is to bridge gaps between remote ideas or situations.

As for gap bridging in the literal sense, a spectacular example is provided by a scene in chapter 9 of Conan Doyle's *The Lost World*. In order to get across a gorge, the heroes fell a tree that reaches exactly to the opposite side. Later this ready-made bridge is used by their adversary, who cuts them off by throwing it down the abyss.

Most machines ensure a gain either in force or in information. "Machines of force" make possible something that seems physically unfeasible, for example, various types of triggers, including the gallows in the Jack London story and Eisenstein's fan. One subclass comprises "murder machines," for example, the powerful hydraulic press in Conan Doyle's "The Engineer's Thumb", or the special trapbed with a canopy that comes down noiselessly to stifle the guest in "The Traveler's Story of a Terrible Strange Bed" by Wilkie Collins. Some machines of force are supplied by the world of nature, for example, such ready-made objects as a river, a precipice, or a wild beast.

In Buster Keaton's film *Our Hospitality*, the hosts want to kill their guest, but custom forbids doing so inside the house. Therefore, while indoors, they entertain him properly, but once he steps outside they start shooting at him. The hero tries to escape by riding on horseback, going down the river in a boat, and boarding a train; he fails and has to run back into the house, where there is again a friendly talk; another chase ensues, and so on.

This plot, like the one recalled by Olesha, is an anthology of various machines (social: convention of hospitality; natural: river, horse; machines proper: guns, train). They are arranged into a sort of automatic assembly line along which the action is passed.

"Information machines" are ready-made entities designed to provide knowledge, to find hidden roads and objects. For example, the role of the water pipe in the Lawrence story, the belt that leads the snake to its victims in Conan Doyle's "The Poison Belt", the thread of Ariadne, all kinds of underground passages—as well as more complicated mechanisms of detection, such as Hamlet's mousetrap—are all information machines.

4. Magical and Mixed Machines

Fairy-tale plots often use as machines and ready-made objects various supernatural forces, so to speak, "magic machines". Machines and amplifiers are aesthetically so attractive because, for one reason, they seem to "violate the law of the conservation of energy, . . . producing the impression of magic. . . . The always desirable magic consists precisely in achieving miraculous results by small, in fact, token efforts" [1962d: 169]. If a machine used in a plot is a reification of the art's mechanics, then the use of sorcery is a literal realization of art's magic: in the former case it is the *machina* that is laid bare, in the latter, the *deus*!

Fairy tales use such magic machines of force as flying carpets, seven-league boots, drugs that turn people into birds or dwarfs or bring the dead back to life, various means of fulfilling any number of wishes, and so on, as well as information machines: magic balls of thread, mirrors, omniscient birds or horses, and so forth. Where real machines are missing, fancy creates magic ones to meet the demands of the plot for ready-made amplifiers.

Hybrid formations are also possible. Thus, Conan Doyle's famous hound of the Baskervilles is a natural machine perfected with the help of a technical device (a phosphorescent dye). In science-fiction plots, machines are half-real, half-magic. Magic machines often combine the properties of physical, social, and linguistic machines, for example, when a magic device is set in action (stopped) by the observance or violation of some convention, for example, a linguistic one.

In the plot of Wilhelm Hauff's tale "The Caliph-Stork," much depends on a certain magic powder. "Whoever snuffs of the powder in this box, and at the same time says, in a low tone, 'Mutabor,' can change himself into any animal he chooses, and will also understand the language of brutes. Should he wish to return to his human form again, let him bow thrice towards the east and repeat the same word. But when he is transformed, let him beware lest he laugh; for, should he do so, the magic word will instantly vanish from his memory, and he will remain an animal forever" (Hauff 1858: 20).

Thus, very sophisticated rules of behavior are set forth, whose observation is controlled by a magic drug instead of by a social machine of coercion (as, for example, in *Thérèse Raquin*).

5. A Universal Plot Machine and Denouement Machines

One is, of course, tempted to think of a machine that would alone do all the plot work. Such a machine would, however, completely replace and thus cancel the plot—it should then be built and used rather than described in a literary text. In fact, such artistic machines *are* produced. As far as physical machines are concerned, there are merry-go-rounds, Ferris wheels, and the like—all of which enable the user to run a certain course, complete with beginning, peripeteia, culmination, and denouement. Compare also mazes and other attractions that involve itineraries, for example, those amusement-park rides (notably, in Disneyland) which take you downhill or downstream, past and across various ready-made landscapes, scenes, and happenings. As for social machines based on conventions, lottery games and the like suggest themselves as parallels.

Viktor Shklovsky has compared plot structures to board games like Monopoly and Risk. "The creators of the adventure novel themselves turned attention to this analogy; and in Jules Verne's *Testament of a Strange Man* the . . . accidents and adventures of the heroes are motivated by the fact that they must go where the dice indicate; moreover, the map of the United States of America is divided into squares and becomes the playing board" (Shklovsky 1973: 64).

In the absence of a machine that covers the entire course of action, let us settle for a reasonable approximation of such a universal plot machine. Theoretically speaking, a plot structure can be "reduced" to its nucleus, or central effect. Such a culmination is usually a concatenation of events, which first go in one direction (e.g., for the worse), but then at a decisive turning point lead to the opposite result: a hidden mechanism produces a spectacular reversal. In a sense, such "culmination machines" can be said to *represent the plot mechanism as a whole*. Predictably, most of them are some sort of rotating device— wheels in the broad sense of the word.

In a film based on Eugène Sue's *Les mystères de Paris,* the hero at one point is trapped inside a mill that is filling with water. He tries to escape by setting the wheel in motion. Just when he finds himself directly under the mill wheel, it comes to a momentary standstill, but then passes the dead point and carries him upward to safety.

A similar example comes close to the ideal of a plot completely determined by a wheel:

A medieval illustration to one of the *Carmina Burana* (the poem *Fortunae plango vulnera* . . . "I am lamenting the wounds inflicted by fortune . . . ") shows the wheel of fortune representing the entire circle of human destiny: a man is carried up, the inscription says *regnabo* 'I will reign'; he is at the top of the wheel: *regno* 'I am reigning'; he is carried down: *regnavi* 'I reigned'; under the wheel: *sum sine regno* 'I am without a realm'.

As in other cases, there are less pronounced manifestations of the same principle. For instance, the reversal can use simple ready-made physical objects such as a rock with a gradual ascent and then an abrupt precipice, or more complicated constructions—"mixed reversal machines." The latter combine ready-made psychological motives with ready-made social and physical mechanisms; recall the Eisenstein episode in which the hero is forced first into retreat and then into escape by attacks from all sides but one—the life-saving window (see Chap. 1).

6. Postscript

In [1967b] I summarized my point as follows:

1. The series of limiting cases illustrates the view of the artistic mechanism as a self-evident object that efficiently realizes the given functions.
2. This view corresponds well with the functional approach developed by Shklovsky (1929, 1965, 1969, 1973), Propp (1958), Tynyanov (1963), and Eisenstein (1964–70, 1968, 1975a,b, see also Nizhny 1979), Lévi-Strauss (1960, 1963), and Mazel' (1978).
   I would now add the following:
3. The machines' efficiency (i.e., their amplifying effect) comes, in PE terms, under the heading of expressiveness; more specifically, under that of ED of SUDDEN TURN (see Glossary), that engineers a transition between something improbable and its realization.
4. In my examples the magical equation 'little = much' usually occurs twice. *Syntagmatically*, some 'small' quantity (mother's whisper; dog's actions) is converted into a 'large' one (loud, far-reaching, important speech; execution of a man). *Paradigmatically*, one simple compact object ('little') covers a set of apparently incompatible plot functions ('much'); even when only one function is embodied, something abstract, unreal, hard-to-believe ('much') is converted into a simple, tangible, indisputable reality ('little'). This essay uses the rarer and more special syntagmatic equation as a metaphor for the more essential paradigmatic one.

5. In the paradigmatic sense, *the "machine" is a complex ready-made sign: a sign*, as it is a part of the dictionary of reality and culture (DR), shared by the author and the reader (cf. the remarks in Godzich 1978: 395, on [1978f]); *complex*, if it combines several functions; and *ready-made*, because it constitutes a single entry in the DR. It is the combination of complexity with unity that accounts for the artistic "magic" that makes the reader "swallow" the ready-made object at one gulp.

6. The concept of a complex ready-made construct was patterned in part on the linguist's conception of *word as a complex unit*. Recent developments seem to confirm the fundamental role played by ready-made ("printed") schemata in human perception, knowledge, and so on (the frames and scripts in artificial intelligence research [Minsky 1975; Schank and Abelson 1977]), in linguistic competence (the "questionnaires" of lexical functions in the "Meaning–Text" model of language [Mel'čuk 1974, 1981; Mel'čuk and Zholkovsky 1970]), and in semiotic poetics (the hypograms and descriptive systems [Riffaterre 1978]).

3

Thematic Invariance and the
Concept of "Poetic World"

1. The "-ian"

Readers familiar with an author are able to perceive in a given text not only its immediate message, but also the more comprehensive—if more abstract and elusive—outlook characteristic of the author's entire oeuvre. Critics account for this by speaking of the author's *poetic world* (PW)—an intuitive, but consistent notion that I will try to explicate in this chapter.[1]

From discussions of the single message of an author's oeuvre, several basic characteristics seem to emerge.

1. Attention is drawn to *repetitiousness*, which is praised, not censured. "Shakespeare's work is a whole and he is everywhere true to himself. He is recognizable by his vocabulary. Certain of his characters appear under different names in play after play, and he sings the same song over and over to different tunes. . . . Then, with a tangible certainty . . . the translator becomes aware of the personality of Shakespeare and his genius" (Pasternak 1959b: 141–42). "Why should the repetition of the images of the garden and the Muse in my poems be seen as mannered? On the contrary, in order to reach the core, one must study the 'nests' of constantly repeated images in the poet's verses—it is in them that the personality of the author and the spirit of his poetry are hidden" (Anna Akhmatova, see Čukovskaja 1976: 149).

This chapter is based on material in [1976c and 1977b].

2. The repetitions testify to a *unity*, a *system*, cf. item 1 above and also: "verses, good and bad, do not exist, but there are only good and bad poets, that is, whole systems of thought, which are either productive or which spin in the void." (Pasternak 1959a: 91).

3. The system is a *hierarchy* of invariant entities which can be discovered by a sequence of generalizations about the repetitions. "When from the fabric of a *Madame Bovary*, we gradually, one after another, subtract characters, their development, situations, occurrences, the plot, the subject, the content. . . The second-rate diverting literature will leave no remainder after such a subtraction. But the real creation lets remain the *cardinal:* the characterization of reality as such; almost as of a philosophic category; as a member or link of our mind's universe" (Pasternak 1960: 4). Although Pasternak speaks of the oeuvre of a whole literary epoch, the same seems applicable to a single poet. "In the multiform symbolism of a poetic oeuvre we find certain constant organizing . . . elements which are the vehicles of unity in the multiplicity of the poet's works and stamp these works with the poet's individuality. These elements introduce the totality of a poet's individual *mythology* into the variegated tangle of often divergent and unrelated poetic motifs; they make poems by Pushkin—Pushkin's, those by Mácha—truly Mácha's, those by Baudelaire—Baudelairean" (Jakobson 1975: 1).

4. These generalizations relate the formal characteristics of the author's style to his deep *thematic values*—compare above "the spirit of his poetry," "the philosophical category," "the coherent mythology," and so on. "What we call the splendor and vividness of description is not a feature imputed merely to style, but something far greater, namely, the presence of a new conception and the philosophic sense of life's own oneness and wholeness" (Kayden 1959: vii).

5. This specific world view pervades the author's works and is in some form or other an *obligatory*, if *unconscious*, presence in his every episode, image, line. "This material, accumulated in Pushkin's spirit, constitutes several intuitive and indubitable certainties (*uverennostej*), which are logically connected as if by cobweb threads and form a sort of system. . . . Pushkin's principal idea was like a canon which was always followed obediently, willy-nilly, by his artistic perception" (Geršenzon 1919: 13–14).

In other words, the notion of an author's poetic world is supposed to capture what is common to all his works and distinguishes them from those of others, his specifically "-ian" element—the Shake-spearean, the Pushkinian, the Tolstoyan. The "-ian" is envisaged as the hierarchy of obligatory thematic invariants that underlies the repetitions. The question now arises: How and in what terms does one formulate it?

One extreme is complete renunciation of any metalanguage. The poet and critic Andrey Bely pictured every poet by what he called a "composite quotation" (*sbornaja citata*) from his works (Mandelstam 1970: 66). Anna Akhmatova's poem "Boris Pasternak" seems to furnish an example: it portrays a fellow poet with an entire anthology of authentic and simulated quotations referring to his favorite images, objects, syntactic and compositional structures, and so on. The point of this method is to capture the poet's spirit by not relinquishing the letter of his texts.[2]

Academic criticism ventures, more or less timidly, toward the other extreme—the conscious development of an appropriate meta-language. I am going to take this latter course, believing that its advantages can be gained without losing the quotational method's grip on real texts.

I begin by considering—in a sketchy way—two sets of examples—from Pasternak and from Pushkin.

2. Extracting the Pasternakian

The chase after the "-ian" starts with catching the poet at repetitions. In Pasternak they are no less striking than in Shakespeare. Consider these examples:

(1) (a) Ne znaja vašix strof,
No poljubiv istočnik,
Ja ponimal bez slov
Vaš buduščij podstročnik.

Not knowing your stanzas,
But having come to love the source,
I understood without words
Your future interlinear.

(b) V rodstve so vsem, čto est', uverjas
I znajas' s buduščim v bytu . . .

Having made sure of one's kinship
with all there is
And being familiar with the future
in everyday life . . .

(c) V ego ustax zvučalo "zavtra,"
Kak na ustax inyx "včera" . . .

In his lips "tomorrow" sounded
As in the lips of others,
"yesterday" . . .

Outline of the Theory

(d) Ja vižu . . .
Vsju buduščuju žizn' naskvoz'.
Vse do mel'čajšej doli sotoj
V nej opravdalos' i sbylos'.

I see . . .
All the future life throughout.
Everything down to the smallest one
  hundredth
Has come true and materialized in
  it.

(2) (a) Net vremeni u vdoxnoven'ja.
  Boloto,
Zemlja li, il' more, il' luža—
Mne zdes' snoviden'e javilos' i ščëty
Svedu s nim sejčas že i tut že.

Inspiration has no time. A swamp,
Or ground, or sea, or a puddle—
It is here that the dream visited me
  and scores
With it I will settle now and here.

(b) Kak vdrug on vyros na tribune
I vyros ran'še, čem vošël.

When suddenly he appeared on the
  podium,
And appeared earlier than entered.

(c) Najdis' v èto vremja minuta svobody
U list'ev, kornej, i vetvej, i stvola,
Uspeli b vmešat'sja zakony prirody,
No čudo est' čudo i čudo est' bog.
Kogda my v smjaten'i, togda sred'
  razbroda
Ono nastigaet mgnovenno, vrasplox.

Should there be at that time a
  moment of freedom,
At the disposal of the leaves, the
  roots, and the branches, and
  the trunk,
The laws of nature would have had
  the time to interfere.
But a miracle is a miracle and a
  miracle is God.
When we are in agitation, then
  amidst the confusion
It hits us immediately, unprepared.

(3) (a) Primostjas' na tvoem podokonnike,
Smotrim vniz s tvoego neboskrëba;

Nesting on your windowsill
We are looking down from your
  skyscraper;

(b) On svešivaetsja v okno;

He is leaning out the window;

(c) V detstve ja, kak sejčas ešče pomnju,
Vysuneš'sja, byvalo, v okno . . .

In childhood, I remember it as now,
One used to lean out of the
  window . . .

(d) V kašne, ladon'ju zaslonjas',
Skvoz' fortku kriknu detvore:
Kakoe, milye, u nas
Tysjačelet'e na dvore?

In a scarf, covering myself with my
  palm,
I will shout to the kids through a
  casement window:
My darlings, which
Millennium is there in our
  courtyard?

(4) (a) O bože, volnenija slëzy
Mešajut mne videt' tebja.

O my Lord, the tears of agitation
Prevent me from seeing you.

(b) On mery razoren'ja
Ne zamečaet iz-za slëz
I pristupa migreni.

The degree of destruction
He cannot notice because of tears
And an attack of headache.

(c) Šarju i ne naxožu sandalij,
Ničego ne vižu iz-za slëz.
Na glaza mne pelenoj upali
Prjadi raspustivšixsja volos.

I grope but cannot find the sandals,
Can see nothing because of tears.
Over my eyes in a veil fell
Locks of my disheveled hair.

Similarities are many, especially within each set. The next step is "subtraction"—as suggested by Pasternak himself: abstracting from differences between examples, let us take down—in plain prose—their similarities.

All the fragments cited in (1) share situation (5):

(5) The poet feels very much at ease in the future.

The common denominator of the examples in (2) can be formulated as:

(6) A historical man of genius acts instantly, faster than natural processes.

Whether we will be able to come up with all the relevant generalizations depends on the order of grouping: a set of examples with minimal differences yields the richest common denominator. Thus, the invariant of (3a–c) is:

(7) A man is at the window, leans, and looks out.

Taking into account (3d) as well, we obtain a more abstract generalization:

(8) A man inside the room is at the window, looks out, and through an open aperture addresses the outside.

The same strategy of minimal steps could have been applied to (1). Note an especially close similarity between (1c) and (1d). In both:

(9) The future sounds, in a poet's speech, as familiar as the past.

67

Only (1c) states this in the third person (about Pushkin), whereas (1d) makes it happen in Pasternak's own text by having a past verb CON-CORD with the noun "future." Invariant (9) is intermediate between the "raw" texts (1a–d) and the more abstract generalization (5).

Thus, a hierarchy of abstractions emerges. The next logical step is to turn, for further generalizations, to the obtained constructs themselves. For instance, (5) and (6) yield:

(10) A genius (in art; in history) works miracles with time (penetrates into the future; acts instantly).

Compared with (8), instead of (6), the same situation (5), displays another relevant feature—'contact'.

(11) A man who is in one part of an important sphere of reality (temporally, in the present; spatially, inside a house) is in contact with the rest of the sphere (the future; the outside world)

Thus, (5) combines two still more abstract invariants—(10) and (11), represented separately in (6) and (8), respectively. Another instance of such a combination is (3d); so far it has been considered only under the heading (8) 'contact in space', whereas in fact, it involves a 'contact' between the given moment and whole "millennia."

The network of logical relations discovered, in the course of sub-traction, between the actual fragments and the underlying thematic invariants can be roughly schematized as in Figure 3.1.

Comparisons must continue to cover all other sets of repetitions, e.g., (4), which would yield:

(12) Intense agitation causes an obstruction of vision.

This, in turn, should lead, ideally, to more and more abstract gen-eralizations: 'intense emotional state obstructing perception' → 'over-poweringly intense states' → 'intense states' → . . . At this point com-parison with 'miracle' would result in an abstraction like 'intensity, magnificence', which, together with 'contact', seems to constitute the highest level of generalization—that of Pasternak's most abstract, and yet quite specific, invariant theme:

(13) Θinv: unity and magnificence of existence.[3]

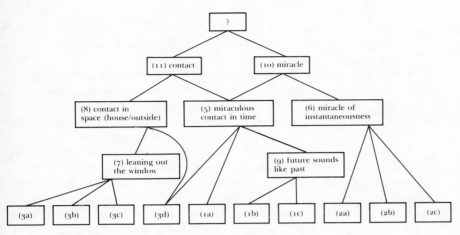

Figure 3.1. Pasternak's PW: A fragment reconstructed

3. Extracting the Pushkinian

Consider the examples:

(14) (a) Tvoj kon' [. . .]
To smirnyj stoit pod strelami
vragov,
To mčitsja po brannomu polju;

Your horse [. . .]
Now stands quiet under the
enemies' arrows,
Now rushes along the battlefield;

(b) Kak bystro v pole, vkrug otkrytom,
Podkovan vnov', moj kon' bežit;

How fast in the field, open all
around,
Newly shod, my horse is running;

(c) Vedut ko mne konja, v razdolii
otkrytom
Maxaja grivoju, on vsadnika neset.

They bring me [my] horse; in an
open expanse
Tossing his mane, he carries the
horseman.

(d) Idët. Emu konja podvodjat.
Retiv i smiren vernyj kon',
Počuja rokovoj ogon',
Drožit. Glazami koso vodit
I mčitsja v praxe boevom,
Gordjas' moguščim sedokom.

He walks. They bring him [his]
horse.
Zealous and quiet is the faithful
horse,
Having smelled the fateful fire,
He trembles. He lets his eyes rove
slantwise

And rushes across the dust of the battle,
Proud of his mighty rider.

I will ignore, for the moment, all the obvious affinities between (14a–d) (all are concerned with the dynamics of horseback riding and use the same verbs, epithets, and metaphors: "open," "zealous," "quiet," "rushes," "carries," "tossing his mane," etc.) and concentrate on more specific similarities between the four fragments.

In (14a,b) the picture frame includes only the 'horse'. His movement is presented as completely autonomous, although wider context makes it clear that both 'horse and horseman' are meant. Yet, the literal meaning of (14a,b) is: 'a horse without a rider rushing along the field'. In (14b) this splitting of the 'horse' from the 'rider' is intensified by the fact that the 'rider' coincides with the speaker (the first person, 'I'), who, as it were, observes from afar the movements of the third person (the 'horse'). In fact, the same is partly true also of (14a), where the 'rider' coincides with the second person ("Your horse . . ."): language opposes the first and the second persons as the participants of the speech event, which takes place "here," to the third person as a nonparticipant of the speech event but a participant of the narrated event, which takes place "there." Thus, in both (14a,b) the 'rider' is not only excluded from the picture encompassed by the poet's vision but is also opposed to the 'horse' through the point-of-view technique.

Unlike (14a,b), (14c) states clearly that the 'horse' does not just race by himself but in fact carries the 'rider'. However, the same paradox,

(15) a man presented as both riding a horse and watching it from afar,

is none the weaker: in (14c) the 'rider' plays at once two opposite grammatical roles—first person ("me") and third person ("the horseman"). The contrast is intensified by the omission of the transitional episode of 'mounting the horse'. This in turn brings about two other contrasts:

(16) abrupt switch in the direction of the horse's movement (first toward 'I', then toward some place in the distance, probably away from 'I');
(17) confrontation between the movements of the horse and the immobility of the observer ('I').

Fragment (14d) is less paradoxical, as the 'rider' appears only in the third person and is clearly distinct from the speaker. Instead, it is richer in dynamics and abrupt switches from immobility to movement and in the direction of movement of the type found in (16) and (17). In this it resembles many other Pushkin scenes, for example:

(18) I, vzvivšis', zanaves šumit [. . .]
Stoit Istomina; ona,
Odnoj nogoj kasajas' pola,
Drugoju medlenno kružit,
I vdrug pryžok, i vdrug letit,
Letit, kak pux ot ust Èola.

And, whirling up, the curtain rustles
[. . .]
There is Istomina standing; she,
Touching the floor with one foot,
Makes slow circles with the other,
And suddenly there is a leap, and suddenly she is flying,
Flying, like down from the mouth of Aeolus.

To return to (14d), almost all of its dynamics concern the horse: as in (14c) the 'mounting' is omitted, while the rider is represented as a passive object of the horse's activity ("rushes . . . proud of his . . . rider"). The rider's passivity is especially conspicuous against the "close-up" of the horse (we discern the play of his eyes). In other words, the invariant of (14c,d) is

(19) a man presented as both actively riding a horse and passively carried by it.

Let us now compare (19) with other scenes of transportation by horse:

(20) (a) Drug milyj, predadimsja begu
Neterpelivogo konja;

My darling, let us abandon
ourselves to the racing
Of the impatient horse [pulling a sleigh];

(b) I dremlja jedem do nočlega—
A vremja gonit lošadej.

And, drowsing, we ride [in a cart]
toward a night lodging—
While time drives on the horses.

The common denominator will be just

(21) passive riding.

'Passivity' or 'sleepiness', as in (20b), is often combined with 'activities' other than 'riding':

(22) Kačajas', lebed' na volne

Rocking, the swan on the waves

Zasnul [. . .]	Fell asleep [. . .]
Vo sne on parus razvivajet . . .	In his sleep, he [the fisherman]
I ryba sonnaja vpadaet	unfolds the sail . . .
V tjaželyj nevod starika.	And the fish, sleepy, falls
	Into the old man's heavy net.

Here

(23) Three agents (swan, fisherman, fish) move (rock, unfold the sail, fall into the net) in their sleep.

Consideration of other fragments, for example:

(24)	(a) Deva nad večnoj struej večno pečal'na sidit.	The maid over the eternal stream sits eternally sad.
	(b) I rečka podo l'dom blestit.	And the river glistens under the ice,

would lead us, via

(25) simultaneous immobility of one and movement of the other of two contiguous objects

and other intermediate generalizations (see Fig. 3.2), to Pushkin's central invariant theme:

(26) Θinv: ambivalent COMBINATION of changeability and unchangeability.[4]

Note, that in the course of subtraction, the specific affinities of (14a–d)—that is, their unusual perspectives and ways of representation, explicitly formulated in (15) and (19), have proved closely related to their more evident properties, the interplay of 'movement' and 'immobility', with which we at first did not want to be concerned but which we then formulated as (16) and (17). The Pushkinian image of 'horse and rider' is consistently based on (25) 'simultaneous combination of immobility and movement' inherent in this dual object (indeed, it is the horse that runs, whereas the rider is in a sense immobile). The effect is often supplemented with (16) and (17) 'dynamic switches and contrasts' and then set in relief by the effects of point of view and signification.

In other words, all the similarities observed in (14a–d) point in one direction: to the central invariant (26). In this respect invariants estab-

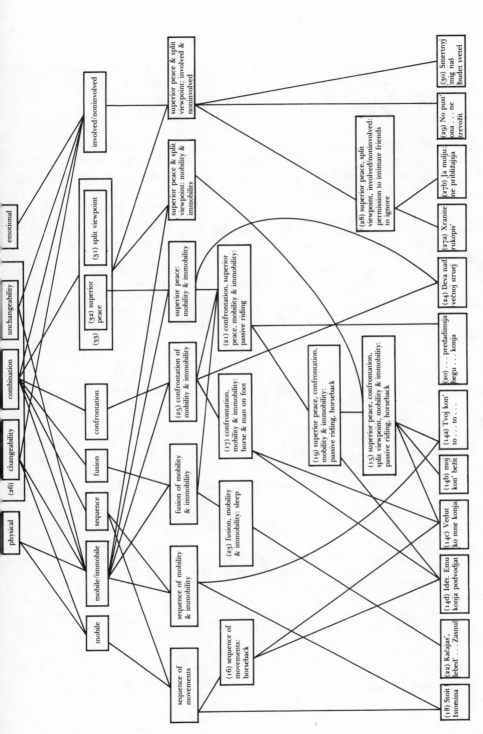

Figure 3.2. Pushkin's PW: A fragment reconstructed

lished in poetics differ from the invariants of linguistic theory. When a linguist, having considered a set of examples, emerges with an invariant (a grammatical category, a selectional restriction, etc.), he does not expect it to explain all the properties of every example. This reflects the fundamental difference between language and literature: whereas the former merely transmits meaning, the latter "infects" the reader with the theme by permeating the text with its manifestations.

To illustrate the point further, I will consider a completely different set of recurrences.

(27) (a) Ja plaxe obrečën . . .
Oplač'te, milye, moj žrebij v tišine;
Strašites' vozbudit' slezami
podozren'e [. . .]
Xranite rukopis', o drugi, dlja sebja!
Kogda groza projdet, tolpoju
suevernoj
Sbirajtes' inogda čitat' moj svitok
vernyj [. . .]

I am doomed to the block . . .
Mourn, dear ones, my lot in silence;
Fear to rouse suspicion with [your]
tears [. . .]
Keep the manuscript, friends, for
yourselves!
When the storm has passed, in a
superstitious crowd
Assemble now and then to read my
faithful scroll [. . .]

(b) Esli rannjaja mogíla
Suždena moej vesne [. . .]
Ja molju: ne približajsja
K telu Dženni ty svoej,
Ust umeršix ne kasajsja,
Sleduj izdali za nej [. . .]
I kogda zaraza minet,
Poseti moj bednyj prax . . . .

If an early grave
Is predestined to my spring [. . .]
I pray: do not approach
The body of your Jenny,
Do not touch the dead lips,
Follow her from afar [. . .]
And when the epidemic has passed,
Visit my ashes . . . .

The two fragments share a very concrete and original pattern:

(28) The "I" splits into two selves—the speaker, occupying a detached posthumous position (beyond the grave in ex. 27a; in heaven in ex. 27b), and the third-person subject of narrated events (the poet's body and scroll in ex. 27a; the girl's body in ex. 27b). The speaker is uninvolved in the fate of the dying self (the poet about to be executed, his works forbidden; the girl about to die), permitting even the closest intimates (friends and readers; the lover) to ignore his/her plight ("Fear to rouse suspicion with [your] tears"; "do not approach . . . Do not touch the dead lips") until the danger for them is over ("When the storm / epidemic has passed").

Elements of (28) are present in many other texts, for example:

(29) Ja vas ljubil: ljubov' ešče, byt' možet
. . . . .

I loved you; love still, perhaps,
. . . . .

No pust' ona vas bol'še ne trevožit . . .	But let it [my love] not disturb you any more . . .

(30) Smertnyj mig naš budet svetel,   Our moment of death will be bright,
I podrugi šalunov   And the girl friends of the playboys
Soberut ix legkoj pepel   Will collect their light ashes
V urny prazdnye pirov.   Into the idle urns of the feasts.

Both share the remarkable

(31) split into two selves expressed by the shift from the first person ("I loved" in (29); "our" in (30), cf. "I" in (27a), "my, I" in (27b)) to the third person ("it" in (29); "their" in (30), cf. "scroll," etc., in (27a), "the body," "her," "the lips" in (27b)) and conveying the attitude of detached noninvolvement.

Further comparisons show that the same attitude of 'superior peace' is often expressed without recourse to viewpoint techniques and constitutes one of Pushkin's most abstract—and at the same time quite specific—invariants:

(32) The hero occupies a position of superior detachment from what usually troubles him; he abstains from using the means at his disposal to control the events "down there" (for more detail see [1980d]).

It turns out that episodes of 'horseback riding' and 'emotional plight' consistently share the point-of-view effect (cf. (15) and (31)), and the element of 'passivity that refuses to use dominance' (cf. (19) and the corresponding features in (28) and (32)). The invariant that cuts across the differences in content is as follows:

(33) combination of changeability and unchangeability expressed through detached "noninvolvement" in the manifestations of the changing pole (movement, passions, troubles), which is often reinforced by a "split view-point" technique.

4. "Poetic World": A Definition

In view of the above discussion, *the poetic world of an author—PW(A)—can be defined as the hierarchy of his invariant motifs ($\bar{M}$inv: situations, objects, linguistic structures, . . .), which is crowned with the central invariant theme (Θinv) and accounts for all that the author's texts have in common.*[5]

As the structure of an individual text is a derivation, PW(A) can also be defined as the common part of the derivations of the author's texts T̄(A), that is, *an invariant derivation of all that is recurrent in his oeuvre.* Or else, it is the derivation of the author's "invariant text"—a construct that emerges quite naturally from the application to the case under consideration of one of structuralism's basic principles. If for Shklovsky all the stories by Conan Doyle are "one story," if for Propp all tales are one tale, and if for Lévi-Strauss all variants of a myth are one myth, then for us all Pushkin's (or Pasternak's) poems are one poem. This logical step is, of course, a difficult one: from the purely formal "oneness" of Shklovsky and Propp it takes us to a more surprising thematic oneness, or else, from the obvious theme-and-plot oneness of a myth to that of a widely diverse poetic oeuvre. The latter is envisioned as the set of all possible alternative expressions of the poet's favorite message (i.e., variations on his Θinv).

A helpful linguistic analogy is a "paraphrastic set" (Hiż 1964), that is, the set of synonymous expressions of the same meaning (Mel'čuk 1974, 1981; Mel'čuk and Zholkovsky 1970). Another useful parallel is the set of different but "synthematic" proverbs discussed in Chapter 5. A PW is then a *hierarchy of poetically synonymous invariant manifestations of the central theme.*

The claim that the poet's oeuvre conveys just one invariant message seems to contradict the fundamental principle of multiplicity of a text's readings due to differences in the readers' varying codes—social, cultural, psychological, and so on. With PWs, involving entire sets of texts, an additional complication arises: texts written under widely different circumstances might not easily lend themselves to one "standard" interpretation.

The general answer is that our concepts are *constructs,* reflecting only certain aspects of the studied phenomena and subject to empirical testing. More specifically, the concepts of theme and derivation apply to particular readings of a text, according to the principle: "for every one reading its own theme and derivation" [1975b:17ff.]. If we are interested in evolving a metalanguage for systematic correspondences between the planes of poetic content and expression, we should be concerned with one reading of a text (i.e., a pair, "text–theme") at a time. For such theoretical purposes, any reading would do, but we can strengthen our case even more: by applying the criteria of "coverage" (of a text by a reading) and "commonness" (to readers), we can isolate, from the set of readings of each text, certain readings that are fairly "representative" [1975b:19ff.].

More help comes from a most unexpected quarter—the principle of thematic invariance. To reduce further the range of "representative" readings of an author's text T(A) we can introduce the criterion of thematic and expressive "unity" of all the texts T̄(A). For each T(A) only one derivation is to be chosen—in such a way that all the derivations for T̄(A) exhibit maximum similarity. The set of derivations thus obtained will form *a derivation and a reading of the entire PW(A).* (Since the operation can, for many reasons, yield different results, a certain—reduced—multiplicity will remain.)

The purpose of the above reasoning has been twofold: to clarify the concepts of "poetic world" and "reading" and their interrelation and to evolve some guidelines for choosing representative readings. No claim is made concerning the uniqueness of any one reading: *each reading of the oeuvre has its own central theme and its own invariant derivation, i.e., its own PW.*

One important aspect of PW as a construct is its deliberately *static* character. Like all derivations (and synchronic descriptions in general), it is a hierarchy of logical relations between the motifs it identifies, purporting to model the poet's literary competence and not his actual creative performance. When a group of texts is traced back to an invariant motif, this means only that they are thematically cognate—no historic or genetic connection is implied. It is only natural that a poet should address similar—his own, typically "-ian"—amorous verses to different women: the similarity does not entitle us to conclude that the verses were addressed to the same person. Nor does the grouping of several texts under a thematic invariant imply the type of factual relationship known as self-quotation, that is, a special—"personal"—kind of intertext.[6]

In a sense, the concept of PW treats all the author's texts, irrespective of the temporal order of their appearance, *as if they were created at the same time*—ignoring differences between periods. But then, $\bar{M}inv$ are deep, "grammatical" entities, apt to remain intact in the course of the poet's evolution. They represent, as it were, the subconscious infrastructure of his artistic personality. Even when a poet's (e.g., Pasternak's) style undergoes radical changes, its thematic base—and quite a rich one!—remains invariant.[7] Also, the description of the base must precede that of its evolution, if only to provide a frame of reference for the latter.[8] Synchronic description permits the scholar to leave aside the complications that would emerge if he took evolution into account—the problems that confront him even at this first stage are formidable enough.[9]

From the content of PWs let us turn to their structure. The derivations of PWs, just like derivations of individual texts, involve a balance of *expansion* and *compression* brought about by EDs VARIATION (VAR) and COMBINATION (COMB) (see Chap. 6).

VARIATION accounts for the rich diversity of motifs incarnating the central theme, that is, for art's tendency to perfuse most different phenomena with a unified poetic vision. This tendency is even more pronounced in PWs (projections of the central theme onto the entire universe) than in individual texts. The opposite principle—that of density and economy—tends to turn every invariant motif into a microcosm of the PW. (In Figs. 3.1 and 3.2, if we read downward, VAR corresponds to diverging lines, COMB to converging lines.)

To implement VARIATION, PWs (again like individual texts) resort to two main sources—the referential and the code spheres of the dictionary of reality, i.e., to, as it were, the general encyclopedia and the special dictionary of linguistic and literary terms. Thus, PW reflects not only the author's recurrent objects, scenes, and so on, but also his favorite "situations" in the world of verbal signs and patterns. It shows how the Θinv permeates both the depicted reality and the codes used in the depiction.

5. Invariant and Local Themes

If PW is a generalized invariant message of the author, this message is so to speak built into his code. The paradox is but an apparent one: the same is true of any natural language, where the semantically relevant grammatical categories clearly belong to the code and at the same time form a kind of obligatory message. In Jakobson's classic formulation (1971: 264), natural languages "differ essentially in what they *must* convey and not in what they *can* convey." In Russian one cannot use a verb without specifying its tense and aspect, that is, specifying whether the denoted event takes place before, at the moment of, or after the speech event, whether it was brought to completion, was punctual, or iterative. In English the speaker using a verb is presented with a different set of options. Every language seems to demand that the speaker fill out a kind of a semantic questionnaire. Tense, modality, number, definiteness, and other such grammatical meanings are obligatorily added to the meaning of the speaker's message proper.

Thus, the integral meaning, or semantic content, $C int$ of a sentence

S is the sum of two components: the "topical" content C*top* the speaker is intent on conveying and the "grammatical" content C*gram* "thrust upon" him by his language:

(34) $\text{C}int(S) = \text{C}top(S) + \text{C}gram(S).$

As a matter of fact, (34) is a formulation of the well-known view that every language "sees" the world in its own peculiar way, corresponding to its *Sprachgeist*. The literary counterpart of this notion is, of course, the poet's "vision of the world," that is, his PW. We can, therefore, split the theme of an individual text T into two components: an "invariant theme" $\Theta inv(\bar{T})$, shared with the author's other texts, and a "local theme" $\Theta loc(T)$, specific for the text.

(35) $\Theta int(T) = \Theta inv(\bar{T}) + \Theta loc(T)$, i.e.: $[\Theta loc(T), \Theta inv(\bar{T})] \xrightarrow{\text{COMB}} \Theta int(T).$

An obvious psychoanalytic parallel to the binomial[10] formulas (34) and (35) would be:

(36) $\text{C}int(D) = \text{C}res(D) + \text{C}neur(D),$

where C(D) stands for the content of the dream; *res* for the day-residues (Freud's *Tagesreste* in *The Interpretation of Dreams,* 1961); and *neur,* for the patient's constant neurosis, or trauma, which he obsessively reads into every situation (cf. Geršenzon's "canon . . . followed obediently, willy-nilly," on p. 64 above).

As, in a sense, the poet's personal "grammar," PW must affect the description of individual texts: if it ignores the system of $\bar{\text{M}}inv(A)$, it becomes as pointless as parsing a sentence without recourse to the corresponding grammar.

The most important implication is the very principle of obligatoriness, or "thrusting." When a language thrusts its questionnaire on the speaker, no particular answers are predetermined. For example, the grammatical category of number by no means compels the speakers of Russian (English, etc.) to perceive everything as 'numerous'. To put it briefly, natural languages are ambivalent about their obligatory meanings. As for PWs, they can be either ambivalent or monovalent, that is, "imposing" on readers quite definite "answers"; see the formulations, (26) and (13), of the respectively ambivalent and monovalent central themes of Pushkin and Pasternak. In particular, with respect to the category of number, Pasternak's PW relies heavily on 'numerousness, plurals, enumerations,' that is, it monovalently prefers one term of the opposition to the other.

In accordance with the principle of obligatoriness and formula (35), the structure of a text can be conceived as a translation of an "everyman's" local theme into the language of the particular PW(A). As a result, derivations acquire a double role: they are now supposed to demonstrate the gradual "grafting" onto the local theme, nonexpressive and not specific to the author, not only of artistic effects but also of the author's invariant motifs. The technical implementation of this program involves two concepts: (*a*) the set $\bar{M}inv(T)$ of those of the author's motifs which are represented in the text; (*b*) the invariant subtheme $\Theta inv(T)$ of the text's integral theme, that is, the thematic invariant behind the set $\bar{M}inv(T)$ that states explicitly what part of the author's PW the given text is devoted to.

One major problem is that of interrelations between the local and invariant entities involved in PE descriptions. The local theme is specific for the text only as compared with the author's other texts. It is usually taken from the common stock of literary themes (such as 'unrequited love', 'coming of spring', 'coronation', 'revolution', 'the art of poetry'). It is, therefore, not so much an "everyman's" as an "every poet's" Θloc that is translated into the given poetic world.

As the local and invariant components of the theme are linked by an additive formula (see formula (35)), that is, as they divide the text's thematic content between themselves, they are by definition *correlative* quantities. This is particularly important for the discovery of the set of the author's $\bar{M}inv$: it should be formulated so as to enable the scholar to demonstrate, in an intuitively satisfactory way, that the theme of any T(A) results from the combination of certain $\bar{M}inv(A)$ and $\Theta loc(T)$. Naturally, the more components of T that are accounted for by invariant motifs, the fewer remain for $\Theta loc,$ that is, the formulation of Θloc depends on the exhaustiveness of the available inventory of $\bar{M}inv(A)$. Comments on an example from Lotman 1978 will illustrate this point.

Consider this draft of an early Pasternak poem:

(37) Kak čitat' mne! Oplyli slova
    Ax otkuda, otkuda skvožu ja
    V ploškax strok razbiraju edva
    Gonit mnoju stranicu čuzuju

How can I read! The words are
    guttered
Oh whence, whence do I blow [like a
    draft]
In the wick-lampions of lines I can
    scarcely make out
The alien page is being chased with
    me

Lotman (1978: 21–23) shows how, as a result of "a deliberate shift from a linguistically and commonsensically predictable set of referents to another, unexpected one, and a parallel substitution of grammatical functions . . . instead of 'the candle gutters' we find 'the print gutters,' 'the words gutter,' or a 'guttering book.' . . . Such lines . . . obliterate the separateness of 'book' and 'candle.' From separate objects they are transformed into facets of a unified whole. At the same time the poet's 'I' and the wind merge." To put it in PE terms, Lotman discovers a major variety of metaphorical contact—the shift of linguistic co-occurrence (see Chap. 7, p. 141). This Minv he opposes to the extra-poetic and extra-Pasternakian, "everyman's" content of the poem, that is, Θloc(T), obtained by subtracting the Minv from the text: "Apparently, the poet's proximate task was to describe an actual situation . . . something like:

(38) I have considerable trouble reading: the candle guttered and the wind scattered the pages.

Yet for Pasternak such a text would have had little correspondence with reality"[11] (p. 22), that is, little correspondence with his PW.

But a close look at (38) shows that this "actual [i.e., referential-sphere] situation" is saturated with Pasternakian motifs. It involves: 'touching, clutching' (wind/"I," the pages, the candle); 'similarity' ("I"/wind: both leaf through the book); 'trembling', 'fast movement' (the pages); 'tenseness to the point of inability to function, over-poweredness' ("I," the candle), cf. formula (12) above; 'exuberance, overflowing' and 'crossing or obliterating the border' (the guttering candle); and some other varieties of (13) 'contact, magnificence'. In addition, all the participants in situation (38)—'wind', 'book', 'candle'—are Pasternak's favorite ready-made objects. Subtracting from (38) all these "referential" Minv, we obtain

(39) I read at night.

This very "spare" Θloc is both *un-Pasternakian and inexpressive*—just the type of theme to place at the beginning of a derivation.

The formulations of local and invariant themes are thus interdependent. There seem to be three major types of correlations between them.

1. They are *clearly distinct or even contrasting*, so that in the course of "translation" Θloc has to be absorbed and overcome by Minv. Com-

pare the Θloc in (39) 'night reading' and the wealth of $\bar{M}inv$ grafted onto it in (37) (a case of mere difference); or the Θloc of "There will be no one in the house . . ." ($\approx$ 'sad winter mood') and its joyous Pasternakian treatment (a case of contrast) (see Chap. 10).

2. The local theme has points of *affinity* with the poet's invariants, which it "attracts" as its closest translation equivalents in the language of his PW. For instance, inherent in 'horseback riding' and 'autumn' are elements of that Pushkinian interplay of 'activeness / passiveness', and 'life / sickness, death' respectively, which are effectively "read into them" in the corresponding poems (see §3 above).

3. The local theme *coincides* completely with the poet's invariants: rather than translating, he just unfolds the picture of his poetic world or of some of its corners, twists, and so on, picking out, as it were, various tunes possible on its keyboard and oblivious to everything external. See the Θloc of Pushkin's "I loved you . . .," formulated as a combination of several $\bar{M}inv$ in Chapter 9 and a similar treatment of an Akhmatova poem in 1982d.

Some of the issues cursorily outlined in this chapter are discussed in detail in Part 3, which is devoted to the description of poetic worlds.

PART TWO

STRUCTURE AND
DERIVATION

4

The Somali Tale
"A Soothsayer Tested"

1. The Object and Aims of Description

The plot of the tale can be briefly outlined as follows:

A king summons a famous soothsayer and orders him to predict what awaits
the tribe in the coming year. The soothsayer tries bead counting but without
success, then leaves for a desert and keeps on trying, but in vain. Suddenly a
snake talks to him; they swear friendship and the snake communicates to the
soothsayer the required forecast (in verse) in exchange for a promised share
of the king's reward. The soothsayer goes back to the king and conveys the
prediction: war is coming. The tribe prepares for it and wins. The king
rewards the soothsayer with livestock, but instead of sharing it, the soothsayer
tries to kill the snake. The snake escapes. Once again the king demands a
forecast. The soothsayer again turns to the snake, who forgives him and
predicts a drought. The soothsayer goes to the king; the tribe makes its
preparations and survives. The soothsayer gets his reward but withholds it
from the snake. For a third time the king wants a forecast. The soothsayer
goes to the snake and brings back a prediction of rain. The tribe prepares
reservoirs and makes full use of nature's bounty. Everybody is well fed and
happy. This time the soothsayer takes all the livestock to the snake, begs
forgiveness, acknowledges the snake's divine wisdom and asks about the
world and life in it. The snake refuses the soothsayer's gifts and friendship
and says: "The world exists, but there is no separate life. This so-called life

This chapter is an abridged translation of [1970c], which also contained a note on the
structure and problems of poetic translation of the tale's verse fragments (omitted
here). The Somali text of the tale ("Faaliyihii la bilkeyday") was published, with extensive grammatical and cultural commentaries, in Galaal and Andrzejewski 1956: 49–61,
109–150; my Russian translation appeared in Žukov and Kotljar 1976: 522–34.

repeats the world's design. When the time of hostility comes, people all become enemies, and in that year of war even you tried to kill me. In a time of hunger, no one will give another a piece of bread, and so you also cheated me out of my cattle. But when the time of prosperity comes, no one will refuse anything to others and thus you too brought me all you had received. And so on every occasion you did what the times bade you."

What is the immediate impression produced by the story? The culmination is, of course, the snake's final speech that sheds new light on the tiresome peripeties of the relations between the characters. The message is both unexpected and well prepared; when the meaning of life, as presented in the tale, is suddenly revealed, the reader experiences a shock of recognition.

How does the tale achieve this effect? To answer this question one should show how the plot in general and each episode in particular "work for" the central effect, bringing it home to the reader as a result of an intense aesthetic experience. In other words, we must point out the functions that the elements of the plot play in the expression of the tale's theme and explain why it is convincing and justified. In my opinion, a consistent solution to this age-old problem of literary criticism naturally calls for a "generative" description that demonstrates how a text can be derived from its theme according to some general principles of artistic expressiveness (see the Introduction and Chap. 1). This approach, which is probably just an explicit ("cybernetic") reformulation of the ideas of Vygotsky (1971), Eisenstein (1964–70, 1968, 1975a,b), and Mazel' (1966, 1976, 1978), aims not at replacing a writer with a computer but rather at evolving a strict method of description, graphically adequate for its complicated object.

I begin (§2) with a tentative ("reader's") formulation of the theme and then (§3–5) list the operations (expressive devices) that develop this initial "preartistic" formula into a more or less full-fledged plot. Though this attempt to follow step by step the invention of all the finds of the plot may strike the reader as overly pedantic, I could only wish for greater precision and accuracy. Still, I hope that even this very rough, slow-motion picture of an imaginary process of composition will help to clarify and elaborate the concept of literary structure.

2. The Theme

Usually the process of critical discovery starts with an intuitive groping for the theme of the text. Our task is somewhat easier, as the tale itself contains a formulation of its message—the snake's concluding statement that "life repeats the world's design," that is, men's actions are not free but determined by fate.

This resembles the theme of the Oedipus myth.[1] In our tale, however, the confrontation is not between two concepts of causality (as in Oedipus: 'fatal inevitability *vs.* freedom of will'). It is not by chance that the snake says "life *repeats* the world's design," not "*is determined by*" it: the soothsayer's actions, connected with the general course of events, are *similar* to, *not caused* by it. The story never so much as implies that the soothsayer attacked the snake because war was going on and he got used to violence, or that he withheld the cattle from the snake because the drought made him needy, or, finally, that he was generous because he had a surplus and saw examples of generosity around him. Only in the end do we find out there was a connection in each pair of events. Still, it was not a causal link in the chain of interactions, causes and results, but precisely a similarity, based not on the impact of one object on another, but on a 'mystical affinity.'[2]

Having identified with the perspective of one protagonist (the snake), we missed an essential aspect of the theme. The snake's final message is presented in the tale not just as an apt or even unexpectedly true observation but as an illuminating truth of the highest order—a 'revelation'. Thus, the theme is:

revelation that human life is not independent, but related to the world's design, and not causally, but by the law of affinity.

In short:

revelation: life is similar to the world's design.

3. From the Theme to an Outline of the Plot

It is logical to start by determining the general plan of the "future" text. To be sure, the plan can result from the application to the theme of any arbitrary devices. Is there not, however, an essential correspondence between a theme's content and the devices suitable for its expression? The explanatory power of generative descriptions would undoubtedly increase if they could rely on such correspondences. Telling examples of how devices can be "extracted" from themes are found in Eisenstein's theoretical works (see the discussion in Chap. 1 of the ecstatic development inherent in the theme).

Let us try to look for devices "contained" in our theme. Three of its components might be active in molding the eventual structure: (*a*) the motif of 'similarity'; (*b*) the status of a 'universal law' accorded to the content of the 'revelation'; (*c*) the motif of 'revelation' itself.

The motif of '*similarity, affinity*' between phenomena naturally calls for comparisons, similes, proportions (ED CONCORD). That the structure should rely on the metaphorical principle is also prompted by the tale's static ("monadic") world view and its interest in mystical relations, based on similarity, rather than causal relations, based on contiguity.

To present a statement as a general law it is best to develop it into a series of situations that illustrate its universality. How can this be done? "How is this statement . . . about 'the omnipotent law of time' [in Ovid's *Tristia*, IV, 6] developed into a convincing artistic image?" [1967c: 173–74]. The answer is: by a special method of selecting the illustrations of the theme: "(1) An ox gets used to the yoke, a horse to the bridle, a lion loses his rage, an elephant submits to his master. . . . (2) Fruits become sweet, grapes become full of juice, an ear ripens. . . . (3) A plough, a stone, a diamond get blunted. . . . (4) Rage and sorrow calm down" (ibid.). The objects are taken from the various domains that "complement each other and together form a broad and complete picture of the entire world," while the "objects themselves . . . display a set of different and often opposite properties . . . and are evenly spread over the respective domains" (ibid.). Both the rhetorical advisability of varying the illustrations of the law and the thematic task of demonstrating its universality suggest the same thing: VARIATION of the theme through different and even contrasting material.

The two considerations are prominent in Eisenstein's analysis of the way Pushkin avoids monotony in illustrating the 'omnipotence of gold' in "The Covetous Knight." The pile of gold is compared to a giant hill from which a king used to survey his territories. "Pushkin . . . distributes the enumeration in two different dimensions. . . . One group of episodes will form the image of the man of power himself. The other—that of his pedestal, the hill of gold." The components of each image are also contrasted: "the feast of virtue and sleepless labour" *vs.* the "bloodied villainy." In the end, "all the tears, blood and sweat shed for all that is hoarded here" are compared to a flood. Once again Pushkin "chooses . . . extreme opposites. 'The mountain' and 'the waters' are a classic pair of contrasting opposites. In Chinese painting the word for 'landscape' is literally 'the picture of mountains and waters'" (Eisenstein 1964–70, v. 3: 123–25).

The device of contrastive VARIATION (VAR*contr*) serves the expression of 'universality' quite often; compare the following fragment from another Pushkin text, *Brožu li ja vdol' ulic šumnyx* ("Whether I roam along noisy streets").

Gljažu l' na dub uedinnennyj,
Ja myslju: patriarx lesov
Pereživet moj vek zabvennyj,
Kak perežil on vek otcov.

Whether I am looking at a solitary
    oak,
I am pondering: the patriarch of the
    forests
Will outlive my forgotten age
The way he has outlived the age of
    [our] fathers.

Mladenca l' milogo laskaju,
Uže ja dumaju: prosti!
Tebe ja mesto ustupaju,
Mne vremja tlet', tebe cvesti!

Whether I am caressing an amiable
    child,
Already I am thinking: farewell!
I am ceding to you my place,
It is time for me to rot, for you to
    blossom!

Here the oak and the child are similar in outliving the speaker ('death' is the theme). But in everything else they are different: the oak is part of nature, the child is human; the oak is taller and older than the speaker, it belongs with his forefathers; the child is smaller, younger, belongs to posterity. The opposition is further refined by a mutual reflection (CONCORD) of the two images: the tree is presented as human ("The patriarch of forests," "the age of fathers"), the humans, as trees and wood ("to rot," "to blossom"). (Thus in painting contiguous objects leave reflexes on each other.) The concluding stanza:

I pust' u grobovogo vxoda
Mladaja budet žizn' igrat'
I ravnodušnaja priroda
Krasoju večnoju sijat'.

And let at the tomb's entrance
Youthful life play
And indifferent nature
Shine with eternal beauty.

combines "youthful life" and "indifferent nature" and thus emphasizes the role of the two images ("child," "oak") as representatives of the entire universe (on VAR*contr* see also note 9 to Chap. 5 and note 18 to Chap. 11).

To return to our generative process, we conclude that the 'universality of the law' can be artistically demonstrated with the help of the EDs of CONCRETIZATION, REPETITION, and CONTRASTIVE VARIATION.

Now let us see what type of structure is "called for" by *'revelation'*. 'Revelation' can be defined as a truth that is first hidden and then suddenly (usually thanks to divine light) becomes known. Therefore, it naturally calls for the plot pattern of 'recognition, or epiphany', based on a well-prepared SUDDEN TURN in the course of events. This device is also quite rich in purely expressive effects (suspense, unexpectedness, etc.). Thus the CONCRETIZATION of 'revelation' yields a 'SUDDEN TURN toward the realization that life is similar to the world's design.'

If we now bring together the devices "extracted" from the three pivotal components of the theme ('similarity', 'universality', 'revelation'), we obtain

a plot with a sudden turn toward the revelation that life is similar to the world's design, a proportion to be concretized and repeated with (contrastive) variation.

The outlined plan of composition poses several further tasks:

1. In order to devise a SUDDEN TURN toward the theme, its opposite—an *antitheme*—must be formulated: the COMBINATION of the two will shape the contrapuntal development of the entire plot.
2. Means of CONCRETIZING the antitheme have to be found.
3. The contradiction between the "static" nature of our theme and the "dynamic" nature of plot development must be resolved.

Let us formulate the opposite of the snake's revelation: 'life as such exists, but no general design of the world does'. The plot then will have to include the depiction of a ' "raw," separate life as such', unrelated to any divine idea or design. Another aspect of the snake's revelation is the emphasis on the static, noninteractive ("monadic") kinship of things. The antitheme will, on the contrary, rely on dynamic plot interactions of the characters. Since causality is seen not as a profound principle of the universe but as an illusory external aspect of life, these causal links should be made superficial, shortlived, and "meaningless." Finally, the inscrutability of the eventual revelation (inherent in the events but concealed from mortal eyes) has to be arranged for by complete but inconspicuous merging (COMBINATION) of the 'world's design' with ' "raw" life'. Thus, on the whole, we obtain the opposition:

the antitheme: "raw," separate life, temporary dynamic plot relations *vs.* the theme proper: eternal static law, poetical, "monadic" world design.

Note that now the contradiction between 'static similarity' and 'dynamic plot' appears in a new light: not as an obstacle to clarity which should be removed or glossed over but as an antithesis that unfolds the theme, and therefore must be emphasized and developed so that its two contrasting poles can be spectacularly COMBINED in the plot. The 'dynamic plot' element will carry the antitheme; as a result, the turn from the antitheme to the theme proper will take the form of a turn from the course of the story to a meditative stasis—a turn, as it were, not *in* the plot but *from* the plot to a plotless lyrical world view. The paradox of form that overcomes the resistance of an "inappropriate" material is considered by some scholars[3] one of the fundamental principles of art. As for the specific pairing of expressive means with the thematic components they convey (the theme proper → poetic proportions; the antitheme → plot motifs) and their ingenious combination, these seem to be peculiar to our tale and constitute its own "artistic discovery,"[4] that is, its original contribution to the art of storytelling.

Thus, we have decided on a

composition with a sudden turn from a meaningless "raw" life involving superficial temporary relations toward a revelation about the proportions between life and the world's design concretized with repetition and contrastive variation.

4. CONCRETIZING the Plot

The obtained compositional outline must now be implemented in concrete situations and interrelations between characters.

4.1. CONCRETIZING *the Theme Proper*

The 'proportion between life and world's design' can unfold into: 'any manifestations of life, for example, men's actions, are similar to the manifestations of the world, for example, divine phenomena'. With a threefold REPETITION this will yield 'action 1 is similar to phenomenon 1, action 2 is similar to phenomenon 2, action 3 is similar to phenomenon 3'.

It is now the time to VARY the 'actions' and the 'phenomena', that is, to spread them evenly over the 'entire universe'. For the 'divine phenomena' this can result, for example, in the set represented in the tale. Indeed, the three 'divine phenomena' that occur in the story form two oppositions, 'social *vs.* natural' ('war' *vs.* 'drought and rain'), and 'good, generous, life-giving *vs.* bad, stingy, deadly' ('rain' *vs.* 'war and drought'). The two natural elements ('drought' and 'rain') and the social phenomenon ('war') are supposed to represent the 'universe', just as 'indifferent nature' and 'youthful life' do in Pushkin's poem. The contrasts within the two oppositions ('natural/social', 'good/bad') and the way each 'phenomenon' participates in both ensure the effect of an even spread and universality.

The same principle of maximum VARIATION is at work with 'human actions 1, 2, 3'. The 'assault on the snake' and the 'failure to pay' are 'violations of contract' opposed to 'paying', that is, 'living up to the contract'; at the same time, 'assault' and 'paying' are opposed to 'nonpaying' as 'action *vs.* nonaction'. As a result, there is a gradual transition from the soothsayer's actively evil to actively good behavior toward the snake, creating an impression that every possible type of action has been represented.

Instead of deriving the VARIATIONS, I have, in fact, analyzed them. Their derivation would comprise three steps.

1. For each term of the proportion, concrete examples are found (ED CONCRETIZATION): 'actions' → 'assaulted, defended, stole, acted greedy, gave a present, betrayed, fell in love . . .'; 'phenomena' → 'war, earthquake, wind, harvest, eclipse . . .'.
2. These examples are spread evenly according to various parameters (ED VARIATION): 'actions' → 'good (defended, gave a present) *vs.* bad (assaulted, stole, betrayed); active (assaulted, stole) *vs.* passive (was greedy, betrayed); violent (assaulted, defended) *vs.* nonviolent (stole, betrayed, fell in love), etc.'; 'phenomena' → 'natural (drought, flood, earthquake) *vs.* social (war, harvest); top (rain, eclipse) *vs.* bottom (earthquake, harvest); good (harvest, rain) *vs.* bad (earthquake, drought); etc.'.
3. Out of the two series of examples (of 'actions' and of 'phenomena') only those are chosen which share common oppositions (ED CONCORD), e.g., 'good (rain, defended, . . .) *vs.* bad (assaulted, earthquake, . . .)' and are most clearly opposed in some other parameters.

One possible result of such a derivation is represented by the actual sets of 'phenomena' and 'actions' in the story.

In the full-fledged text of the story the principle of similarity between actions and phenomena is also evident in the way every phenomenon is presented. In fact, two of these ('rain' and 'drought') easily supply illustrations of this idea, as they constitute 'phenomena that affect the life of people'. The snake's forecasts proceed from descriptions of inanimate nature to plants to animals and finally to people. This progression again stresses the universality of the event and the similarity between 'world' and 'life'. Unlike the two elemental phenomena, 'war' belongs to the human sphere and thus does not easily lend itself to exemplification of the theme 'actions *vs.* phenomena'. And yet the prophecy about war manages to implement this opposition-proportion. It begins with the mention of "the time of diabolic villainies and of Iblis' eight-year term" which forebodes "wives donning their mourning garments" and "warriors whose corpses are pecked by birds," and so on. In other words, 'war' is first presented not as a form of human behavior but as a law of the universe, reflecting the "will of Iblis"; only in its second half does the prophecy proceed to specific military actions: "men have made their noisy preparations . . . saddled their well-fed horses for the assault . . . soon in a savage horde . . . will they launch their attack."

Thus, in the three episodes the 'divine phenomena' are split into 'manifestations of the world's design' and 'manifestations of life': 'drought' → 'scarcity in nature + the tribe's famine'; 'rain' → 'generosity of nature' + 'contentment of the people'; 'war' → 'the time of war + hostilities'. And within each pair the same kind of similarity is maintained as between 'phenomena' and 'actions'. Additional REPETITION and VARIATION are made possible by presenting each 'phenomenon' ('war,' 'drought,' 'rain') twice: first as a forecast and then as reality. The repetition is saved from monotony by contrasting the forecast to the events as: (*a*) verse *vs.* prose, and (*b*) anticipation *vs.* fact. The latter opposition is highlighted by suspense in the plot: Will it come true or not? Will the forecast help the tribe or not? Will the soothsayer keep his promise to the snake or not? and so on.

This multilevel system of proportions, oppositions, comparisons, and repetitions creates the poetic element that was chosen as the embodiment of the theme proper—'similarity'.

4.2. CONCRETIZING *the Antitheme*

It has been decided to develop the antitheme through plot. One quite common story pattern has the 'protagonist first commit some wrong actions and then mend his ways'; compare a Russian fairy tale analyzed by Propp (1958: Chap. 9, §b), in which the little girl is first arrogant toward a stove, an apple tree, and a river and thus fails to enlist their assistance; later she changes her attitude and they save her and her brother from the geese. How can one make such a story line convey the idea of 'raw, meaningless life'? To do so we only have to undermine its purposefulness, for example, by discarding the causal links between the change in behavior and the circumstances. That, in fact, is what actually takes place in our tale: the snake ignores the soothsayer's misdeeds, agrees to help him again and again, and in the end dismisses with a shrug the gifts it seemed to have expected all the while.[5]

4.3. COMBINING *the Theme Proper and the Antitheme*

One of the requirements of the SUDDEN TURN is that manifestations of the two subthemes be COMBINED all along the plot line. That is, the antitheme should be embodied in those very motifs that already embody the theme proper. These motifs, which have been linked by similarities, have now to be linked on the plane of contiguity as well, that is, shaped into a story. For instance, the 'human actions' can be presented as those of a protagonist.

Let us COMBINE 'aggressiveness' and 'stinginess' with the 'protagonist's wrong actions' and 'generosity' with his 'correct actions'. Then we will have him 'acting wrongly = aggressively and stingily' and then 'acting correctly = generously'; let him 'do this respectively in the times of war, drought, and rain'. Let us further COMBINE 'revelation' with the turning point of the SUDDEN TURN construction: the 'revelation' will be the denouement. We thus arrive at the following approximation of the actual story:

a plot with a sudden turn from the story of a protagonist who in the time of war and drought commits wrong actions (attacks, is stingy) and then in the time of rain changes for the better and is generous, to a revelation that it is not this that matters: all human manifestations (aggressiveness, stinginess, generosity) are similar to divine phenomena (war, drought, rain).

5. Ensuring the Unexpectedness of the Reversal

To make the reversal from ignorance to knowledge unexpected and well prepared, the story should unfold in such a way as to contain from the start all the evidence and even the very pattern of the eventual revelation while concealing that evidence from the reader. If in the end the protagonist's actions 1, 2, 3 will prove similar to phenomena 1, 2, 3 respectively, then in the narrative they should seem as much unlike them as possible.

In a sense, this is again a contrastive VARIATION. But up to now the device was without artifice, inviting the reader to enjoy, consciously from the start, the effect of similarity projected onto variety (e.g., the property of 'outliving the poet' is shared by a child and an oak; that of 'being a divine phenomenon' is shared by war, drought, and rain; etc.). Now we have to turn a similarity not just into a difference or a contrast but into a complete unrecognizability—in order that the recognition be the more astounding.

The opposition 'life *vs.* world's design', inherent in the theme, was unfolded into the antithesis 'one man's actions *vs.* phenomena involving an entire people and nature as a whole'. This antithesis, however, does not suffice for the current purpose. The 'unrecognizability' is primarily a compositional problem and it is best solved by compositional means. For instance, the similarity between the terms of the antithesis can be concealed by distancing them as far as possible from each other in the narrative space of the tale. We can resort to the widespread device that splits the plot into two stories: an outer, or framing, story and an inner, or framed, story, which suddenly merge in the denouement. This pattern is a ready-made object (see Chap. 2) ideally suited for our purposes: if the 'actions' and the 'phenomena' are distributed between the two structurally different story lines, they will become so disparate and incongruous that their fundamental similarity will be impossible to detect.[6]

The framed inner story is usually introduced by the motif of 'communication (song, order, letter, etc.)'. Our plot already includes 'revelation' and can naturally motivate 'presentiment' or 'prediction'. In CONCORD with the theme's cosmic scale (world, king, etc.) it is natural to cast the protagonist as a 'soothsayer' (other plots might have, say, 'correspondents exchanging letters'). His actions will form the outer story; the objects of his forecasts, the framed story. The protagonist's actions (the framing story) must be both linked with the inner story and separated from it—in time, space, and motivation.[7] Here is how this is done in the actual plot.

To provide a minimum of characters necessary for the framing story, the soothsayer is split into 'soothsayer proper' and 'oracle'; in CONCORD with the categories of 'stinginess / generosity' and 'wrong / correct behavior', the motifs of 'contract', 'king's order', and 'reward' are chosen from the stock of folklore motifs. They provide additional links making the narrative chain longer and more flexible, so that its ends ('actions' and 'phenomena') can be dissociated as much as possible. Moreover, in the tale the compositional dissociation of the outer and inner stories is supported by three other kinds of dissociation: *motivational* (two lines of action: contract between the soothsayer and the oracle; the prediction of events according to king's order); *spatial* (two scenes of action: the desert; the tribe's territory); and *temporal* (the soothsayer's meetings with the snake take place before and after the predicted events, never at the same time).

Now that the similarity between 'soothsayer's actions' and 'divine phenomena' has been made undetectable, the direct formulation of this similarity, saved up for the denouement (see §4.3), will come as a necessary and long-awaited revelation, shedding light on the design of the world and of the tale, not as a moral appended to the text.[8]

The motifs of 'contract', 'order', and 'reward' help develop the motif of 'raw life' and get the reader interested in the superficial external aspect of the 'actions and phenomena': Will the soothsayer manage to produce a forecast? Will he get the reward, escape punishment? etc. Though the tale in fact treats the destinies of an entire people, the world's design and fate itself ("I am not a snake, I am Fate," says the oracle in the end), the narrative seems to center around an ordinary man's ordinary problems (avoiding punishment, getting rewards, sharing or not sharing them with a partner).

A more challenging task is the projection of the antitheme ('meaningless, superficial, transient, raw life') onto the story line of the 'divine oracle'. Here is how the tale accomplishes it: (*a*) The oracle is made a character of the outer story and tied with the soothsayer by commercial interests ('contract', 'reward'). (*b*) The oracle's prophecies, correct and important as they are, are made into specific forecasts for one year only, applying to the content of a single (inner) story and predicting individual events, not formulating the design of the world; their problematic character is used to build up suspense (will they come true?). As a result, the oracle's forecasts contrast with his final revelation as: 'connected with earthly interests *vs.* sublimely disinterested'; 'particular, specific, temporary *vs.* general, eternal'; 'referring to a part of the plot *vs.* encompassing it all'; 'numerous, inconclusive *vs.* one, exceptional, final'; 'problematic *vs.* indisputable' (unlike the forecasts, which "look forward to" and await a confirmation, the revelation "looks back" on the events that have already happened and therefore strikes the reader as absolutely correct).

Let us state the obtained plot:

A soothsayer motivated by an order and a reward makes a contract with an oracle, whom he contacts in a separate place and at a special time, about forecasts. He obtains forecasts of war, drought, and rain, each of which comes true, involving the world and the lives of men. The soothsayer gets rewards and is on the three occasions respectively aggressive, stingy, and generous toward the oracle. In the end the oracle reveals to him that human actions in general and his own in particular repeat universal phenomena: life is similar to the world's design.

As on some other occasions (cf. [1967d, 1970b]; Chap. 1), I refrain from trying to "generate" the complete text of the tale or even its plot as summarized in the first section of this chapter. I think that for reasons of both theoretical and descriptive interest a discussion of the thematically pivotal and artistically most ingenious core of the plot should suffice.

6. Postscript

I stand by the above description (only slightly edited from [1970c]) and would add only one essential observation. To incorporate it, however, I would have to change the order of the derivation, that is, to rewrite a considerable part of the chapter. It will probably be both more honest and more instructive to admit this failing, state the correction, and see how it affects the derivation.

One of the principles of PE description is that every effect is derived (i.e., singled out and accounted for) by a separate step, assigned its logical place in the overall hierarchy of effects. An effect overlooked by the scholar will either be completely absent from his derivation or "smuggled" into it at one or several points, that is, tacitly bundled together with other effects, thereby making the corresponding steps something other than elementary. As a result, the derivation will fail to show "how it turned out so well" and thus forfeit its claim to explicitness and explanatory power.

The effect in question here is that of 'a false turn preceding the final real one'. This device (RECOIL MOVEMENT, i.e., a zigzag whereby the denouement is arrived at after a move in the opposite direction, see Glossary) is often employed in plots, cf. false solutions in detective stories (e.g., Lestrade's and Dr. Watson's solutions that set off those of Holmes). The device is put to original use in our tale: the 'false turn' takes place *in* the plot, whereas the 'real one' is a turn *from* plot to plotlessness. Let us see how this is (mis-)represented in the derivation.

The groundwork for the 'false turn' is first laid in §3, where it in fact says that the 'real turn' will be not *in* but *from* the plot. This contrast, as yet purely conceptual, can later unfold into a sequence of two actual turns mutually opposed in the spirit of §5; in other words, it predisposes (cf. §3) RECOIL MOVEMENT. Another thematic element that prompts the same is the 'unexpectedness of the final revelation' (treated in §5): the more complete and "closed" the line of 'raw life events' (and such should be the effect of a falsely "final" turn), the less probable a further—really final—reversal.

In the actual derivation, however, the 'false turn' is neither anticipated in §3 nor generated in §5. Instead, it is inconspicuously introduced in §4.2 as a by-product of an allegedly random CONCRETIZATION of the antitheme. In reality the chosen motif ('a protagonist mends his ways') is not all that neutral: (*a*) it involves a 'turn in the plot from bad to good', which will, in the light of the final 'turn from the plot', prove 'false'; (*b*) its terms ('good *vs.* bad') are ideally suited for the ensuing COMBINATION, in §4.3, with 'bad and good phenomena'; that is, yet another device (CONCORD) is employed implicitly.

The inaccuracy is thus twofold: on the one hand, more EDs are actually applied than is announced, so that unwarranted effects are achieved; on the other hand, this is done at the wrong moment and without proper artistic motivation. A correct strategy for generating this effect would be as follows:

1. A 'false turn' is prompted in §3.

2. A completely neutral motif is chosen in §4.2, e.g., 'a protagonist commits a causal series of acts'.

3. These 'acts' are COMBINED with the 'actions' from the line of the theme proper, yielding much the same results as in §4.3 but without any chronological order of the events.

4. The actions are arranged into a 'false turn' in §5, providing a more convincing explanation of the way 'revelation' is embedded in the structure of the tale.

5

Deriving Poetic Structure:
A Somali Proverb

1. Proverbs and Poetics

Proverbs provide a rich source of material and a perfect testing ground for the method of description proposed by the poetics of expressiveness. Although situated in a no-man's-land somewhere at the crossroads of linguistics and folklore, proverbs exhibit an indisputably artistic organization; some are small masterpieces of the genre. Therefore proverbs constitute a legitimate and desirable object for poetic studies.

Because proverbs are short, they promise the realization of the structuralist's dream of an exhaustive description. Because they are thematically transparent, the separation, presupposed in PE, of themes from texts is less difficult than it is with more complex literary genres. In fact, for proverbs the problem has been solved independently of any concerns of poetic analysis. Owing to the work of G. L. Permjakov, we have at our disposal standardized 'nonexpressive' formulations of the themes of all existing and potential proverbs.[1] As a result, PE description can concentrate on derivation proper as a path from an already established theme to the proverb's text. Finally, the structural homogeneity of proverbs helps one to avoid ad hoc solutions in descriptions and to make sure that similar—"stereotype"—effects are accounted for by similar moves in the derivations.

Of special interest is the abundance of synonymous, or, rather, "synthematic", proverbs, that is, different artistic variations on one

This chapter is an abridged version of [1978g].

and the same theme. Consider proverbs (1b–k), which can be grouped under the same heading—(1a) (see Permjakov 1968: 232–33).[2]

(1) (a) One should think over one's actions.
   (b) "Even in jest choose your words carefully" (Tartar).
   (c) "First—thought, then—action" (Osetin).
   (d) "First think carefully, and only then speak" (Tibetan).
   (e) "Think two times, speak once" (Turkish).
   (f) *Measure thrice, and cut once* (English).
   (g) *Sem' raz otmer', odin raz otrež'* (Russian, lit., "Seven times measure, one time cut").
   (h) "Measure seven times, cut once; only a fool acts first and thinks later" (Tibetan).
   (i) "Chew before you swallow; listen before you speak" (Amharic).
   (j) "A dog will run around a place three times before it lies down; a man must think thirty-five times before he speaks" (Vietnamese).
   (k) "Man has two ears and one mouth; therefore, listen twice, speak once" (Turkish).

Differences between these synthematic texts are due, in derivational terms, to the choice, number, and implementation of expressive devices applied to the theme, (1a). Let us see how expressiveness gradually accumulates from (1b) to (1k).

None of the proverbs settles for an unadorned, purely linguistic CONCRETIZATION of the theme, that is, for a sentence like (1a). Proverb (1b) is a result of a CONCRETIZATION ('think' → *choose words*), AUGMENTATION ('think' → *think carefully*), and CONTRAST (['in normal speech'] → *even in jest*).

In proverb (1c) (and in the rest of the examples) a different course is adopted: DIVISION into two subthemes ('thought'; 'action') with subsequent CONCORD (parallelism) of the parts. In (1c) the CONCRETIZATIONS are quite trivial; (1d) adds two AUGMENTATIONS (trivial again: *carefully; only then*); (1e) introduces a numerical realization of the AUGM and CONTR (*2:1*); (1f) uses another manifestation of the same EDs (*3:1*) and a more original CONCRETIZATION of the two central terms ('thought' → *measure;* 'action' → *cut*); (1g) is remarkable for the way the CONCORD is implemented: the syntactic parallelism, common to (1c–f), is echoed by elaborate phonetic, prosodic (‿ ́) and morphological symmetries between the key verbs *otmér'* (lit., 'measure off') and *otréž'* (lit., 'cut off').

With proverb (1h) a new expressive pattern is added—VARIATION, doubling the number of illustrations of the theme. Unlike in (1i), the VARIATION is not accompanied by CONCORD: the first illustration uses a numerical pattern (7:1), the second, a sequential pattern (*first/later*), and instead of CONCORD there is an additional CONTRAST (*only a fool does otherwise*). In (1i) the VARIATION involves two CONCORDED illustrations (*chew/swallow; listen/speak*), with most of the CONCRETIZATIONS new (except *speak*). Finally, (1j) adds to VARIATION both CONCORD *and* CONTRAST, this time a numerical CONTRAST between the illustrations (3:35). The last example, (1k), involves both VARIATION and CONCORD (*2:1/2:1*) and, in addition, a complicated play that lays bare the parallelism: the "therefore" is, in fact, a non sequitur.[3]

The above sketch of derivational description shows, among other things, how constructs, posited as intermediate stages in the derivation of a complex text, can be attested by simpler texts, for which they are the terminal structures. This bears out both the principle, sometimes called into question,[4] of representing poetic structure as a series of approximations and the adequacy of actually proposed approximations.

2. A Somali Proverb: Formulating the Theme

I will now attempt a detailed derivational description of a Somali proverb, which is, to my mind, a genuine small masterpiece. Here it is, in the original with word-for-word glosses, (2a), and in literal, (2b), and standard, (2c), English translation:

(2) (a) *Caano aan fiiqsi loo   dhamin iyo   hadal aan fiiro*
      Milk   not a-sip one-in drinks and talk   not attention
      loo   odhan feedhahaaga ayyay   wax yeelaan .
      one-in speaks ribs-your   do-they harm

   (b) The milk that one does not drink in sips and the words that one speaks without attention harm your ribs.

   (c) Gulped milk and careless words harm your ribs.

Like any poetic text, it loses many of its effects in translation, but the description is meant to capture them all.

Derivation starts with the formulation of the text's theme. As I have said, this is greatly facilitated by the availability of Permjakov's formulations. But I have also pointed out [1978g: 314–18, 321–27] that some modifications are in order, dictated by a stricter separation of theme from expressiveness and a more precise formulation of themes. One departure from Permjakov that I am going to introduce will abolish a thematic distinction; the other will add a new distinction.

(*a*) It is clear that proverb (2) has roughly the same theme as proverbs (1b–k). It differs, however, in that it "proves" the theme by means of a *reductio ad absurdum:* it implies that 'thinking is right' by showing that 'thoughtlessness is wrong'. Such proverbs are widespread:

(3) (a) "Don't cut without measuring" (Persian).
    (b) "Don't swallow without chewing, don't talk without thinking" (Vietnamese).

In fact, the negative pattern is there already in (1h), in which it forms the second term of VARIATION ("only a fool acts first and thinks later").

For Permjakov the difference between the proverbs in (1) and (3) is a thematic one, and he distinguishes accordingly between positive and negative themes. I see the two sets of proverbs—(1) and (3)—as absolutely synthematic, differing only in expressiveness. Therefore, in the description of (2) I will proceed from the positive formulation, (1a), leaving the negative transformation to EDs in the derivation (see §4).[5]

(*b*) A thematic distinction of a different kind, however, seems to be relevant for proverbs about the importance of 'thinking'. Some of them apply to situations of 'unthought-out speech', but not to 'unthought-out acts'. Compare the Russian proverb

(4) (a) *Slovo—ne vorobej, vyletit—ne pojmaeš'* "A word is not a sparrow, if it flies away you won't catch it",

whose theme is, approximately:

(4) (b) One should think over one's words.

Accordingly, the word *slovo* 'word' that appears in its text is a direct CONCRETIZATION of the thematic element 'speech'.

As for our Somali proverb, it applies to any kind of 'unthought-out acts'[6] so that its theme is

(5) = (1a) One should think over one's actions,

and the word *hadal* 'talk' in its text is (just like *caano* 'milk') a CONCRE-
TIZATION of the thematic element 'action'.

Let us now consider how this theme is artistically expressed in the
text of the proverb—by what "tricks" an unadorned thesis is transformed into a miniature work of art.

3. A 'Universal Law': AUGMENTATION and VARIATION

Unlike many examples in (1), our Somali proverb does not involve a
parallelism between 'thought' and 'actions' but concentrates instead
on the parallelism between the two illustrations ('milk/talk').[7] Indeed,
in both cases the 'action' part of the situation ('gulped milk'; 'said
words') and the 'thought' part ('sips'; 'attention'), instead of being
clearly separated into two independent, similar and coordinated constructions (cf. proverbs (1c–1i)), form an asymmetrical structure. It is
subordinate and comprises three main constituents: a qualified noun,
a verb in the attributive clause, and a preverb-governed noun. In ED
terms, this means that the derivation of proverb (2) does not begin
with DIVISION of the theme into 'thought' and 'action' with subsequent CONCORD of these subthemes.

On the other hand, like most other examples, our proverb does
involve an AUGMENTATION. Most of the proverbs in (1) AUGMENT
'thinking' by stressing either the 'intensity of thought' (one is advised
to think 'carefully and/or many times') or the 'priority and/or strict
necessity of thought' ('think first and only after that act'). Our
proverb emphasizes the importance of 'thinking' in a different way—
by underscoring the 'universality' of the law. The implementation of
this strategy consists of three major operations.

1. The very decision to use this kind of AUGMENTATION constitutes
a first step:[8]

(6) One should *always* think over one's actions.

2. For the artistic expression of the thematic element 'always, universally', literature has devised a subtle and effective method: the
universality of a propounded law can be "proved" by demonstrating
that it applies to widely different phenomena. When (as is the case
with proverbs) brevity is sought, a minimum of two contrasting il-

lustrations suffices. To highlight both the contrast and the basic unity of the two illustrations they are made to look as similar as possible. Technically this is handled by the EDs VAR*contr*[9] and, subsequently, CONCORD. Note that recourse to VAR*contr* is not arbitrary: the expressive device is brought in as a way of embodying the idea 'always, universally'. In other words, this is an instance of CONCRETIZATION of a thematic element via an ED (see Introduction, Glossary). Our proverb shares the VAR*contr* pattern with a number of other examples, such as (1i), (1j), and (3b). In the derivation this common property is reflected by the following, as yet very abstract, approximation of the actual text:

(7) two illustrations[10] of (6), contrasting (and similar) in one or several features.

3. The next step is to CONCRETIZE the contrastive relationship. In this respect our proverb once again follows a stereotype, using the oppositions 'physical/spiritual' and 'motion into (the body, from the outside) / motion out of (the body, from the inside)'. This yields formula (8), common to our proverb and to proverbs (1i) and (3b):

(8) *Illustration 1:* One should think over one's physical actions involving motion into the body from the outside; *Illustration 2:* one should think over one's spiritual actions involving motion out of the body from the inside.

In fact, the common denominator of the three proverbs is even richer, as the only way to CONCRETIZE these illustrations is through the ready-made objects 'food' and 'speech' (a limitation imposed by the dictionary of reality, which supplies the CONCRETIZATIONS of EDs):

(9) One should think over the intake of food; one should think over the letting-out of words.[11]

One by-product of this forced CONCRETIZATION is that the two 'actions' are not only opposed but also similar to each other: both are 'located in the mouth'. This similarity is not very prominent in our proverb (and still less so in proverbs (1i) or (3b)), but it is relevant in the light of the structural importance of 'location' elsewhere in the text, in the derivation and in the body (see below about 'ribs'). Thus a first step toward CONCORD of the two illustrations is taken. Systematic implementation of this CONCORD, envisaged in (7), is considered in §§5 and 6.

4. A Comic Plot: SUDDEN TURN and "Failure of Pretensions"

There is a certain ring of truth to our proverb, due probably to the fact that it relates certain happenings, events, and causal links between them, so that two *plots* emerge. This sets our proverb apart from the rest in examples (1) and (3), which mostly consist of slogans and injunctions. Only once, (1j), is there a rudimentary narrative ("A dog will run around a place three times . . .") and twice, (1j and 1k), a semblance of causal linking. In (1k) ("Man has two ears and one mouth; therefore . . .") the causality is faulty and thus comical. In all these cases, however, the links are logical inferences between illustrations rather than causal links inside them. In PE terms the plot structure of (2) involves the complex ED of SUDDEN TURN (S-TURN). As for the proverb's comic bent, to account for it, the derivation will include a *comic figure,* namely, "Failure of pretensions." The two patterns—S-TURN and "Failure"—are in several respects similar and form a compact and stable construction underlying plots with comic reversals.[12]

Using such a plot in our case means that the thesis formulated in (9) will be "proved" by a comic *reductio ad absurdum:* an instructive ridiculous failure of the opposite attitude will show that (9) is true. In terms of EDs this means that (9) is subjected to CONTRAST, yielding:

(10) One should not take food in without thinking it over, one should not let words out without thinking them over; one should think over the intake of food, one should think over the words one lets out.

In view of the obvious tautology, the second, "positive" formulation is usually either omitted from S-TURN-cum-"Failure" plots (by means of ED REDUCTION) or survives as an appended moral. The first, "negative" part becomes the centerpiece of the plot and develops into a miniature drama.[13]

First of all, an explicit element of *narrative 'failure'* is introduced: 'one should not', from (10), is CONCRETIZED as 'bad things will happen to one'. This entails a clear-cut DIVISION of the extant material into two consecutive parts: 'wrong behavior—bad results'.

(11) Bad things happen to a person who does not think while taking in food; bad things happen to a person who does not think over the words he lets out.

To make the eventual 'failure' less expected and thus more striking and complete, the s-TURN construction begins with an episode portraying, by contrast, some 'successful activities' of the character. For the sake of instructiveness (as well as general expressiveness) these 'successes' should be the very same actions that embody the character's 'lack of thinking'. (These two tasks are handled respectively by EDs RECOIL and COMBINATION, which form part of SUDDEN TURN.) In our case the element of 'apparently successful careless behavior' is CONCRETIZED as 'carelessly consuming much food; producing much careless talk'. In addition, to create a comic impression the character should behave in this way not because of mere 'carelessness' but because of some 'enthusiastic involvement, blinding passion, or absurd pretensions' (a requirement specified by the comic figure "Failure"[14]). In our proverb these elements are represented by 'hungering for food' and (to a lesser extent) 'garrulousness'. As a result, at this point we obtain:

(12) Bad things happen to a person who consumes much food greedily and in a hurry; bad things happen to a person who talks carelessly and too much.

Let us now look at the way 'failure' is developed. As yet it has the very abstract form of 'bad things happening'. The next steps will be concerned with (*a*) imparting to it some comic traits (as required by "Failure") and (*b*) CONCORDING it in an instructive causal way with the plot material already generated (i.e., with 'consumption of food', 'greediness','careless words', etc.). Constraint *a* is realized by the farcical element of 'physical discomfiture', constraint *b*, by modeling the 'failures' on ready-made moralistic plot patterns dealing with 'food' and 'talk'. 'Failure of greedy eating' follows the pattern of 'harm through excess' (of the 'to bite off more than one can chew' type); 'failure of talkativeness' assumes the form of 'harm through unguarded words' (of the 'your tongue is your enemy' type). Thus the next approximation of the proverb's plot is reached:

(13) One who consumes much food greedily and in a hurry suffers physically as a result; one who talks too much and carelessly comes to physical grief invited by the contents of his words.

Further CONCRETIZATION of plot elements goes hand in hand with (and is in fact determined by) the development of new symmetries between the subplots.

5. Identity in Contrast: CONCORD and COMBINATION

As we recall, the two contrasting VARIATIONS on the theme were designed to convey 'universality' by showing that the "law" holds true even under extremely different conditions. To set off the contrast and emphasize the unity, numerous similarities (CONCORDS) between the opposites are now to be introduced.

Some similarities are in fact already there. The two subplots share: (*a*) the thematic complex (9), supplemented with the elements 'failure' and 'success' (see (11) and (12)); (*b*) the 'location of intake of food / outlet of words—mouth'; (*c*) the element of 'physical grief' tacitly introduced as a by-product of 'farcical comicality' in (13).

At the same time the two story lines contrast with each other in being respectively (*d*) 'physical / spiritual' and (*e*) 'directed into / out of the body'. In elaborating the causal links in each subplot, we have, in fact, AUGMENTED the opposition 'into / out of' into that of (*f*) 'processes inside the small space of a human body / processes in the wide space of social relations'.

This latter spatial contrast is now set in greater relief by an additional, very elegant spatial symmetry. A double CONCORD is introduced: the two 'physical griefs' will now affect the characters 'in one and the same part of the body' and, like the starting point of both subplots ('mouth'), it will be placed 'at the body's boundary'. The happy find of the derivation at this point is *feedhaha* 'the ribs', an area close to the body's surface, proverbially connected in Somali with beating and quite plausible as a localization of pain from hurried swallowing. The symmetry between the subplots thus attained is almost perfect (see (14) and Fig. 5.1):

(14) When one greedily and hastily consumes much food, it passes in through the mouth to the inside and then comes back to the boundary of the body hurting one in the area of the ribs; when one talks much and carelessly, the words pass out through the mouth to the outside and then come back to the boundary of the body in the form of beating, provoked by the content of the words, in the area of the ribs.

Still greater symmetry is achieved by deletion from the text of the differing parts of the two subplots, that is, of the specific mechanisms that bring about the 'stomach pain' and the 'beating' respectively. This REDUCTION heightens not only the parallelism between the stories but also the reader's involvement in the situation, since now it is

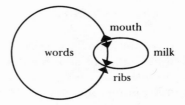

Figure 5.1. The two routes

up to him to supply the missing parts of the plot.[15] Together with
REDUCTION of some other obvious details, this yields:

(15) Food swallowed greedily causes pain in the ribs; words uttered carelessly
cause pain in the ribs.

This formulation invites yet another deletion—this time by fusing
(COMBINING) the two finales (and consequently the two subplots) into
one.[16]

(16) Greedily swallowed food and carelessly uttered words cause pain in
one's ribs.[17]

The omission of all other specific details of each 'failure' leaves the
role of a single common denouement to the 'ribs', so that they accu-
mulate most of the finale's expressiveness. This effect is further reinforced by CONTRAST between the very tangible 'ribs' and the pointedly colorless verb *wax yeelaan* 'they harm'—a noncommittal
compromise between 'stomach pain' and 'beating'. As a result, the
'ribs' stand out as the sole symbol of 'failure'.

Further CONCORDS and other EDs spread from the referential
sphere (of events and objects) into the code sphere and thus determine the definitive linguistic shape of the proverb.[18]

6. Code Sphere: CONCORD and AUGMENTATION

As a result of compression, the four-part structure (two subplots,
two parts in each) has become tripartite (two initial parts, one finale).
This raises a compositional problem: how to emphasize the importance of the finale as an equivalent and counterbalance to the two

beginnings. One way of AUGMENTING the third part is purely quantitative—by making it twice as long as the two first, according to the
widespread 1 + 1 + 2 pattern of 'summarizing symmetry'.[19] In a
sense this would recapture the essentially four-part articulation of the
plot. Another way is to AUGMENT the third component qualitatively,
turning it into a real denouement—short, occurring toward the end
and effectively summarizing (solving) the preceding development. In
this case the quantitative articulation is closer to 1 + 1 + 1, but the
"weight" of the third 1 in a sense "equals" 2. It is this latter pattern
that is used in our proverb. It corresponds well to the fused plot,
obtained in (16), with two subplots and a common finale, as well as to
the thematic perspective of 'nonthinking, punishment, and belated
realization of the truth'.[20]Also, tripartition is common in the shorter
forms of Somali folklore and poetry.[21]

The pattern consists of several EDs that implement the conflicting
effects of 'triple symmetry' and 'summarizing finale'.

1. The third part is directly AUGMENTED in various respects, forming a clear-cut INCREASE as compared with each of the initial parts.

2. It is also AUGMENTED indirectly—by CONCORDS of the two first
parts, excluding the third. The effect of such an *a a b* sequence is that
of two symmetrical "halves" followed ("concluded") by an asymmetrical "whole."

3. CONCORDS running through all three parts promote the general
parallelism in the triplet and more specifically the unity of the third
part with the other two; this, in the context of the EDs in 1 and 2,
supports the effect of a 'unifying and summarizing whole'.

Let us see how this pattern is realized in our proverb. I list the
corresponding code-sphere structures and details without attempting
to arrange them in a derivational sequence. I also find it convenient
for the exposition to reverse the order of operations 1–3.

Triple CONCORDS. Syntactically, the text consists of three clauses with
approximately the same set of components (actants, phrases, words).
Metrically, each of the three parts is eight or nine syllables long.
Phonetically there is first of all the alliteration, traditional in Somali
verse (Andrzejewski and Lewis 1964: 42ff.), of the initial sounds of
full words, in this case of *f-: fúqsi, fúro, feedhahaaga,* and also the
overall phonetic parallelism of the three lines—alliteration in /f-/, /l-/,
/-n/ and assonance in repeated short and long /a/.

Double CONCORDS. On the morphological and syntactic levels the two initial parts form an ideal parallelism. Each contains a noun with a zero (i.e., indefinite) article plus a negative relative clause. The clause in each case consists of the negative particle *aan;* the impersonal pronoun *la* 'people', conjoined with the preverb *u* 'for, by' (*la* + *u* = *loo*); a noun with a zero article governed by the preverb *u;* and a negative verb in the subjunctive. Both the word order and grammatical details are the same throughout.

The syntactic parallelism is echoed on the metrical and phonetic levels. The corresponding words are perfectly similar in the number of syllables (2 - 1 - 2 - 1 - 2), the verbs, in inflection (-*n*); the nouns governed by the preverbs—*fiiqsi* 'sip' and *fiiro* 'attention' (embodying the theme of 'thinking')—are similar phonetically (*fii-;* ending in a vowel) and prosodically (a long and short syllable). The common phonetic denominator of the two lines is roughly as follows:

(17) *a - aan - fii - loo - dh - n*

The vocalic series *a - o - i* is both opposed and similar to its *a - e* counterpart in the third line, with the common *a* forming the link needed for triple symmetry.[22]

INCREASES. First of all, sequentially, the denouement of the plot is naturally placed at the end and is thus emphasized. Syntactically and morphologically, the denouement is accorded the role of the main predication of the sentence (with a sentence-forming particle *ayya* and an affirmative verb in the indicative) and thus clearly opposed to the "noun phrase–attributive clause" structure of the initial parts (with their dependent negative verbs in the subjunctive). The INCREASE in 'grammatical directness' is evident for every feature involved (predication, indicative mood, affirmation). A similar INCREASE occurs with respect to the categories of number and definiteness. The third clause is in the plural ('they harm') with the plural subject (*ay* 'they') referring to the sum total of the singular objects in the preceding lines ('milk' and 'talk'), adjoined by a coordinating conjunction (*iyo* 'and'). As for definiteness/indefiniteness, there are four indefinite and one definite noun respectively.

Moreover, the morphological composition of the definite noun (*feedhahaaga*) involves yet another INCREASE of the same sort, this time resulting in a striking shift of point of view. While the opening clauses use the third-person indefinite pronoun (*la* 'people' = Fr. *on* = Ger. *man*), the last clause switches to the second person—the generic, that is, still impersonal, 'thou'.[23] The effect is again one of INCREASED directness, of a, so to speak, "grammatical close-up." This effect is further enhanced by the following subtle COMBINATION. The second person is represented by its possessive particle *-aa-* 'thy' (*feedha - h - aa - ga* 'ribs-thy-these'),[24] so that the reference to the addressee (albeit purely formal) is fused into one word with the 'ribs'. With the 'ribs' having accumulated all the pain of the 'double failure', their verbal fusion with the addressee produces the impression of a 'blow delivered to the ribs of the reader'.[25]

I have tried to trace the elaborate and thorough implementation of the underlying theme, purely informative and commonsensical, on many levels in both the referential and code spheres of the proverb. My aim was twofold: to gauge the expressive richness of this particular specimen of verbal art and to illustrate the techniques, advantages, and difficulties of derivational description in general.

6

Pun and Punishment: The Structure of a Bertrand Russell Aphorism

> In a man whose reasoning powers are good, fallacious arguments
> are evidence of bias . . . displaying the distorting influence of a
> desire.
>
> —Bertrand Russell (1950:67)

The text under discussion consists of two simple sentences:

(1) *Many people would sooner die than think. In fact, they do.*[1]

Laconic as it is, the aphorism displays characteristic features of the
Bertrand Russell image:

(2) philosopher's stance, aristocratic poise, militant rationalism.

This is a tentative formulation of the theme of the analyzed text. As
such it is bound to form the starting point of a derivational description of the text's structure. The question, however, arises, Where does
the scholar get this formulation from in the first place? It is, of course,
the result of an intuitive literary-critical analysis of the work. But, in
the case of a PE scholar, the intuition is disciplined and even guided
by his bearing in mind that the eventual formulation will have to serve
as the starting point of a derivation.[2] I begin the discussion of our text
with an informal search for its theme and only then proceed to the
description proper.

This chapter is a revised version of [1980a].

1. A Reading of the Text

The two elegant sentences are in fact rich both in content and in literary craftsmanship. Let us consider them more closely.

1.1. *Aggression*

The microplot, (1), features, as philosophic aphorisms usually do, Man in general, or, rather, a certain class of people (*many people*). Their story centers around the two lexically full words—the verbs *think* and *die*. However, we are not presented with philosophic reflections on death like *Memento mori* or with a variation on the theme of *Cogito ergo sum* (although, in a sense, our text can be read as an inversion of the Cartesian formula: aphorism (1) $\cong$ *Non cogitant ergo non sunt*). Once the double entendre on *sooner* has been revealed (first it reads figuratively, as 'rather', and then the literal sense 'before than' is suddenly understood), it becomes clear that the author has in mind human stupidity and the futility of life devoid of thought. In a word, we are dealing with a skeptical saying of the genre:

(3) "They were born, suffered and died" (Anatole France).

Yet, Russell's tone is different, it is one of mockery rather than compassion. If one is going to quote France, a closer parallel would be example (4) (from *Penguin Island*), also based, like (1), on word play:

(4) ". . . our free-thinkers, who, as a rule, do not think freely for the reason that they do not think at all."

Russell is even more pitiless, for his pun (unlike (4)) concerns the dead (about whom, as the saying goes, *aut bene aut nihil:* note the compassion that softens death in (3)). The heartless jesting over a gaping grave combines the effects of (3) and (4) into black humor of the type exemplified by (5a,b).

(5) (a) *King. "Where's Polonius?" Hamlet. "At supper (. . .) Not where he eats; but where he is eaten: a certain convocation of politic worms is e'en at him"* (Hamlet, IV, 3).
(b) *Obit anus, abit onus.* 'The old hag dies, the burden is cast off' (Schopenhauer on the death of the woman whom he had crippled by throwing her downstairs and to whom he was to pay a life pension; quoted from

Russell [1965:727], who, though ostensibly indignant, clearly relishes the joke).

This cruel laughter, somewhat unexpected from a renowned philosopher and pacifist, is nevertheless in full accord with the militant rationalism of the author of *Why I Am Not a Christian.* Moreover, Russell's mercilessness is not confined to irreverence toward the dead. The pun on *sooner* is supplemented with the play upon the words *would / In fact, . . . do:* the 'dying' that occurs in the second sentence is thus represented as the 'fulfillment of the heroes' wishes'. Russell assumes, in relation to them, the role of a god who, taking men at their words, punishes them for their foolish wishes by fulfilling them to the letter. One is reminded of King Midas who wished that everything he touched would turn to gold and almost died of hunger.

A further macabre effect is added to the literal wish fulfillment by the play on the word *do,* which is not only an auxiliary, but also the most general verb of action. As a result, the characters' obstinate adherence to the philosophy of 'not thinking even in death' acquires yet another dimension: their very 'dying', which they prefer to 'thinking', is represented as an 'action', that is, the opposite of 'thinking' in terms of the 'thought/act' dichotomy. The equation *die = do = act (≠ think)* is also supported by the existence of the proverbial phrase *Do or die* and by the rhymelike interplay of the two monosyllables in *d-.*[3]

Incidentally, the motif of 'punishment through wish fulfillment' is relevant to our discussion not only in the mocking arrogance of its *Tu l'as voulu* logic but also in its characteristic literalness. The stress laid on formal correctness of statements, on the strict correspondence between statements and events they describe, and on the fidelity to the principle *A = A* reflect the rationalist stance of one of the classics of formal logic. The motif of 'pitilessly taking one literally' is widespread in literature and folklore, and it is not limited to situations of wish fulfillment or divine intervention. Compare the behavior of Shylock, who insists—in strict agreement with the contract—on being paid with a pound of the debtor's flesh. The characteristic features of the situation—namely, principled rejection of the commandment of mercy; hatred, openly professed by Shylock as his motive; desire to push its realization to the extreme, that is, to taking a life; imprecision of the contract (concluded, as it were, as a joke) and the mocking insistence on fulfilling it to the letter are all relevant for fully comprehending Russell's attitude in (1).[4]

The element 'hate' has, in fact, already been touched upon implicitly when we spoke of Russell's militant non-Christianity. The word "militant" sounds like a trite and almost self-evident attribute of rationalism. But what it actually means is a relentless war of exter-mination, rooted subconsciously in aggression, hate—the killer in-stinct. These thematic elements are quite appropriate for the descrip-tion of deep human motives in general and of those of humor in particular.[5] They can be perceived with sufficient clarity (although with some effort and astonishment) behind the impenetrable bril-liance of Russell's wit.[6] Indeed, aphorism (1) brings to mind not only the aphorisms quoted above, which are objective, factual statements (however caustic they may be), but also the following type of pragmat-ic (to the point of cannibalism) injunctions:

(6) "You are in fact longer than I by a head, but if you keep reminding me of it, I'll deprive you of this advantage" (Napoleon to one of his generals); "If the enemy does not surrender, he must be annihilated" (Maxim Gorky).

Deliberately—"unrealistically"—cruel is also the very dilemma "Think or die", patterned on *Patria o muerte*, "Your money or your life" and the like. Its spuriousness pushes to the extreme both the obstinacy of the fools and the aggressiveness of the author, who alone could have presented them with this absurd choice.

1.2. *Sublimation*

In trying to pinpoint the shocking element of 'hate, mockery' in Russell's saying, I have perhaps overstated my point. The murderous content is actually presented in the flawless form of "English" humor.

Indeed, humor as such, in a sense, is a product of compromise between aggressive-defensive instincts and the censorship imposed on civilized behavior (see note 5). Thus, the implausibility of the carica-tures ('ready to die for the right not to think'; 'never once thought in their lives') not only testifies to the extent of the author's venom but also displays its fictitiousness. The speaker's own posture itself—one of reason, philosophy, and aristocraticism—prescribes restraint. Rus-sell (unlike Napoleon in (6) and Dionysus in the Midas legend, unlike Hamlet and Shylock), does not assume the punitive function himself. Punishment in (1) materializes on its own—in conformity with the arrogant indifference of the thinker, who is above soiling his hands with despicable fools, certain that they will bring about their own deserved downfall.

Furthermore, the kind of retribution that befalls them—death—is actually not a specific one designed for those who refuse to think. Obviously, one of the propositions implicit in (1) and reconstructed in the course of its comprehension is the well-known "philosophical" truth

(7) *All men are mortal. (Socrates is a man. Therefore, . . .).*

Thus the outcome that is natural and inevitable for every human (such exemplary thinkers as Socrates not excluded) is deliberately presented as "capital punishment." The arbitrariness of this twisted interpretation serves a twofold purpose. On the one hand, it lays bare the author's aggression: he does not stop at a logical inaccuracy for the pleasure of pronouncing a death sentence on his characters (cf. the epigraph). On the other hand, this aggressiveness is muffled and sublimated by being channeled into a purely mental sphere.[7]

1.3. *Verbalness*

That the retaliation is imaginary is also underscored by the central role played in it by pun, that is, the most superficial, "nonserious," purely verbal of all means of mental equation. As a result, the word-play serves as yet another embodiment of the two contrasting attitudes—the heartless mocking (of the dead) and its sublimation onto a purely verbal plane. In general, the linguistic form of the witticism is rich in effects that work toward a sublimation of the author's aggressive drive. Thus, the paucity and paleness of the second sentence, consisting of only three items, all of them function words, tend to obscure the ruthlessness of the fools' final undoing by carrying it out, as it were, behind the scenes (in accordance with the rules of classic drama). At the same time this paucity is a sort of verbal equivalent of the 'deathlike life devoid of thought', that constitutes the plot content of the second sentence (cf. situations like that in ex. (3), "They were born, suffered and died," based on the paradox 'life = nonlife').

There is, however, another side to the second sentence. Being completely pronominal, it requires a whole series of logical operations in order to be comprehended: (*a*) retrieving all the antecedents (*many people* for *they; die sooner than think* for *do; would* for *in fact*); (*b*) discovering all the wordplay couplings—firstly, the literal meaning of *sooner*—and also (*c*) the difference between the figurative and the literal meanings of the phrase *would . . . die;* and (*d*) the play on the pair *die/do* and the implied phrase *Do or die!*; (*e*) understanding the logical relations between the wish (*not to think*) and the obligation tied to it (*to die*); (*f*) taking into consideration a rule of linguistic communication, namely, the *presumption of novelty,* which helps one to discard, as a possible antecedent of *do,* the verb *die* taken alone (otherwise we would only obtain the truism *Men are mortal*); and finally, (*g*) reconstructing the deleted but implied links of the logical chain, in particular, the textbook example (7). Thus the second sentence (portraying, as plot, the punishment of stupidity and, as a poor sentence, the poverty of life devoid of thought) embodies, by its entire elliptic structure, a feast of the speaker's and the reader's triumphant intellect— although it does so in a muted, allusive, sublimated manner.

2. From Reading to Derivation

The above impressionistic analysis of the witticism must now be rewritten in explicit derivational form. In the course of the discussion, I have, in fact, isolated and labeled quite a few elements, attitudes and motifs that convey the speaker's 'aggression' and 'sublimation' ("real" and "verbal").

1. '*Aggression*': 'stupidity'; 'futility of not thinking'; 'mercilessness'; 'cruel laughter'; 'wish fulfillment'; 'mocking arrogance'; 'rationalistic literalness'; 'militancy, hatred'; 'humor'; 'arbitrary imposition of a cruel dilemma'.
2. '*Sublimation*': 'English humor'; 'restraint'; 'humor as compromise with censorship' (= 'venom' + 'fictitiousness'); 'the speaker's self-effacement from the plot (i.e., from the punitive action)'; 'passing off natural death for capital punishment (aggression made purely mental)'.
3. '*Verbalness*': 'pun' = 'mocking the dead' + 'pure verbalness'; 'linguistic paucity of the second sentence' = 'a veil for the ruthless punishment' + 'verbal equivalent of the deathlike life devoid of thought'; 'ellipsis' = 'logical operations' = 'feast of reason'.

All these elements must now find their place in the description of the thematic-expressive structure of (1), that is, in its derivation from (2). This will, of course, call for further development, detailing, and hierarchization of the observations made—a heuristic process upon which I will not dwell. The derivation splits into three successive approximations of the text: "deep design" (DD), "deep structure" (DS) and "surface structure" (SS).

3. Deep Design

DD is a very general program for evolving the text. It reflects the most abstract expressive characteristics that the text in question has in common with a vast number of other synthematic texts. The derivation of the DD of our witticism from the theme is shown in Figure 6.1. A few remarks will suffice to make the figure clear.[8]

3.1. *Theme*

The derivation starts with a modified version (2′) of (2), in which the same thematic elements are regrouped and connected by a 'contrast' relation and a new explicit generalization (2b) 'nonmilitant attitudes' is introduced.

3.2. *Primary Unfolding of the Theme*

(2′a,b) → (8a,b): the opposition 'militant/nonmilitant' AUGMENTS into 'hate/sublimation'.[9]

(2′b′) → (9a,b): CONTRAST yields the pair 'stupidity, passion / reason, restraint', where the second term is the dominant one (as it corresponds to the initial 'rationalism').

(2′b″) → (10), (11): 'aristocratic' VARIES as 'aloof' and 'refined'.

(2′b‴) → (12): 'aphorism' is one possible CONCRETIZATION of 'the philosophical' in the sphere of literary genres.

3.3. *CONCRETIZING and COMBINING 'Aggression' and 'Sublimation'*

(8a), (9) → (13): the 'domination' relationship is pressed into the service of 'aggression', yielding 'cruel defeat of stupidity by reason'.

(8a), (10) → (14): COMBINATION of 'hate' and 'aloofness' produces 'arrogance, humiliation'.

(8a), (8b) → (15a,b): one way of COMBINING (reconciling) 'aggression' with 'sublimation' is 'humor, ridicule'.

(8), (10) → (16): 'sublimation' COMBINES with 'aloofness' into the principle of 'withdrawal of the aggressive character from the plot, i.e., from participation in the actions undoing stupidity'. Since 'sublima-

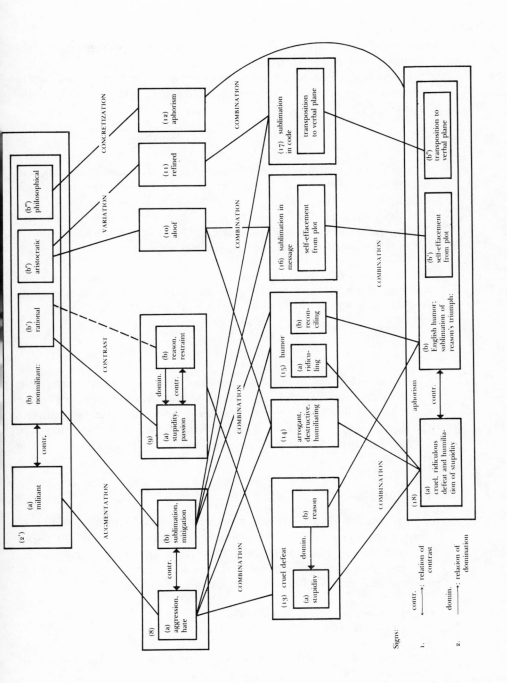

(2') (a) militant — (b) nonmilitant:

contr.

(b') rational · (b'') aristocratic · (b''') philosophical

CONTRAST

VARIATION

CONCRETIZATION

(10) aloof

(11) refined

(12) aphorism

(9) (a) stupidity, passion ← domin. → (b) reason, restraint

contr.

AUGMENTATION

(8) (a) aggression, hate ← contr. → (b) sublimation, mitigation

COMBINATION

COMBINATION

COMBINATION

COMBINATION

(13) cruel defeat (a) stupidity — domin. → (b) reason

(14) arrogant, destructive, humiliating

(15) humor (a) ridiculing · (b) reconciling

(16) sublimation in message self-effacement from plot

(17) sublimation in code transposition to verbal plane

COMBINATION

COMBINATION

(18) (a) cruel, ridiculous defeat and humiliation of stupidity

contr.

aphorism

(b) English humor: sublimation of reason's triumph:

(b') self-effacement from plot · (b'') transposition to verbal plane

Signs:

1. contr. ←——→ : relation of contrast

2. domin. ——→ : relation of domination

tion' implies its 'base' counterpart, formula (16) represents both 'sub-limation' and 'aggression'.

(8), (11) → (17): another solution to the same problem is to 'transfer aggression into the code sphere of the text, preferring purely verbal effects'.

3.4. *Deep Design*

(13a), (14), (15a) → (18a): 'cruel defeat of stupidity', 'arrogant, humiliating', and 'aggressive aspect of humor' COMBINE into an integral aggressive pole, (18a).

(13b), (15b), (16), (17) → (18b): 'sublimation' will rely on (18b') 'self-withdrawal from action' and (18b") 'transfer into verbalness'.

On the whole, the deep design provides for

(18) an aphorism in which the cruelly ridiculous defeat of stupidity is, in the tradition of English humor, veiled by the withdrawal of reason's triumph from the plot action and by its transfer into pure verbalness.

4. Deep Structure

DS is the next major approximation of text (1) and thus represents a narrower class of synthematic texts. Namely, those that share (*a*) the same principal expressive devices and figures involved in carrying out the deep design (expansion of the structure); and (*b*) the way these are COMBINED into a compact artistic pattern (compression of the structure).

4.1. *Expansion*

Implementation of DD introduces an array of complex constructions: two "Caricatures," "Punishment by wish fulfillment". "Passing off (one thing for another)" and "Pun" (see top of Fig. 6.2).

"*Caricature*" is a comic figure[10] defined as a grotesque AUGMENTATION of the ridiculed quality, in this case of (19) into (19'):

(19) stupidity, unwillingness to think
(19') passionate wish, obstinate desire not to think.

The 'obstinacy' further motivates recourse to a specific variety of "Caricature", which can be called "Caricature through *even*":

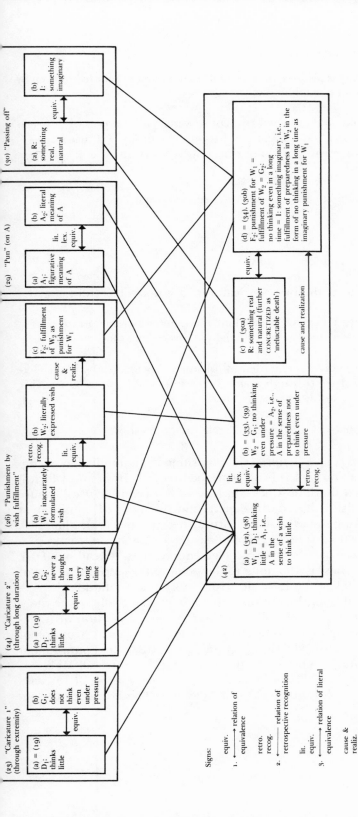

Figure 6.2. The deep structure

(20) the stupidity is pictured as so durable that it remains unaffected even by circumstances most conducive to change.[11]

Russell's joke makes use of two contrasting VARIATIONS of "Caricature through *even*"—"Caricature through extremity" ("Caricature 1") and "Caricature through long duration" ("Caricature 2"): the *many people* both

(21) refuse to think even when threatened with death

and

(22) never think once in their lives.

At the DS level the two "Caricatures" are not yet as full-fledged:

(23) "Caricature 1": . . . refuse to think even under extreme pressure
(24) "Caricature 2": . . . never a thought in a very long time.

Note that (23) conveys the idea of 'obstinacy' twice: (*a*) by being, like (24), a "Caricature through *even*" and, additionally, (*b*) by portraying the characters' stubbornness as

(25) a deliberate challenge to unfavorable circumstances.[12]

"*Punishment by wish fulfillment*" ("Punishment") is another comic figure implementing the 'ridicule' specified by DD. In point of fact, it COMBINES two more abstract constructs—the comic figure "Failure (of pretensions, wishes, desires, etc.)" and the motif of 'punishment through taking inaccurately formulated propositions literally'. "Failure" (see note 10) is based on the complex ED SUDDEN TURN,[13] a common means of AUGMENTING elements such as 'defeat' (see DD). "Failure of wishes" is also quite to the point in (1), since the object of 'ridicule' has taken the form of 'wish, desire (not to think)'.

The motif of 'punishment through taking . . . literally', quite widespread in literature (e.g., Shylock), lies at the intersection of (COMBINES) several components of DD—'cruelty', 'arrogance', 'triumph of reason over stupidity'. Merging with "Failure," the 'punishment through taking . . . literally' acquires a comic flavor (recall Midas—a classical example of "Punishment"). For the *many people* of Russell's aphorism, in conformity to the principle of 'self-withdrawal', an "objective" version of "Punishment" ("Punishment$_{obj}$") is meted out: the chastisement accomplishes itself without the interference of any triumphant personage.[14]

The abstract format of "Punishment$_{obj}$" is represented by (26) (see Fig. 6.2). Formula (26) explicitly distinguishes between (*a*) the real wish W_1, inaccurately formulated by a personage, and (*b*) wish W_2, which in reality is not his wish but constitutes the literal (i.e., in a sense also "real") meaning of his words. In accordance with the logic of SUDDEN TURN, only W_1 is stated in the text directly, whereas W_2 comes to light in retrospect when (*c*) its fulfillment F_2 proves unexpectedly to be a punishment. (The relations of 'literal equivalence' and 'retrospective recognition' between W_1 and W_2 and of 'precedence, causality and realization' between W_2 and W_3 are shown in Fig. 6.2 by arrows.)

"*Pun*" is yet another comic construction involved in the implementation of 'ridicule'. It COMBINES this function (which it shares with "Caricatures" and "Punishment") with that of channeling 'ridicule,' that is, 'aggression', into a purely verbal sphere. Both principal puns in (1),

(27) *sooner* = (*a*) 'rather than'; (*b*) 'earlier than'
(28) *X would sooner* (or *rather*) *die than Y* = (*a*) 'X wishes very strongly not to Y';
(*b*) 'X prefers ceasing to live to Y'

are instances of

(29) equating the figurative meaning of a word with its literal meaning.

It is the abstract formulation (29) that is arrived at on the level of DS (see Fig. 6.2). That the equation of meanings is based on the mere coincidence of lexical shapes makes, as we recall, for the effect of 'verbalness'.

"*Passing off* (one thing for another)" is a construction most often used comically (see note 10). In (1) it is concerned primarily with embodying the 'purely mental, imaginary, unreal, "it's-just-a-game"' status of the 'stupidity's cruel defeat' (which in turn CONCRETIZES 'sublimation'). At the same time, "Passing off" is yet another way of displaying 'intellectual sophistry', that is, a manifestation of 'reasons's triumph'. The abstract (deep level) formulation of the "Passing off" construction in text (1) is

(30) mental equation of something real (R) with something imaginary (I) or vice versa (see Fig. 6.2).

This operation, in fact, permeates all three figures so far discussed. "Caricatures" pass off a real quality ('not much thinking') for its grotesque hyperboles; "Punishment" passes off a real wish (W_1 = 'not to think') for a wish (W_2 = 'to die') that on the one hand is unreal (unintentional) and, on the other, is even more real than the former, since it is the literal meaning. Thus, 'passing off real for imaginary' runs in two opposite directions simultaneously and is in this sense double. The same by definition holds true for "Pun".[15]

Apart from these three figures, "Passing off" is responsible for the effect of

(31) conferring the role of (*a*) imaginary punishment upon (*b*) something real, natural, and even inevitable (in the actual text, death) and thus making punishment fictitious.

4.2. *Compression*

The structure has grown into a number of fairly complex patterns (five constructions with eleven distinct components linked by seven relations) and is in need of compression. This seems advisable in view of general considerations of artistic economy and also the desirability of creating optimal conditions for eventual REDUCTIONS. These latter will serve to necessitate 'logical inferences'—an embodiment of the 'feast of reason' (see end of §1.3).

Compression of the numerous items (see top of Fig. 6.2), generated in the course of expansion, into a compact definitive DS (see bottom of Fig. 6.2) is achieved through term-for-term superimposition of the extant constructions. A pivotal role in the COMBINATION is played by the "Punishment" figure: within its framework a place is found for almost every component of the other constructions.

The role of the inaccurately formulated "real" wish (W_1) is assigned to the "real" component common to both "Caricatures":

(32) W_1 = desire to think little.

The role of the literally expressed wish (W_2) is assigned to the hyperbolized, that is, imaginary, component of "Caricature 1," yielding:

(33) W_2 = conscious desire not to think even under extremely cruel pressure.

The role of 'fulfillment of W_2, enforcing punishment', is assigned to the hyperbolic component of "Caricature 2":

(34) punishment for W_1 = fulfillment of W_2 = never a thought in a very long time.

As a result of the three superimpositions, the purely mental operations of 'passing off a defect for a grotesque hyperbole' find themselves clothed in the garb of factual plot relations:

(35) the ridiculed wish W_1 is connected with its hyperbole W_2 by the spectacular plot relation of retrospective recognition of their equivalence: the wish W_2 turns out to be the real, factual aspect of W_1
(36) the same wish W_1 is connected with its other hyperbole F_2 by the plot relation of instructive punishment
(37) the two hyperboles—two separate, purely mental VARIATIONS of grotesque ridiculing—are now connected by the plot relation of literal realization, coming true.[16]

In the course of the superimpositions the equivalence relation between real and imaginary things (envisaged by "Passing off") has naturally assumed the form of the 'literal equivalence' of the statements of W_1 and W_2. The task of expressing these wishes is now assigned to the lexical meanings involved in "Pun":

(38) W_1 is to be expressed by the figurative meaning A_1 of the word A
(39) W_2 is to be expressed by the literal meaning A_2 of A.

In other words,

(40) literal equivalence is narrowed down as punning lexical equivalence.

The 'imaginary' component of "Passing off"—(30b)—has coincided neatly with a component of "Punishment," resulting in:

(41) hyperbole in "Caricature 2" = fulfillment of W_2 = imaginary punishment for W_1 for which something real is passed off.

But this very 'real, inevitable, and so on, something', i.e. (30a), remains a separate component within the definitive form of DS (see

(42c) = (30a)), so that the superimposition of "Punishment" and "Passing off" is at this point incomplete.

The structure produced by all these COMBINATIONS is formula (42) in Figure 6.2. Stated in a discursive and somewhat simplified terms, it reads as follows:

(42′)(*a*) The real wish to think little is inaccurately expressed by the figurative meaning of a word (*b*) whose literal meaning expresses, as is later realized, the exaggerated conscious determination not to think even under extremely cruel pressure. This results in (*d*) the fulfillment of this determination in the form of no thinking even over an extremely long time, which is (*c*) something real, natural, and inevitable but (*d*) is presented as if it were a punishment for the initial real wish.

The multiple mutual COMBINATIONS have compressed the structure considerably. As a result, each of the three principal components of "Punishment" (in the form it has assumed in DS (42) in Fig. 6.2), as well as most of the relations connecting them, is a "threefold" COMBINATION—(42d) is even fourfold. Among other things, this prepares the ground for the eventual REDUCTION of all the elements reconstructible from the numerous equivalences. One component of "Punishment" has, in fact, been slated for REDUCTION from the start, namely, (42b), 'the literally expressed wish W_2'. It will depend for its retrospective reconstruction on the equivalence of the figuratively expressed wish W_1 with its literal fulfillment F_2.

Formula (42) forms but the skeleton of DS obtained by elaborating and superimposing constructions (23), (24), (26), (29), (30). The complete DS includes also the decisions to

(43) effect REDUCTIONS
(44) effect COMBINATIONS implied by equivalences
(45) use, as a common pivot for various COMBINATIONS, the thematic element 'death' (which goes back to 'irreverent laughter at the dead', discussed in §1.1 but omitted from the simplified derivation of DS (42)).

Solutions to these "problems in COMBINATION and REDUCTION" form the substance of the next, surface, stage of derivation.

5. Surface Structure

SS is the last approximation of the actual text. It represents a very restricted class of synthematic texts that share with the one under derivation most of its expressive characteristics. This is especially true of the SS of our very short text (1), because the multiple constraints imposed on the components of DS by equivalences and other relations leave little room for variance in implementing the structure. As a result, the SS of (1) specifies practically all its linguistic characteristics, so that the range of possible textual realizations of the SS boils down to just one—text (1). This should not come as a theoretical surprise; rather, it is a way of accounting, within the framework of derivational description, for the popular notion of a text's "uniqueness."

The transition from DS to SS is almost completely confined to compression; practically no expansion occurs at this point. The compression involves two major stages—first COMBINATIONS and then REDUCTIONS.

5.1. *COMBINATIONS*

In accordance with (45), the motif of 'death' is introduced into every term of DS (42). As a result, all the terms unanimously, so to speak, sentence the characters to death. 'Punishment' is CONCRETIZED as 'death of the characters'. The 'wish W_2', whose fulfillment must, by definition, lead to this punishment, therefore, yields 'death wish, desire to die'. 'Something natural', in (42c), is accordingly CONCRETIZED as 'ineluctable death'. Both grotesque components in (42) share the element W_2, which has now taken the form of 'death wish'. Thus they both must include 'death'. This is done by resorting to a standard COMBINATION of "Caricatures" (see note 11): "Caricature 1" is sharpened into

(46) "Caricature through death": (*a*) they do not want to think so much that (*b*) they refuse to think even if threatened with death.

"Caricature 2", is sharpened into:

(47) "Caricature through a lifetime": (*a*) they think so little that (*b*) not a single thought occurs to them before death (= during a lifetime).

Finally, 'death' finds its way into the 'wish W_1, not to think' as well. It must be expressed inaccurately, that is, figuratively, in such a way as to have the literal meaning coincide with 'wish W_2, to die'. In the context of (46) this automatically points to the idiomatic phrase:

(48) *I would rather die than . . . (think).*

That (48) has the figurative meaning A_1 expressed by an idiom is fortunate for several reasons. An idiom usually (and this one by all means) COMBINES a high degree of emotion ((48) expresses a 'wish') with the naturalness of a colloquialism. This 'naturalness' not only enhances the credibility of the artistic invention but also helps to 'pass off the grotesque for reality'. The idiom (48) in particular is a godsend inasmuch as two of its components simultaneously take part in the figurative/literal play:

(49) (a) *would* = (a) 'wish W_1, not to think'; (b) 'wish W_2, to die';
    (b) *die* = (a) pure emphasis on W_1; (b) the very essence of the 'wish W_2'.

A further task of "Pun" is to implement the 'literal equation' of *rather* in (48) with the 'death wish W_2'. The solution is supplied by the two meanings of *sooner* and the element 'before (the moment of death)' on which already hinges the COMBINATION of the two "Caricatures" (see (47b)):

(50) *sooner* in its two meanings simultaneously: (a) 'rather'; (b) 'before'.

The emotional choice of death over thinking has, through the casualness of a colloquialism, acquired a degree of credibility. To bolster it still more,

(51) the deliberate choice made by the characters is disguised as (passed off for) objective observations on their behavior and assumptions about their—probably unconscious—motives.

This is implemented by a shift to third-person narrative:

(52) *Many people would sooner die than think,*

which can be construed both as an indirect rendering of the characters' direct statement of desires and as a surmise of a detached and uninformed observer.

5.2. REDUCTIONS

The multiple COMBINATIONS just effected facilitate REDUCTIONS. One component of "Punishment"—W_2—has long been earmarked for deletion. Another element that can as well be left implicit is the 'ineluctability of death'. Also, the "real" fact of 'thinking little' can be deleted from both "Caricatures" as reconstructible from its grotesque exaggerations. After these REDUCTIONS we obtain:

(53) *Many people would sooner die than think, and their wish is fulfilled literally in the sense that the people die sooner than they have a thought.*

In (53) the entire "Punishment" has shrunk to its two "nuclear" components, that is, to, so to speak, a 'crime' and a 'punishment' (COMBINED respectively with grotesques G_1 and G_2) (see note 15). This fairly symbolic skeleton of the witticism is further bared by the following two operations.

1. Maximum REDUCTION is applied to the common elements of the two components. For example, there is no need to repeat the punning word A (*sooner*) first as A_1 and then as A_2. The same goes for . . . *die than think* and *die . . . than they have a thought*. Also, the abstract scaffolding of "Punishment"—*their wish is fulfilled literally in the sense that*—can now be removed: the construction has been embodied in the flesh of concrete facts and postures. All such elements are either deleted completely or replaced by pronominal lexemes.

2. All and only pronominal lexemes are chosen to form a separate sentence—the second (*In fact, they do.*). This serves to set in greater relief, by code-sphere means, the bipartite compositional pattern as well as to convey its instructive essence. Indeed, the first sentence brings together all the 'criminal stupidity and passion', while the second shows the subsequent 'punishment', namely, the 'paleness of their lives; death taking place behind the scenes; the murderous power of intellect looming behind all this'.

Appendix
Russell: Biographical Quotations

In section 1 of the present Appendix, Bertrand Russell speaks about himself, thought, intellect, life, death, ulterior motives, desire, love of power, hatred of mankind, cruelty and punishment (in general, and by wish fulfillment, in particular). To have Russell convict himself I permitted myself—in Russell's own vein—some juggling in the arrangement of quotes: invectives he levels at others backfire. In section 2 a similar picture of Russell is drawn from quotations of external observers.

Bertrand Russell's statements are quoted from Russell 1950: 67, 173–174, Seldes 1966: 605ff., Kenin and Wintle 1978; D. H. Lawrence's letter, from Kenin and Wintle 1978: 645; Sidney Hook's opinion, from Hook 1976: 54.

1.

Men fear thought as they fear nothing else on earth—more than ruin, more even than death.

Thought is great and swift and free, the light of the world, and the chief glory of man.

. . . those who fear life are already three parts dead.

In a man whose reasoning powers are good, fallacious arguments are evidence of bias . . . displaying the distorting influence of desire.

All human activity is prompted by desire.

Much that passes as idealism is disguised hatred or disguised love of power.

The pursuit of knowledge is . . . mainly actuated by love of power.

Power is sweet.

I have a perfectly cold intellect, which . . . respects nothing. It will sometimes hurt you, sometimes seem cynical, sometimes heartless.

I like mathematics because it is not human.

The infliction of cruelty with a good conscience is a delight to moralists.

The reformative effect of punishment is a belief that dies hard, chiefly . . . because it is so satisfactory to our sadistic impulses.

In superstitious moments I am tempted to believe in the myth of the Tower of Babel, and to suppose that in our own day a similar but greater impiety is about to be visited by a more tragic and terrible punishment. . . . And what simpler method could he [God] devise than to let them [the nuclear physicists] carry their ingenuity to the point where they exterminate the human race? If I could think that deer and squirrels, nightingales and larks would survive, I might view the catastrophe with some equanimity, since man has not shown himself worthy to be the lord of creation.

2.

In a letter to Bertrand Russell (September 1915) D. H. Lawrence wrote: *The enemy of all mankind, you are, full of the lust of enmity. It is not the hatred of falsehood which inspires you. It is the hatred of people, of flesh and blood. It is a perverted, mental blood-lust.*

Sidney Hook in his review of two of Russell's biographies is concerned with the problem of which deep passion underlay Russell's political inconsistencies and tergiversations (e.g., he was said to declare that it was better to be red than dead, a flagrant contradiction to the idea of a holy war against the Soviet Union). Hook writes: *It cannot be his pacifism, which was never principled with him, as is indicated by his support of the war against Hitler and his willingness to sacrifice a half-million lives to insure Stalin's downfall. . . . The passion was his hatred of mankind, of its stupidity and viciousness, of its persistent refusal to listen and follow the counsels of wisdom he had offered it throughout his life. . . . "I hate the world and above all the people in it." . . . No one who felt so keenly about intellectual freedom . . . could have been so calmly resigned to the victory of Communism except as a punishment for a world whose policies had contributed to that victory.*

PART THREE

THEMATIC INVARIANCE

7

'Window' in the Poetic World
of Boris Pasternak

Air, light, the noise of life, reality, things and essences burst into his
poetry from the street as through an open window. The outside
world, everyday things, nouns, crowded in and took possession of his
lines, driving out the vaguer parts of speech.

—Boris Pasternak (1958: 284)

1. The Problem

If we were to ask ourselves in what pose it would be most natural to
imagine the figure of the poet which emerges from Pasternak's
verses, one of the most suitable answers would probably be: by a
window (recall for instance the pose of 'leaning out of the window'
discussed in Chap. 3). The words quoted in the epigraph are about
Pushkin, but essentially this is a poetic portrait of Pasternak himself.
It is typical of him to list objects and to divide them into objects of the
external world and objects of everyday use, which exist for him *na
ravnoj noge* "on an equal footing" and which enter into contact with
each other. It is Pasternak who loves to depict various kinds of contact
between the street and the room; and of such situations one of his
most favored is the picture of light and air, the noise of life, things,
essences, bursting into a room through a window.

In his collection of poetry *My Sister Life,* the word *okno* 'window' is
twenty-first in frequency.[1] But besides the window as such, we find in
Pasternak's verses: windowlets, window sash, window embrasure,
sash, rows of windows, windowsill, casement window, casement

This chapter has been previously published as [1978f].

hinges, casement frame, window frame, simply a frame or frames, transom frames, shutters, folding shutters, glass, panes, colored panes (i.e., stained glass), balcony windows, balcony blinds, portiere, curtain, muslin, gauze, drapes, awning, train or carriage window. In other words, the 'window' as a favored object of Pasternak's occurs more often than the actual word *window,* which is merely one of the ways of introducing this object into the consciousness of the reader.

In the opening lines of the poem "August," the window is the compositional center of a landscape that is arranged on either side of the window:

> As it had promised, without deceiving,
> The piercing sun at daybreak trained
> A slanting strip of saffron
> From the curtain to the counterpane.
>
> It covered with burning ochre
> The wood next door, the houses in the village,
> My bed, the wet pillow,
> And the patch of wall behind the bookshelf.

On the purely verbal level, the window is represented here only by the word *curtain.* In other cases, when it is present as an object, the window or its component parts are not mentioned at all in the text and have to be guessed at from the context: "I will go in, remove my coat, come to, / Will be lit up by the lights of the streets"; "From the garden, from the swing, out of the blue / A twig rushes in to the pier glass"; "When we light the lamp at night / And mark the leaves like napkins . . ."

This concern for the window runs not only through Pasternak's poetry but through other genres as well. What he says about Pushkin is a kind of literary portrait. In his play *The Blind Beauty* (Pasternak 1969) the insurrection scene is constructed as the invasion of rebellious peasants into the master's house through a window—a symbol of the collapsing social barrier (particularly eloquent is this remark: "The house seems less and less shut off from the country outside," Pasternak 1969: 63). In the novel *Doctor Zhivago* the study with a large window becomes a symbol of poetic creativity and undergoes several plot peripeties: the poet, Pasternak's *alter ego,* first envies the owner of the study, then himself comes to occupy it and there creates his famous poems.[2]

In commenting on the epigraph I tried to suggest in what sense the image of 'window' is suitable for Pasternak's artistic purposes. To substantiate this guess I will show in detail how the window works in Pasternak's texts, which of its components and characteristics play a part in fleshing out the poet's favorite themes and how the window relates to Pasternak's other recurrent images. These questions can be answered more or less formally—in PE terms—by using the concepts of "ready-made" object and "poetic world."

"Ready-made" object was defined in Chapter 2 (see § 6) as a unit ("entry") in the "dictionary of reality and culture" (shared by the writer and his readers) that covers a certain set of functions. It is ready-made in itself in the sense that it is one "solid" object that has fused the individual properties in question into a "whole." It is ready-made with respect to the poetic task it is called on to fulfill—that of expressing a given set of functions—in the sense that its constitutive properties (i.e., those defined already in the dictionary) cover the entire range of functions required by the poetic structure. To take our linguistic analogy (functions to be expressed, dictionary, entry) to the extreme, art is a "language of objects" that manages to take seriously the Laputan Academy's project of a universal language: "since words are only names for *things,* it would be more convenient for all men to carry about them such *things* as were necessary to express a particular business they are to discourse on . . ." (Swift 1940: 197–98). The art of speaking by demonstrating objects is painting; yet in a certain sense this applies to all forms of art, and in particular to literature, if one agrees that its main purpose is "to infect" the reader with the author's thoughts and feelings, as Tolstoy used to say, but not so much by means of direct declarations and calls to action as according to the principle "just watch what I do."

How does this correlate with the concept of "poetic world" (see Chap. 3)? That concept assumes that all the texts by one and the same poet say, basically, one and the same thing, constituting as it were, a set of type variations on an invariant central theme. It is these type variations, or invariant motifs, that form the functions to be covered by ready-made objects. The notion of "ready-madeness" thus acquires yet a new dimension: a poet's favorite object is ready-made with respect to an invariant set of functions in the sense that it is repeatedly used by the poet for this set as if it were part of his personal poetic vocabulary. Interesting theoretical problems arise concerning the interrelation between the general and personal dictionaries,[3] but I will have to concentrate here on a more specific one—the role played by the window in the poetic world of Pasternak.

The properties of 'window' to be reflected in a general dictionary of reality are obvious: a window is designed so that while preserving the internal room in isolation from the external environment (the glass as part of the wall), it can allow into the room light and, if so desired, air and sun, for which purpose it may be opened; the penetration of light is also controllable—using shutters, curtains, or blinds; normally the frames of a window are quadrilateral in form; and so on. As for the functions 'window' is to be matched against, we have to turn to Pasternak's invariant motifs. In introducing the concept of "poetic world" in Chapter 3, I have, in fact, discussed some recurrent window scenes and sketched a general outline of the Pasternak world. In order to put the window in the right perspective we will now need a more detailed description of the hierarchy of Pasternakian motifs. Still, it should be borne in mind that what follows is but a tentative and cursory exposition.[4]

2. Pasternak's World: Central Themes, Their Varieties and Combinations

In what terms does Pasternak view the world? What are his favorite ideas? What themes and motifs pervade his texts? One of his central themes is that of 'unity, or contact' between the small-scale, everyday manifestations of man and the large-scale manifestations of life and the universe, while another is the theme of 'magnificent intensity' of existence.

In terms of content, the theme of 'contact' may be interpreted in roughly the following way: man is the equal partner of such macrocosmic elements as the sky, the distance, eternity. This is expressed in a great variety of different ways, pervading every aspect, every level, and every element of Pasternak's poetry.

Man's contact and unity with nature are at the basis of the famous Pasternakian *imagery*. In the natural world, Pasternak distinguishes the features of the human face: "The face of the azure sky breathes above the face / Of the unbreathing beloved one, the river. . . . / One moment the wind carries the laughter of the lucernes, / Like an airy kiss, along the heights, / Or, treated to wild rose from the swamp, / It creeps and stains its lips with mare's-tail / And brushes the river on the cheek with a twig. . . . / If the perch's fins should miss a beat. . . ." With the aid of the metaphor, that which is small and human—the face, laughter, lips, a cheek, a kiss—is, as it were, imposed on the macroworld—the sky, the river, the field, the wind, the swamp (cf. the epigraph from Lenau to the book *My Sister Life:* "The forest roars, storm clouds swarm across the sky, and then in the movement of the storm I discern your maidenly features").

This tendency to equate the small-scale and everyday with the grandiose, massive, and exceptional is just as consistently effected through *phonetic techniques: šljuzy žaljuzi* 'the shutter's sluices'; *nezasteklënnyj nebosklon* 'the unglazed horizon'; *I vzamen kamor—xoromy, / I na čerdake—čertog* 'And instead of box rooms—palaces, / And in the attic—a mansion'. 'Man = landscape' metaphors are often supported by phonetic similarities, resulting in paronomasias; compare "The boat thumps in the drowsy breast, / The willows hang down and kiss on the collarbones, / On the elbows, on the rowlocks." Out of three metaphors here (boat = heart, river = breast, rowlocks = collarbone), two are reinforced by phonetic superposing: *lodka* 'boat' ≃ *kolotitsja* 'thumps'; *uklyučiny* 'rowlocks' ≃ *ključicy* 'collarbones'.

What is sometimes done by means of the metaphor (for example, the superposing of a human face on a whole landscape) may be done without it—by bringing the two into direct *physical contact:* "It was you, going out / Beyond the fence, placing your face against the field"; " . . . the mist, / Kissed the thick eyelashes"; "Night rubbed itself against [my] elbow"; and so on. The *varieties* of such physical, or plastic, *contact* are elaborated in Pasternak's verse with great detail. They are different variants of the realization of a link between objects, different CONCRETIZATIONS, as it were, of the very fact of linkage. Here are some of these:

'Illumination, lightening' "The bright stage from below / Pours its light on the hem."
'The leaving of a trace' "Like ointment, the thick blue of the sky / Lies down in dapples on the earth / And stains our sleeves."
'Touching, clutching at' "Spurge, / Wormwood and genista were catching at [his] canehead, / Impeding [his] steps."
'Clinging' "She as if by a wave of fate from the depths / Was fastened to him."
'Penetration' "The fine-ribbedness of partitions / I will pass right through, will pass through like light."
'Reflection' "And noon from the steep bank / Flung the clouds into the pond, / Like a fisherman's seine nets."

'Enveloping' "Just as the reeds get drowned / By waves after the storm, / To the bottom of his soul plunged / Her features and forms."

'Similarity' "In the house is hubbub and the fuss of housekeeping. / Just the same fuss and hubbub are in the distance."

'Loving contact' "The willows hang down and kiss on the collarbone"; "The sand all round is blotched / With the damp kisses of jellyfish"—a combination of a metaphor of a kiss and the 'leaving of a trace';

'Acquaintance, kinship' "My sister life."

'Self-sacrifice, giving' "Life after all is also only a moment, / Only a dissolving, / Of ourselves in all others, / As if as a gift for them"; "You rubbed yourself out entirely for the make-up, / The name of that make-up is the soul."

These then are typical CONCRETIZATIONS of the idea of contact. Another essential aspect of the classification of contacts is the typical *pairs of contacting partners*. In this respect Pasternak is remarkably consistent. What are the constant pairs, then?

In the first place, it is 'man and the macroworld,' but we have also:

'Earth–heaven' "When else did the stars grow so low / And midnight was plunged into the grass?"

'The near–the far' "Figures grow in the wind . . . / And, bent over like a chimney, / The horizon greets them."

'The inside of a house–the world outside' "For us the forest is still—like a hallway."

'The temporary–the eternal' "Throughout many long winters / I remember the days of the solstice, / And each one was unrepeatable / And countlessly repeated itself anew."

'The concrete, corporeal, tangible–the abstract, incorporeal, intangible' "And the midnight would be dipped into the high grass"; "Like butter, the horses were churning the space."

What is common in all these pairs is the disparity—to be overcome by contact—between the small, the immediate, the nearby, "the here and now," and the distant, the eternal, the infinite "out there."

In connection with the problem of 'window' I will be mostly concerned with physical variations of contact. As for its verbal manifestations, they too have many variations: phonetic similarities; paronomasias; an extended, explicit comparison; a metaphor proper; an intentional change in lexical co-occurrence of the type "Into Peter's eyes welled up, / Making them water, coves full of sedge" (in Russian, only *tears* can *well up*, hence, *coves* = *tears*); a peculiarly Pasternakian enumeration of totally different objects ("There are many of us at table, / Place settings, stars, candles"; "the wind . . . rocks the eyelids / Of branches and stars, and streetlamps, and milestones, / And of the seamstress gazing from the bridge into the distance"); and a number of other such variations. Without stopping to study them in detail, I will outline briefly the general correlation between verbal and physical contact in Pasternak.

These two ways of expressing the theme of 'contact' basically belong to two distinct levels of poetic language. The physical contact is contact between objects that are present in the "reality" depicted by the poet, in those pictures of life, albeit invented, that he "describes" in verses. Verbal techniques permit the poet to draw into this description other objects, which are not present in the depicted scene but are thought into it by semantic, lexical, syntactic, phonetic, and other associations. (One might clarify the distinction between these two levels by a comparison with painting, in which there is a clear distinction between the posing figure, even when that figure has adopted a pose indicated by the artist, and the possible ways of transforming it on canvas.)

In actual texts the varieties of contact which belong to the two different levels often occur simultaneously, in correspondence with the artistic principle of COMBINATION. In the quotation involving "the face of the azure sky" I have drawn attention to the metaphors that superpose a human face on the landscape. But this image is full of physical contacts as well: in it there is not one face, but two ("The face of the azure sky breathes above the face / Of the unbreathing beloved one, the river"), so that we now have the possibility of 'clinging' and of 'loving contact' ("an airy kiss"); or further on, "treated to wild rose," is an example of 'giving'; "stains its lips with mare's-tail"—an example of the 'leaving of a trace'; "brushes the river on the cheek with a twig"—an example of 'touching'.

Metaphors themselves are often introduced in such a way as to heighten the capability of the objects for physical contact. Thus, in the example from the poem "St. Petersburg" ("Into Peter's eyes welled up, / Making them water, coves full of sedge"), the metaphor equating coves with tears permits the water of those coves to come into direct physical contact with the eyes of Peter (the variations 'clinging', 'enveloping', and to some extent 'touching, clutching at', if we count the irritant effect which the sedge has on the eyes, making them water). In other words, metaphors do not simply coexist with physical contact (as is in principle possible with "pure" COMBINATION) but form with it a single construction, outside which this type of physical contact would be impossible.[5]

Variations of physical contact may be COMBINED one with another as well: "As with f\am, at midnight, on three sides / Suddenly the cape is lit up." Here the 'clinging' of frothing surf to the shore is COMBINED with another variety of contact, that is, 'illumination'. A characteristic feature of Pasternak's poetry is that when he COMBINES two (or more) varieties of contact, he usually names in the text only the one which for the given situation is the more unexpected, the more "information-laden." Thus, for the situation 'surf' the fact of the wave clinging to the shore is an obvious feature, so that it is carried in the subtext, while 'illumination', which is possible only at night, is named directly.

This kind of structure is possible only in cases in which the depicted situation contains, if only latently, at least two varieties of physical contact. Otherwise the second, more unexpected variation has to be introduced, "forced in" with the aid of a metaphor. Thus, "the willows hang down and kiss on the collarbone" is a case of 'clinging' or 'touching'; metaphor (willows and boat = lovers) makes it possible to introduce a further variety of physical contact, that is, 'loving contact' ("kiss"); "the blue sky / Lies down with sunlight dapples on the earth / And stains our sleeves" is a case of 'illumination' and, thanks to the metaphor, of 'leaving a trace' ("sunlight dapples," as it were, "stain the sleeves"); "a rush of unextinguished summer light-ings / Nailed this scene to the wall for me" is a case of 'leaving a trace' (a shadow) plus 'metaphorical clinging and clutching' ("nailed"), cf. also "And the fire of the sunset has not cooled down, / Since the time when the evening of death / Hastily nailed it to the wall of the Ma-nège" (same varieties and same construction).

The tendency to pile up manifestations of 'contact' is so great that Pasternak sometimes twice introduces one and the same variation of physical contact in a single situation, for instance, 'leaving of a trace': "As if like a piece of iron / Dipped in antimony, / You were dragged in a groove / Across my heart," where antimony leaves a trace on the piece of iron and the iron leaves a double—dye and groove—trace on the heart.

Another most important theme in Pasternak's poetry is that of daz-zling brightness, intensity of existence, where everything seems to be in the highest possible state of elevation and tension. I call this the theme of 'magnificence' or, in Pasternak's own words, 'the highest phase' (". . . as if having reached the highest phase, / The sleepless odor of marigolds . . ."). I will point out those of the numerous variations of 'magnificence' that are crucial for explaining the role of the window.

'Shivering, trembling, swaying'. "Like the fact that muslin is in asthma, / Like the fact that even the mezzanine shook / At the sight of your shoulders"; "The trembling piano will lick the foam from [its] lips"; "The garages of the car yards tremble"; "The shivering contour of the glacier"; and so on.

'Morbid states'. Critics have noted the preponderance of images of illness in Pasternak (Tynyanov 1978:34ff.; Levin 1966: 205). Clearly, for Pasternak, sickness and certain intense biological processes (with which in everyday life and speech unpleasant associations tend to be linked, such as the secretion of sweat or saliva, and so on) are yet one more type of 'intensity', that is, a variation on the theme of 'magnificence'. Here are some examples: "And the forest peels and in droplets / Sprinkles pouring sweat . . . / The garden feels sick with the miles of calm, / The tetanus of angered glens . . . / The storm is near. The garden gives off a smell / From its parched mouth . . . / The garden's mouth is full of damp nettles"; the poem entitled "The earth's diseases"—"With mother of pearl, / With the waterfall of bacilli, / With a wet hum, with a mass of staphylococci . . . / And the incisors shine in the lightning flashes, . . . / The tetanus tightens with a trembling the shadows, / And tetanus dusts the grass snakes. / Here's the downpour. The gleam of rabies, / A whirlwind, gusts of rabid spittle . . . / One has at least to be in delirium, / To give one's consent to be the earth."

'Tears, weeping'. This motif, which occurs very frequently in Pasternak's poems, seems to fulfill the same function (along with a number of others). Some examples of this motif are: "Verses are made up in a sob"; "Oh, God, the tears of anguish / Stop me from seeing Thee"; "What breaks into life, and is refracted in a prism, / And is glad to play in tears."

How do the two basic themes of Pasternak's poetic world relate to each other? On the *content plane,* the question boils down to how the themes of 'contact' and 'magnificence' are linked into a coherent picture of the world. One possible interpretation is as follows: 'magnificence' is the main theme, while the theme of 'contact' is subordinated to it—all objects are in such a highly intense state that they emerge from themselves and merge with each other in powerful ecstasy. In Pasternak's own words:

> "A multitude of fluttering ['trembling'], watchful souls would stop one another, would flow together and, as people would say in the old days, would 'commune' together ['contact'], thinking aloud. . . . The infectious communality of their ecstasy ['higher phase'] obliterated the boundary of man and nature. In that famous summer of 1917 in the interval between the two revolutions, it seemed as if not only people, but roads, trees and stars were holding meetings and making speeches ['man and the macroworld', 'the near and the far off', 'earth and sky']. . . . This sensation of the ordinariness of a history which could be observed at every step and yet was still in the process of becoming, this feeling of eternity, which had come down to earth and met the eyes everywhere ['temporary and eternal'], this fairy-tale mood . . . was what I was trying to communicate in my book of poems" (Pasternak 1965: 631).

Another possible interpretation of the link between the two themes would be that the main one is 'contact': everything small-scale and everyday is in contact with the vast and great, and thus full of power and significance; in other words, the state of 'highest phase' is but a special manifestation of 'contact'. When Pasternak speaks of the "vastness of [his] apartment" and of how "during a walk before dinner / An absolutely awesome darkness will fall," then essentially he is expressing his sense of the immensity of every small interval of time and section of space.[6]

To be sure, the two proposed interpretations are not mutually exclusive.

On the *expression plane* the link between the two themes is naturally manifested in their frequent COMBINATION in concrete objects, images, and situations. Some of the typical constructions are: 'contact leads to trembling' ("But suddenly across the portiere / Will run the trembling of intrusion: / Measuring silence with your steps, / You will enter like the future"; "The horses churned the space like butter"); 'contact leads to tears' (recall the sedge coves in Peter's eyes); and so on. A loose combination of both themes is also possible: "Midday will crash down . . . in a lattice of trembling sunlight's dapples," where the "sunlight's dapples" are a case of 'contact' ('illumination' and 'leaving of a trace'), and the "trembling" is a case of 'magnificence' ('trembling'), but there is no causal connection between them.

To conclude this section on Pasternak's poetic world, I will give an example of the "poetic synonymy" of fragments from different poems. Compare "If the perch's fins should miss a beat" and "The boat thumps in the drowsy breast." In both lines (already quoted above) the poet is in fact saying one and the same thing: 'contact' is expressed

1. metaphorically: the boat / perch $\simeq$ heart beating in the river, thanks to similar shifts in lexical co-occurrence—only the heart can "miss a beat" or "thump" in this sense (or as we saw earlier, only tears can "well up")
2. phonetically: *lódka* 'the boat' $\simeq$ *kolótitsja* 'thumps', *ókunja* 'perch' $\simeq$ *ëknut* 'miss a beat', in both of which cases the noun is a name of an object that stands metaphorically for the heart and is phonetically similar to the verb, which can be collocated only with the word "heart"
3. 'contact' is COMBINED with 'magnificence': "thump" and "miss a beat" are manifestations of 'trembling'.

3. Pasternak's World: Ready-made Objects

Thus, Pasternakian motifs are typical variations of the two basic themes—'contact' and 'magnificence'. And it is these motifs that constitute the functions "exchanged" for concrete objects and situations. As we might expect, for each pair of partners and for each variety of contact there will be particular ready-made objects, which are especially suitable for the corresponding functions.

For the pair 'earth–sky', when the 'reflection' variety of 'contact' is being used, the obvious ready-made object is 'the surface of water': "A star would dive and float like a wick / In the icon-lamp of the waters of the Kama"; "Flung clouds into the ponds . . . / The vault of heaven sinks like a seine-net"; "He does not know the sirens' scales / And could anyone believe in a fish's tail / Who, just once, had sipped from the chalices of their kneecaps / The reflection of the stars, lapping as if against the ice?"
Such varieties of 'earth–sky' contact as 'touching, clutching at' and 'leaving a trace' regularly use 'trees, fences, and haystacks': "On the bushes grow the fragments / Of dispersed clouds"; "This disc gone wild that had chipped off its horns / On the fence, has now / Knocked down the palisade with its butting"; "And the sky, covered with clouds

like with down . . . / Has got stuck in the branches up above, / And cannot move for the heat"; "A haystack rears like a hayloft / Where the moon, like a passing traveler, / Had snuggled down for the night . . . / The new day gets up from bed / With chaff and straw in its hair." Note that in practically all these cases the physical contact is motivated by metaphors: clouds grow, the moon has horns and spends the night, the day has hair. The first two examples express also the theme of 'magnificence': "gone wild," "had chipped off," "has now knocked down," "butting," "cannot move," and so on.

Other ready-made objects that manifest contact between the heavens and earth are 'mountains', 'birds', and 'precipitations of rain and snow' ("Snow is falling, snow is falling, / As if it is not flakes that fall, / But the vault of heaven coming down to earth. . . .").

The contact in the pair 'the temporary–the eternal' is manifested by ready-made objects of two main types:

1. 'recurrent phenomena' of all kinds, which are both now and always, such as 'festivals, seasons, dates in the natural calendar' (as in the earlier example "I remember the days of the solstice")

2. 'deeds of great men', in particular, creative artists, who have left a trace in time. There are many examples of this, but here are just two that are based on 'leaving of a trace': "Their tracks lie unerasable, / On time and on the sailor" (referring to the famous admirals Naximov and Ušakov); "Others will trace, step by step, / Your living footsteps."

The contact in the pair 'interior of a house–external world' is expressed through

1. ready-made objects which combine elements of the home and of open space, such as 'ruins' ("Like lilac, . . . / Gleaming brightly through the gaps / In the walls of crumbling castles . . . / Earth in every stony cavity, / Grass in front of all the doors"), or 'unfinished buildings' ("The jay flies screeching / Through the deserted birch-grove, / Like an unfinished building, / It rears hollowly"), or by the custom of 'lunch on the grass' ("A garden table beneath the fir tree. / On the fresh shashlik / The breath of the waterfall . . . / On the bread and meat / The fumes of its avalanche")

2. metaphors which either describe the house in terms of the external world ("The cool of the garden is in the apartment"), or the external world in indoor terms (cf. the verses about the moon spend-

ing the night in the haystack, quoted earlier, and also: "But the pines . . . / Rented their corners to squirrels and wood-peckers . . . / And the ravine by the door sheltered a hoopoe . . ."; "July with storms, the July air / Rented the room from us").

Prominent among those typical features of the home which get linked with the macroworld are 'eating' and 'love, intimacy'. Obviously, 'eating' is one of the most domestic and everyday activities of man, one of the symbols of the home in its intimate, undemanding, microcosmic aspect. Therefore, the contact of a dining table with the external world can demonstrate the home—macroworld unity with particular eloquence.

A ready-made object that is particularly suitable for this construction is the custom of 'lunch on the grass' (compare the example quoted above and also "Windfallen fir trees, / The precipitous sheep's path, / We are many at table, / Place-settings, stars, candles"). Another ready-made object which combines the elements of the home and the external world and therefore allows the poet to present a picture of eating "in plain sight of everyone" is the 'balcony or outside veran-dah'. "At the windows and balcony, / Where the potato fritters were frying / The whole southern slope gazed / In its silver frame." Note the striking similarity of these lines with the 'lunch on the grass' lines quoted earlier. The next stage is when the dining table is moved completely into the room, but elements of the external world 'pene-trate' there through the 'window': "We would unstopper / The mildewed window like a bottle, / And in would rush . . . / . . . the sun / And pour the oil from the asphalt / Over the salad"; "The sun goes down and, like a drunkard, / From far away, with aims trans-parent, / Reaches through the window / For some bread and a glass of brandy."[7]

A different variation on the motif 'food—the macroworld', this time realized through a metaphor, is instanced by the lines: "The roads have turned to porridge, / I pick my way along the edge. / I turn the ice sour, like dough, with clay. / I plod through the thin gruel." Note that whereas previously the everyday had become great owing to its contact with the macrocosmos, now it is the reverse: in the mac-rocosmos (the countryside during a thaw), through the comparison with porridge, dough, and gruel, the everyday quality is emphasized, its accessibility to man. A characteristic detail here is "I pick my way along the edge," which corresponds to the motifs of simplicity, mod-esty, everyday quality, even provincialism (see note 9).

Another typical manifestation of the indoor life is of course 'love, intimacy'. Pasternak is so devoted to the idea of contact between the home and the external world that the desire to shut oneself off from the space outside and into one's own microworld does not arise in his hero even in the most intimate moments. The backdrop to (and participant in) scenes of lovemaking (which represent 'loving contact') is often nature (cf. the already quoted "Oars at rest": "The boat thumps in the drowsy breast, / The willows hang down and kiss on the collarbone, / On the elbows, on the rowlocks . . . / The splendor of crushed daisies in the dew . . . / This means—to embrace the vault of heaven . . .").

In *Step'* ("The steppe") it is a heap of straw (*omët*) in the open field that is turned into a semblance of dwelling place (cf. "The garden table beneath the fir tree"): "Could this be a haystack in the mist? Who knows? / Or is it our straw heap? We go up—It is. / We found it! The very one.—The straw heap, / The mist and steppe on all four sides . . . / Open, open on all four sides."

The poem *Dožd'(Nadpis' na Knige stepi)* ("Rain [An inscription on The book of the steppe]") is one of those which do not easily yield a literal reading. One may read the situation it depicts as follows: in a room are the poet and his beloved ("She is with me"); outside the window is the rain ("Weave like a silkworm / And beat against the pane"); everything going on in the room is constantly equated with everything going on outside ("Melt, flow like an epigraph. / Pour, laugh, tear the gloom. / To a love which is like you . . . / The downpour is a comb for her . . . / And [throw] entire trees / Into her eyes, her temples, the jasmine"); the final quatrain presents the picture of actual physical contact between the lovers and nature: "Now let us run and pluck,/ Like a groan from a hundred guitars, / The St. Gotthard of the garden, / Washed with the mist of lime blossom."

We find the same motif of openness to the external world in the poem *Svad'ba* ("Wedding"), dedicated to a form of 'love intimacy' which is fully institutionalized and, as it were, has an officially registered address: "And at daybreak into the deepest slumber, / When all one wants to do is sleep and sleep, / Once more the accordion struck up . . . / And yet again, again and again / The vernacular of the comic song / Came bursting in from the party / Straight at the slumberers in bed." Note that this invasion by the external world is not undesirable: it is regarded by Pasternak as an indisputably positive phenomenon from which the broadest generalizations should be drawn in the spirit of 'contact', 'giving', and 'self-sacrifice': "Life too is but a moment, after all, / Only a dissolving / Of ourselves in everyone else, / As if we gave ourselves to them. . . ."[8]

Such are the typical ready-made objects and constructions expressing the contact between the home and the world outside. The 'window' has a natural place among them, owing to its position on the boundary between the home and the world outside, where they naturally make contact. The various properties of the window and of its component parts help to express contact between the home and the objects in the world outside and to realize several varieties of 'contact' and 'magnificence'.

4. The Function of the Window as a Ready-made Object

The 'window opening' and the 'casement' are apertures through which 'penetrate': air, odors ("There's a scent of acacias / And the windows are flung open"); sounds ("A pair of casement hinges, / Echoes of February . . . / The hubbub broke in like a ramrod"); birds, clouds ("In through the wide-open windows and onto their embroidery / Settled the clouds, like doves"); lightning ("Like the rustle of a fire-ball . . . / Like this bundle of storm, / Flying smokeless into the room"); the seeds of plants, and so on ("July, carrying in his clothes / The fluff of dandelions and burdocks, / July, coming home through the window"); even people ("Kicking in the window with her heel, / She flew across into the arms of the crowd / And in their arms, beyond the clouds").

The 'windowpane' is the medium through which 'penetrate' visual impressions ("The winter day in the open embrasure / Of the undrawn curtains"; "They would put a crescent moon in either pane"; "Then winter during a snowstorm, / Piercing the gloom with her snowflakes, / Would peek into the house from the garden"); or else rays of light come in (cf. "August", quoted in § 1, and also: "Who gushed in toward the bookcase / Through the sluices of the shutter"; "From the kitchen the flaring oven / Threw the monstrous hands of the skivvies / Onto the snow beyond the sledge").

'Windowsill' and 'balcony' are open to the outside world, and may carry elements of the inner world of the room, such as people (cf. "In childhood, as I still recall, / You'd lean out through the window" and fragments in ex. (3) in Chap. 3); a candle ("And lit like a laid-out corpse / By a swaying candle from the windowsill"); and plants, which belong simultaneously to nature and to the home ("And the swellings

of those same white buds / Both on the sill and at the crossroads";
"Toward the white stars in the snowstorm / Stretch the geranium
flowers / Across the window embrasure").

'Windowpanes', 'frames', and 'sill' are surfaces making possible 'illumination', 'penetration', and 'leaving a trace'. These presuppose
such partners as rays of light, raindrops, branches of trees: "And
bunches of fowl-cherries in bloom / Washed the transom frames with
their leaves"; "The trembling outline of a glacier / Washes the sill with
lilac"; "the elm / Throws into a tremble the canvas of the blind / And
maps the twigs upon the gauze."

'Panes', 'shutters', and 'curtains' can tremble, rattle, sway (the 'magnificent trembling'): "There's laughter in the house and the windows
ring"; "All night it [the garden] bumped against the window / And the
shutter rattled"; "And the curtain in the wind / Waves against the
window." As the examples show clearly, the theme of 'magnificence' is
often combined with 'contact'; the 'trembling' is due to the impact of
the world outside, for instance, the wind.

The 'panes' may be covered with raindrops or condensation from
the room, so that metaphorically an image is created of the 'window in
tears or sweating' (variations of 'magnificence'; raindrops at the same
time express 'contact', namely 'leaving a trace'): "The sunset from the
garden doused the panes / Of glass with September's bloody tears";
"Perspiration ran in streams from the balcony windows / As if from
the thighs and backs of shivering bathing girls"; "And when the poul-
tices are put on, / The inside windowpanes weep."

Thus, the 'window' is a ready-made object that expresses, either
one at a time or in various COMBINATIONS, a set of functions essential
to Pasternak's poetic world:

1. contact between the house (man, furnishings, candles, crockery,
food and so on, as well as parts of the window itself) and the world
outside (wind, odors, plant seeds, sounds, clouds, lightning, sunset,
the sun, streetlights, winter, snowflakes, snowdrifts, the earth, playing
children, mountain slopes, buds, branches, leaves, flowers, raindrops), involving the following varieties of 'contact': 'penetration',
'clinging', 'leaving a trace', 'similarity', illumination';

2. 'magnificence', in its varieties: 'trembling' (shutters, windowpanes, and curtains), 'sweat' and 'tears' (metaphorical on the
glass).

The place of 'window' among other ready-made objects and motifs in
the overall system of Pasternak's poetic world is shown in Figure 7.1.

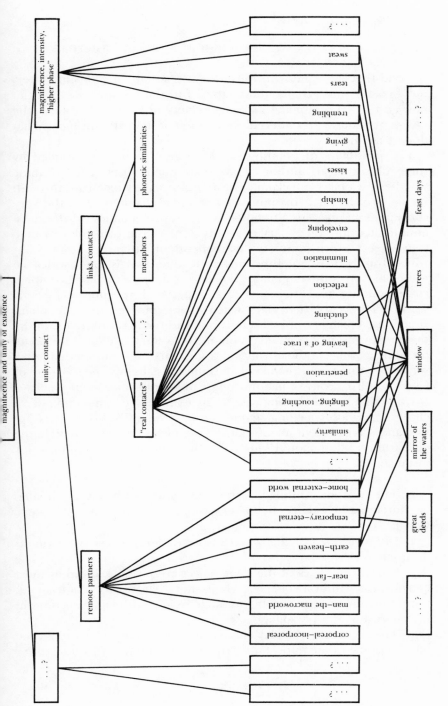

Figure 7.1. Pasternak's PW: The place of 'window'

5. The Unity of the 'Window' Motif in Pasternak

I said that the window fulfills a certain set of functions in Pasternak's poetry, and I then outlined these functions in some detail. I can now go further and make a stronger claim: in Pasternak's poetry the image of window has internal unity and constant significance. What does it mean?

The possibility of pointing out a range of functions fulfilled by some object in an author's texts does not in itself predetermine whether the object can claim to be a single image which runs through his oeuvre. In fact, this possibility is already contained in the very concept of an object as a bundle of constitutive qualities which can be enumerated in a dictionary of reality. One can in principle envisage some object which occurs quite frequently in an author's works but which fulfills different functions each time, that is, ones which lie within its constitutive qualities but do not form a constant complex corresponding to certain essential aspects of the author's poetic world. This occurs particularly when an object merely serves auxiliary functions, which are only distantly and indirectly connected with the theme. For instance, rain might on one occasion make someone break his journey, on another bring on a good harvest, on another slake someone's thirst, and then explain someone's absence, be a symbol of God's wrath, or convey an atmosphere of longing, and so on. In order to claim that we are dealing with a single image (i.e., something like a character, whose personal name serves to identify his various appearances as different manifestations of one and the same entity), the object in question should satisfy certain quite strong conditions, for instance:

1. The functions fulfilled by the object must not be merely auxiliary, but must be related to themes which form the author's poetic world.

2. Different uses of the object must be more or less synonymous (synthematic).

3. Contrasting uses of the same object are possible, but they must be contrasts within a coherent whole (not a very strict requirement, but intuitively understandable by analogy, say, with contradictions in the character of a personage).

4. The object should play some constant role in the composition, plot, or some other important structural component of the author's works.

Let us see whether the 'window' in Pasternak meets these requirements. The concept of poetic world implies that of "poetic synonymy", that is, the existence of segments of text which are equivalent with respect to the functions they express and only differ in having these functions realized by different concrete objects (see example at the end of §2). In fact, the structure of a poetic world involves a whole hierarchy of levels of synonymy (see Chap. 3, §4). It stands to reason that if the object in question occurs in a hierarchy of synonymous constructions of this kind, its image acquires consistency and unity.

In an overwhelming majority of cases the 'window' in Pasternak fulfills the same set of functions: it expresses the 'contact between the house and the external world' and, quite often, the theme of 'magnificence' as well. Since these are the most important if not the only themes that define Pasternak's poetic world, the thematic weight of the 'window' image is beyond question: it could in no way be called a secondary or auxiliary element. In this role the window is synonymous (on one level or another) with other typically Pasternakian objects and situations.

1. As a ready-made expression of 'contact' in general the window turns out to be a poetic synonym for 'trees', 'mountains', and the 'mirror of the waters' (contact between earth and heaven), 'feast days', 'seasons', and the 'deeds of great men' (contact between the temporary and the eternal), and so on.

2. In the pair 'house–world outside', the window is a more precise synonym for such ready-made objects as 'lunch on the grass', 'balcony', and 'door'. Compare two different realizations of the single construction 'contact between the world outside and the house leading to trembling', one with a window ("And the curtain in the wind / Waves against the window"), another with a door ("But suddenly across the portiere / Will run the trembling of intrusion").

3. The window itself, with its component parts, regularly appears in completely synonymous constructions barely distinguishable in referential terms. Compare, for instance, the following realizations of the construction mentioned in the previous paragraph: "And the curtain in the wind / Waves against the window"; "And seizes the curtain like a dancer, / Whisks it upward to the ceiling"; "the elm / Throws into a tremble the canvas of awning"; "All night it bumped against the window / And the shutter rattled." Another recurrent construction is 'man's contact, thanks to penetration, with the street without leaving the room' (recall the 'leaning out' series of

examples). With plants in place of people and metaphorical in place of physical 'penetration', we get the lines: "Toward the white stars in the snowstorm / Stretch the geranium flowers / Across the window embrasure."

As for the window's role in the macrostructure of Pasternak's poems, the composition of many poems is built around the unfolding of the very 'contact' whose metaphorical and plastic variations underlie the various separate images we have been examining. Isolated contacts cohere into a plot scheme. In the lines "And the swelling of the same white buds / Both on the window and at the crossroads, / In the street and in the workshop," the 'contact between the house and the world outside' is presented in the form of a static 'similarity': the twigs with buds on them in the window are "the same" as those in the street. Dramatized, this situation develops into the plot of *Devočka* ("The little girl"): "From the garden, from the swing, out of the blue / A twig rushes into the pier glass . . . / But look, they're bringing the twig in in a wine glass / And placing it by the pier glass frame."

At first, the twig is outside the window and belongs to the external world, to that garden which can so often be glimpsed in Pasternak's lines beyond the window, sends its sounds and scents into the room, touches the frame and windowpanes ("washes the sill with lilac"), tries to squeeze in ("All night it bumped against the window / And the shutter rattled"). The twig's first contact with the room is via the mirror, a pier glass, so that by being reflected, it turns out to be not just in the room but on the side opposite the window, that is, in the innermost part of it, furthest from the external world. The mirror is a kind of second, more inner window on the garden, also consisting of glass, frame, and "sill"—the dressing table. It is on this "sill" that they place the twig brought in from the garden, so that before our very eyes we see it turn from an element of the external world into an element of the world of the room, a visible proof that a plant in the house is "the same as" a plant in the street.

The plot of the poem is put together out of a sequence of varieties of 'contact' between the garden and the room using more or less synonymous ready-made objects ('window', 'mirror', 'door'): metaphorical 'penetration' through the window; 'reflection' in the mirror; physical 'penetration' into the room, presumably through the door; and, finally, 'clinging to' the mirror. The transition from metaphorical to physical penetration and from disembodied 'reflection' to direct 'juxtaposition' and 'clinging' is an increase in the power of 'contact', offering a sense of closure, of a realized initial impulse.

Plots which are built on movement between the inside and the outside of a house are quite numerous and varied according to a number of features, in particular:

1. The *type of movement*, which includes actual physical movement ("Measuring the silence with your steps, / You will enter, like the future"), imagined physical movement ("I long to go home to the immensity . . . / I will go in"), a visual route (". . . in a straight / Path into the garden, the tree trunks and chaos / The mirror runs toward the swing . . . / And into the background, into the gloom, through the gate / Out to the steppe, into the scent of drowsy medicines / Streams like a path, in knots and whorls / The glittering hot quartz"), or an acoustic route ("In the house there's laughter and the windows ring . . . / The forest, mockingly, flings / This noise onto the precipitous slope"; "Over the roofs of the city apartments / The valkyries' flight thundered like a storm"), or a purely metaphorical route ("Now let us run and pluck . . . / The St. Gotthard of the garden," that is, after the exit into the garden, instead of continuing a real path out into the steppe, there is a metaphorical leap to the Alps).

2. *The shape of the trajectory*, either (a) unidirectional, from outside into the house ("The little girl," *Groza* ["The storm"], "*Nikogo ne budet v dome* . . . ," ["There will be no one in the house . . . "], etc.) or vice versa (*Zerkalo* ["The mirror"], *Dožd'* ["Rain"], *Rassvet* ["Daybreak"]: "And I run down the steps, / As if I'm going out for the first time / Into those streets deep in snow . . ."); or (b) round trip, from inside the house to outside and back in again (*Veter* ["The wind"], *V bol'nice* ["In the hospital"]: "Then he looked gratefully through / The window behind which the wall / Like a spark from the blaze / Was lit up from the town. / There in the glow shone the gates / And in the reflection of the town a maple / Bade with a crooked branch / A farewell bow to the patient"—a visual route from the room through the window into the garden and then to the town, then back through the window into the room via the metaphorical gesture of the maple), or from outside into the house and back out ("*Mne xočetsja domoj, v ogromnost'* . . . " [I long to go home into the hugeness . . . "]; or *Muzyka* ["Music"], where first a piano is carried into the room "over the vastness of the city's sea" and then its music flies out "over the roofs of the city apartments").

3. The *ready-made object* that unites the house with the external world: 'window', 'balcony', 'door' and its varieties ('porch', 'steps', 'verandah'), as well as their less precise synonyms uniting the garden or courtyard with a more distant and extensive world such as 'paths', 'gates', and 'holes in fences'[9] ("In childhood, as I still recall, / You'd lean out through the window, / In the street, like in a quarry, / It's dark under the trees at noon . . . / Beyond the gate faint paths / Would lead you away to an overgrown garden"; "Backyards with a broken stile"; "There is a pass broken through the garden fence. / It disappears in the birch-wood"; cf. also "The mirror" with its "path into the garden," "back gate," and "path out to the steppe," all reflected in the mirror).

As we see, a class of plots in Pasternak elaborates the contact between the house and the world outside. In the course of this archeplot the boundary between the two spheres is crossed by different varieties of contact. The role of this regularly transgressed boundary occupying a constant position in the plot is played by the window and its synonyms.

So far I have treated the 'window' as a means of linking the house with the world outside and I have concentrated on open, transparent, and unshuttered windows. But Pasternak's poems also contain windows that separate—that are closed, shuttered, or snow-covered. Can this be reconciled with my assertion about the unity of the window image as a vehicle for the theme of 'contact'? Sometimes even in a picture of an impenetrable window it is the contact that is stressed, cf. "The snowstorm patterned the pane / With the lace and arrows"— 'leaving a trace', a type of contact repeated later on in the poem within the room as well: "The wax from the nightlight like tears, / Dripped on the dress," resulting in 'similarity'. But this is a special case. What usually happens is as follows.

It is characteristic of Pasternak's poetic world that he not merely depicts contacts, particularly those between the house and the world outside, but evaluates them positively: *in the normal beautiful universe that Pasternak celebrates, both the elements engaging in the contact and the very fact of contact between them are all good.* What, then, occurs in those (relatively rare) cases when the poet feels he is in conflict with what he is depicting? Images emerge of a 'negative contact', that is, either 'hostile and destructive' or else 'frustrated, unrealized, abortive'. Negative phenomena for Pasternak are the motifs of 'parting' (i.e., anticontact), 'insincerity', and sometimes 'death'. In the poem *Razryv*

("The break") the beloved's hypocritical farewell kisses are compared to leprosy: "O sorrow, infected with lies from the start, / O grief, leprous grief . . . / But why are you making a farewell gift to my soul / Of this most bodily disease?" Here Pasternak has used with a negative sign his favorite varieties of contact—'leaving a trace' and its spiritual correlate, 'giving' (cf. the characteristic "positive" image: "You rubbed yourself out entirely for the make-up, / The name of that make-up is the soul"); thus, leprosy is a ready-made object that combines destructiveness with 'giving' and 'leaving a trace'.

In the pair 'house–external world' this negative state of the poetic world is manifested in the following. Everyday objects (generally dear to Pasternak, cf. "A cup of cocoa steams up the mirror"; "The Caucasus was right there as if in my palm, / Right there, like a rumpled bed"; etc.) undergo a negative reevaluation: Pasternak adopts a hostile, "unmasking" stance toward the home, everyday objects, and comfort, "where cosiness lies and flatters, simpering." Contact with the world outside turns out to be destructive for this kind of domesticity: "And with all that the ravines have breathed for centuries, / With all the darkness of the botanical sacristy / He [the poet] will exhale into the typhus-laden yearning of the mattress / And will spatter with the chaos of the thickets." The same image of the "typhus-laden yearning of the mattress" reappears in a poem written fourteen years later and addressed to another woman, and only the direction of the movement changes: "Out of the typhus-laden yearning of mattresses / Let's rush right out into the immaculate air of latitudes . . . / Our honor is not beneath the shelter of a home."

As the attitude to the world changes, then, so does the sign of contact. And with it changes the role of the window: now it symbolizes yearning, parting, and death; it is therefore shut fast, contact with the street is cut off, or if it does take place, threatens death ("I ought to write while we are apart . . . / But the sadness of lonely melodies . . . / Is like the sterility of a lowered blind / Leading the violet into deceit"; "When through the hoarfrost on the window / You can't see the light of God's day, / The inescapability of the yearning / Is like the emptiness of the sea twice over"; "Well, go to others, do good. / *Werther* has already been written, / Nowadays even the air smells of death: / Opening a window is like opening a vein"). Thus the dual use of the window—as linker and separator—corresponds to the two mutually opposed states of Pasternak's poetic world—the "positive" and the "negative"—and therefore does not break but rather reinforces the unity of the image.

In the overwhelming majority of cases the window is used within the range of functions I have indicated. Sometimes, however, the window has little bearing on the expression of 'contact'. Take, for instance, the lines "To the alarm of the serried windows"; "Rows of windows, / Unlit late in the evening, / Looked like horsecloths / With slits for the horses' eyes." One can speak of contact here only insofar as these lines are metaphorical, and in any case the contact is hardly between the house and the world outside. But on the whole such uses of the window, deviating from its unified image are infrequent and may be regarded as exceptions that prove the rule.

In several cases the window's rectangular shape takes on a more or less auxiliary role of creating the pictorial effect of a frame ("The window embraced in its square / Part of the garden and a patch of sky"; "The wintry day in the open embrasure / Of the undrawn curtains"; "And the windows with their double braid / Of branches in the silver of the lace" [that is, the branches are seen on the surface of the window like a pattern on a braided collar, while, presumably, the "double braid" refers to the two sections of the window]. "They would put a crescent moon in either pane" [as in a frame]).

This kind of framing also occurs in poems that have nothing to do with 'window' (cf. "It [tomorrow] walked with a strip of frame like a framemaker. / The trees, buildings, and churches / Had an otherworldly look / Inside the hole of the inaccessible frame. / Like a three-tiered hexameter they were / Displaced to the right across the square. / The ones displaced were carried out in a dead faint, / And no one noticed the loss"). Although this function is auxiliary and purely expressive, it serves to underline the theme of contact by presenting the external world as if it were part of the house, a sort of picture in a frame on the wall.

The consistent use of the window in various synonymous constructions and plot schemes which express the central themes of Pasternak's poetic world, the correspondence between its openness/closedness and the positive/negative view of the world, and the negligibility of "deviant" uses, all seem to warrant the recognition of the 'window' as a single image running through Pasternak's poems, a sort of recurring character, alongside such images as the 'beloved', 'artistic creativity', 'spring', the 'garden', 'night', 'rain', the 'candle', the 'train', and some others.

8

Pushkin's Invariants

The literature on Pushkin is vast. But although the problem of describing his invariant motifs has been posed,[1] no comprehensive description of Pushkin's poetic world (in the sense defined in Chap. 3) exists. I will outline one possible reading of his PW. I assume that the reader is by now familiar with the idea of such descriptions and with Pushkin's invariants (see Chaps. 3 and 7), and therefore I will be brief, keeping examples and comments to a minimum. As a result, the exposition might sound somewhat dogmatic.[2]

1. The Overall Picture

1.1. *The Central Theme*
Pushkin's Θinv can be formulated as

(1) an objective view of reality seen as the field of interaction between the two ambivalently evaluated poles: changeability, disorder *vs.* unchangeability, order (the ambivalent opposition "changeability / unchangeability," or simply, "changeability / unchangeability"); compare Chap. 3, §3, formula (26).

There are two main subthemes of (1):

(2) the very category of changeability/unchangeability
(3) the objective view and ambivalent evaluation of these two poles.

Subtheme (2) states the content of Θinv (1), subtheme (3), its structural aspect. In actual texts, the former is represented by more con-

Earlier versions of this chapter appeared as [1976d(1) and 1979g].

crete oppositions fashioned out of the material of the referential and code spheres; the latter is responsible for the various types of interaction between the contrasting poles. The application of the interaction types to the material produces the invariant manifestations of the central theme as a whole.

1.2. *Manifestations of 'Changeability/Unchangeability'*

The CONCRETIZATION of subtheme (2) involves all the major zones of the referential sphere.

In the physical zone, 'changeability/unchangeability' is represented by the oppositions 'movement/immobility', 'chaos/order', 'stability/destruction', 'gaseousness, liquidity, softness/hardness', 'lightness/heaviness', 'heat/cold', 'light/darkness', and several others; in the biological zone, by 'life/death' and 'health/illness'; in the psychological zone, by 'passion/impassivity', 'immoderation/moderation', 'inspiration / absence of inspiration', 'author's longing for fame and response / indifference to the opinion of others'; in the social zone, by the opposition 'freedom/bondage'.

This classification into zones is, of course, very rough; compare, for instance, the borderline situations arising as a result of constraints society imposes on passions:

(4) "Of restraining status / How quickly she accepted the artifices"; "And regardless of [lit., past] all the conventions of the world / [She] rushes, till her strength gives out, / Like some lawless comet / In the calculated realm of luminaries."

As the example in (4) shows, the motifs of one zone can serve as tropes for those of another zone. Compare the metaphorical cross between the 'immobility', 'movement', 'destruction' (the physical zone) and 'impassivity', 'bondage', 'freedom', 'passion' (the psychological and social zones) in

(5) (a) "Who, O waves, brought you to a halt, / Who shackled your mighty gallop, / Who to a speechless and dreaming pond / Turned your rebellious flow? / Whose magic wand has defeated / In me hope, grief and joy / And my stormy spirit . . . / With the dozing of idleness, lulled to sleep?

(b) Play, winds, dig up the waters, / Shatter the fatal bulwark— / Where art thou, storm—symbol of freedom? / Rush above the captive waters."

In the code sphere the central opposition 'changeability/unchangeability' is CONCRETIZED as: 'light, simple syntax / heavy constructions'; 'dynamic and intense intonation / slowed down intonation, pauses'; 'tropes / lack of tropes'; 'direct, "involved" description / detached, "noninvolved" view from the outside'; and in a variety of other ways.

1.3. *Manifestations of 'Objectiveness, Ambivalence'*

The types of interaction that implement subtheme (3) can be characterized in terms of extant 'relationships' between the poles and of the 'outcome' of the interaction.

The 'relationships' involve the 'presence / absence / degree of antagonism' between the interacting participants and the 'degree of their mutual autonomy'. As for 'autonomy', we find (in decreasing order): two completely autonomous objects ('the lyrical hero and his beloved', 'the wave and the rock', etc.); two states of one object ('the sadness and the joy of the poet'); an abstract phenomenon and its aspect ('the orderliness of the rippling movement [of a military formation]'). The range of 'antagonism's' manifestations includes such pairs as: 'two duellists', 'a wild horse and a horse-trainer', 'horse and rider', 'horse-drawn carriage and rider', 'embracing lovers'.

The 'outcome' is—in accordance with the ambivalence of Θinv (3)—in favor of now one, now the other pole. The "balance of force" can be (*a*) 'graded' and (*b*) characterized by the 'mode of its textual manifestation'. 'Grading' ranges all the way from the 'victory' of one pole to the 'harmony' between the poles. Among the more subtle grades of balance we find motif (6), discussed at some length in Chapter 3,

(6) superior peace: positively evaluated detachment and rest enjoyed by the "winner" who abstains from reaping the fruits of his "victory," e.g.: "I am above all desires; I am calm; / I know my power: I am content / With this awareness."

and

(7) showing through—of the "defeated" pole through the fetters imposed by the "winner," e.g.,
    (a) "And the river glistens under the ice." "The sad forest and the faded vale . . . / The day peeps through—and already it's dark."
    (b) "And maybe at my own sad sunset / Love will shine with a farewell smile"; "Restrained not without effort, / We like to hear sometimes / The rebellious language of others' passions / And it stirs our hearts for us."
    (c) "Through the cast-iron railings / Poke your wondrous dainty foot"; "O,

tell me please, how wives there can / Love with piety demurely combine, / Tell me how a letter drops from behind a grille"; "Love and friendship will reach / To you through grim prison latches."

As is easy to see from (7), the 'showing through' pattern applies to the material of the various zones. In (7b) the same physical landscape as in (7a)—'the setting sun peeping from behind the clouds'—serves as a metaphor for a similar situation in the emotional zone; in (7b,c) emotions 'show through' psychological, physical, and social controls (restraint, railings, grille, prison latches).

'Modes of manifestation'. The 'victory' of one pole over the other can be conveyed (*a*) by a direct approval / disapproval of one pole by the poet; (*b*) by an objective statement of actual 'victory'; (*c*) by an indirect suggestion, for example, by the temporal replacement of the "loser" by the "winner." COMBINATIONS of two or even all three modes are possible. Especially interesting are contrapuntal combinations, where, for instance, the "winner" on the plane of evaluation is the "loser" on that of temporal order or actual victory. Such counterpoints are typical of Pushkin's ambivalent universe. Consider, for instance, fragment (5). Its first part, (5a), depicts a 'real transition from movement, passion, and freedom to immobility, impassivity, and bondage'; the second part, (5b), is an 'imaginary transition in the opposite direction'. In both cases 'movement, passion, and so on' are evaluated positively, 'immobility, and so on', negatively. Both types of situation have numerous analogues in Pushkin: compare (5a) with M*inv* 'the cooling down of passions' and (5b) with 'the awakening of passions' and 'the coming of inspiration to the poet' (cf. (36b), (39) below). But there are also situations similar to (5a) and (5b) in the order of succession but opposed to them in the distribution of evaluations (cf. (8a,b)):

(8) (a)"With your meek and loving power / You pacify my stormy dreams"; cf. also "Restrained not without effort" in (7b).

(b) "Who in his hostile power / Summoned me from nothingness, / Filled my heart with passion, / Disturbed my mind with doubt?"

Table 8.1 shows four characteristic superpositions of evaluation and temporal order; the pluses and minuses represent, respectively, the "victories" and "defeats" of 'passion' in the given manifestation mode.

Table 8.1. 'Passion': principal patterns

Order of replacement	Evaluation	Example	Situation
−	+	(5a)	'negative cessation of passions' ("deadening")
−	−	(8a)	'positive cessation of passions' ("moderation")
+	−	(8b)	'negative awakening of passion' ("disturbance, worry")
+	+	(5b)	'positive awakening of passion' ("inspiration")

As has been said, the varieties of the central theme (1) as a whole are COMBINATIONS of the types of 'material' and of 'interaction'. I concentrate only on the most important motifs, proceeding from one type of material to another.

2. Motifs of the Physical Zone

Pivotal for this zone is the opposition '*movement/immobility*', involving such motifs as 'immobility', 'movement', their alternation or simultaneity, and alternation of different 'movements', ready-made moving objects as 'sea', 'ship', 'horse'.

(9) positively evaluated immobility: "She rests modestly / In her solemn beauty."
(10) negatively evaluated immobility: ". . . the exiled hero, / By the torment of tranquillity / Punished in the seas at the behest of tsars."

It is worth noting that examples (9) and (10) are not quite "pure," for the 'immobility' involves the psychological and biological zones as well; for some examples of strictly 'physical immobility' see (15).

(11) positive movement: "How swiftly over the plain, open all around / Once shod again, my steed races."
(12) abrupt switches from one positive movement to another to a third, etc.: "From the Lycee's threshold / You stepped across to a ship lightly. / And since then your road has lain at sea, / O favorite child of waves and storms"; "He returned and straightway came, / Like Čackij from the ship to a ball. . . ."

Situations of the type in (12) are often supported in the code sphere by

(13) syntactic construction *ešče—uže* 'while still—already': "Still cupids, devils, serpents / Leap and roar on stage; Still . . . [enumeration of other processes follows, occupying ten lines],/But Onegin is already off. / He's riding home to dress [for the evening]."

Of course, the motif of 'abrupt switch' may itself express 'changeability', even if it links not 'movements' but other phenomena. Compare

(14) 'regularity of change': "One dawn to replace another / Rushes on, allowing night just half an hour"; "Over the fallen ranks a new line / Closes the ranks of bayonets"; "In their evenly rippling ranks"; "Dressed, undressed and once more dressed."

The element of 'regularity' in (14) represents the 'unchangeability, order' pole of the central $\Theta inv(1)$. Thus, (14) COMBINES both poles of (1).

Another characteristic COMBINATION of poles is:

(15) alternation of immobility and movement (in any order and with any distribution of evaluation): "Whether I circle with the rebellious crowd, / Whether I taste sweet tranquillity . . . "; " 'Hurry, hurry!' But the nettlesome steed / Suddenly shook his plaited mane / And halted. . ."; "Hark! . . ./ The ship raced into the Neva—and there amidst the swell, / Floats, rocking, like a young swan"; "So dozes, unmoving, the ship in the unmoving moisture, / But hark!—the sailors suddenly rush, and clamber . . ./ The mass heaves and cuts apart the waves."

In between (14) and (15) is situated

(16) transition to fast movement not from complete immobility but from "running on the spot": "And indeed: the horse is before me, / It paws with its hoof all aflame, / . . . / The horse reared up and off it carried me"; cf. also the ballet example, (18), in Chapter 3.

On the other hand, the 'halt, cessation of movement', is also not always a complete one; compare the penultimate example in (15).

Up to now we have been dealing with situations of 'switch, replacement, alternation'. No less numerous are those characterized by

(17) simultaneous COMBINATION of immobility and movement:

(a) "There's no movement, said the bearded sage. / The other fell silent and began to walk around before him"; "Gurgling, the stream still runs beyond the mill, / But by now the pond is still."

(b) "And dozing we drive to our lodging, / And time drives on the horses"; "Dear friend, let us abandon ourselves to the gallop / Of the impatient horse."

In (17a) 'immobility' and 'movement' are distributed between different objects, whereas in (17b) they involve different aspects of one and the same object. The latter, closer type of COMBINATION is achieved with the help of such ready-made objects as 'dozing' and 'riding in a carriage or sledge'; compare (20) and (22) in Chapter 3.

Real 'immobility' and potential or subdued 'movement' often COMBINE to produce situations of 'superior peace'. In the physical zone this usually involves the motif of 'height, vertical top'; compare (18):

(18) "The Caucasus is beneath me . . . / Here the clouds pass submissively beneath me; / Plunging through them, the waterfalls roar . . ."; ". . . I've read somewhere / That a tsar once ordered / His warriors to bring handfuls of earth to a heap, / And a proud hill soared up—and the tsar / Could happily survey from its crest / The valley covered in white tents, / And the sea where his ships ran / . . . / I can gaze on all that is in my power."

The main features of the pattern of 'superior peace and immobility in a vertically high position' are present in the situations of 'horse-riding' as well (cf. Chap. 3, § 3). In still another type of physical manifestation of 'superior immobility and peace' the 'superiority' is expressed— instead of through 'height'—through 'geographical distance':

(19) ". . . how quiet the sky is; / Unmoving the warm air—. . . etc . . . . And far away to the north—in Paris— / Perhaps the sky is covered with clouds, / A cold rain falls and the wind blows.— / But why should it matter to us?"

Let us now consider some other physical manifestations of 'changeability/unchangeability'. 'Immobility and order' are sometimes emphasized as 'stability, durability, heaviness', whereas the opposite pole appears as 'destructive (or simply fruitless) energy'. Among the various COMBINATIONS of 'victory' and 'evaluation' are motifs (20)–(22):

(20) positive destruction: "But, inconquerable, you [the sea] began to

play, / And a flock of ships sinks"; "And mighty and free would I be, / Like a whirlwind digging up the fields, breaking the forests . . .";

(21) negatively (or ambivalently) evaluated destruction: "The earth is disturbed—from the tottering columns / The idols tumble! The people, driven on by terror, / Beneath the raining stones. . . ."

(22) positive indestructibility: "There stands a gray crag, in vain the banks tremble, / In vain the thunder rumbles and the waves growing turbid / Rush past and break. . . ."

Motif (22) is evidently related to psychological and social situations of 'superior peace', cf. (31b) and (44). In (21) worth noting is the way opposition 'movement/immobility' is developed into the motif of 'heavy immobile masses being set in motion', which has certain analogues in the psychological zone.

We have so far discussed in considerable detail the *dynamic* aspect of the physical zone. The central opposition (1) manifests itself also in other aspects of this zone, namely; those of

1. *temperature and light:* 'heat / cold', 'burning / cooling', 'blaze / darkness', etc.

2. the *state of the substance:* 'hard / liquid, powdery or gaseous'

3. *biochemical characteristics* connected with the biological and psychological zones, e.g.: 'water / wine / poison'; cf. the 'sober flow of water' (38c) / 'noisy Bacchus's liquid' (38c) / 'magic poison of desires', etc.

4. *sound characteristics:* 'noise / noiselessness', 'speech / silence', etc.

The evaluation in these cases is again variable. For instance, there are situations of both 'negative cold' ("Either the plague will seize me, / Or the frost petrify") and 'positive cold' ("With her cold beauty / She loved Russian winter"). Especially typical is motif (23), bordering on the biological zone:

(23) positive COMBINATION of cold (snow, etc.) with light and/or heat (blood coursing, roses); "Frost and sun, a wondrous day . . . / Glittering in the sun, the snow lies"; "But northern storms harm not the Russian rose. / How hotly the kiss burns in the frost . . ." "I love the still air and frost / Of your relentless winter, / The running of sleighs along the wide Neva, / The girls' faces brighter than roses."

3. Motifs of the Biological Zone

In this zone the poet seems to concentrate on hybrid situations that COMBINE— in some way or other—*'life'* and *'death'*. Of special interest is the search for convincing motivations for a positive attitude to 'death':

(24) the half-dead living (with variable evaluation): ". . . Evgenij / Sat unmoving, deathly pale / . . . And as if bewitched, / As if rooted to the marble, / Could not stir!"; "I'm drawn to it [the fall], / As, I suppose, you are sometimes drawn / To a consumptive girl. Doomed to die / The poor thing declines, without grumbling or anger. / A smile can be seen on her faded lips; / She hears not the yawning of the grave's abyss; / A crimson color still plays on her face. / She's still alive today, tomorrow gone"; "Old Derzhavin noticed us / And, coming down into the tomb, gave his blessing."
(25) the dead that seem alive or half-alive or act as if they were alive; leaving the grave; conversations from beyond the grave; "the dead grabbing the living": "Long the dead man mid the waves / Floated, rocking, like one alive"; "Your friend Voltaire . . . / Has still not calmed down in his home beyond the grave, / And wanders still from cemetery to cemetery"; "The lively conversations of dead acquaintances" (i.e., books); cf. also the scenes of rendezvous and conversations with the dead beloved (37c); "The bone threatened me with death!"

One type of COMBINATION of 'life' and 'death' is the following motif (widely used in other zones as well, such as the psychological and the social).

(26) abyss, entrance, door, etc., leading to the territory of the unchangeability pole; on one side of it are light, warmness, air, movement, life, freedom; on the other, darkness, coldness, hard vault, immobility, death, imprisonment; the evaluation is variable: "Terrible is the cold of the subterranean vault, / The entrance to it is open for all. / But there is no way out from it"; "We will all descend beneath the eternal vaults / . . . / And let young life be playing / By the entrance to the grave, / And indifferent nature / Shine with her eternal beauty"; "The vaults of Tartarus tremble / . . . / There is immortality, there oblivion . . ."; "The dungeons will collapse and freedom / Will greet you joyfully at the entrance. . . ."

In an example in (24) ("She's still alive to-day, tomorrow gone") we may see a manifestation of the motif

(27) rapid replacement of life by death (often accompanied by 'replacement of movement by immobility' in the physical zone; cf. exx. 14–16): "He ran upon my sword and died / Like a dragonfly upon a pin"; "They rush, come to blows in a general uproar . . . / Delibaš is already upon a lance / And the Cossack headless."

In (27) the contrast between the opposite states that replace one another is accentuated by the instantaneous switch from maximum liveliness to complete deadness. Another way of intensifying the contrastive relation between 'life' and 'death' is COMBINING them in a simultaneous situation. In such situations 'life' and 'death' are either distributed between different people or characterize one and the same person. In the latter case the COMBINATION is often psychologically motivated by M*inv* 'relishing the perilous danger', which resembles structurally the situations in (23), where 'heat' is caused by 'cold'. Cf. a direct formulation of this structural principle, derived from the juxtaposition of these very situations of the physical (winter) and biological (plague) zones, in the Chairman's song in *A Feast in the Time of the Plague:* ". . . merry is the winter's heat of feasting . . . / As from mischief-making winter / Let's lock ourselves against the Plague as well! / Let's light the fires, fill the goblets. . . ." And further on: "All, all that threatens death, / Holds a mysterious charm / For the heart of a mortal. . . ."

These last lines already take us into the next M*inv:*

(28) boisterous liveliness on the brink of death (one's own or others'); (*a*) relishing the perilous danger; (*b*) love at the price of death; (*c*) love against the background of death:

(a) "I will see blood . . . / The death-dealing lead / Will whistle around me. / And how many powerful impressions / For my thirsting spirit!"; "There is an intoxication in battle, / And on the brink of the gloomy abyss . . . / All, all that threatens death / Holds a mysterious charm / For the heart of mortal man— / A promise, perhaps, of immortality! . . . / And we drink the breath of the rose-maiden— / Filled, perchance, with plague!"

(b) "'I'll die', says Tanya, / But death from such poison is kind"; "Tell me, which of you will buy / My night for the price of life?"

(c) "As long as I am not hanged, / Then I will be at your feet / In the shade of the Ukrainian cherry trees"; "And the lady of the house awaits her dear one, / Not the dead one, but the living"; cf. also the love scenes in front of a corpse in "The Stone Guest" and "The Golden Cockerel", discussed by Jakobson (1975: 158–59).

The opposite type of 'aquiescence in death', also typical of Pushkin, is not through emotional excitement but, on the contrary, through seeing

(29) death as the way to the desired rest (the links with the psychological zone are evident); cf. (35b), (37c): ". . . The graveyard of a clan / Where sleep the dead in solemn peace; / Where the undecked graves have ample space"; cf. 'death as rest and eternal sleep' in the lines about Voltaire in (25); "Perhaps with my burial shroud / I shall cast off all earthly feelings . . . / I shall know no regrets. / And forget love's yearning?"; cf. also 'love of death-like beauty' in (24) and in (37c).

One could say that, if (28) is 'death exciting', then (29) is 'death appeasing', and that both are evaluated positively—or at least ambivalently.

4. Motifs of the Social Zone

In the social domain, the central theme 'changeability/unchangeability' manifests itself as the opposition '*freedom, riot, chaos/bondage, prison, bridle, rigid order, stronghold*', which in its turn is VARIED through application of manifold types of interaction and evaluation. Particularly characteristic are situations (30)–(32):

(30) negative bondage, positive freedom; positive escape from imprisonment and/or destruction of fetters, prisons, and strongholds: "An enemy of restricting conditions and fetters, / I had no difficulty in giving up feasts, / Where . . . / The cold of decorum smothers all ardent truth"; "I sit behind the grille in a dump dungeon / . . . / 'We are free birds; 'tis time, friend, 'tis time! / . . . / Whither we sport, the wind . . . and I!'"; "Arise, O Greece, arise / . . . / The land of heroes and gods / Has burst the slave's fetters."

(31) (a) negative freedom, negative riot, positive bondage; (b) positive submission to moderation, bridle; positive image of a stronghold:

(a) "My hateful freedom . . ."; "O rose-maiden, I am in shackles; / But I am not ashamed of your shackles"; "Forgetting his grove and his freedom, / The captive siskin above me / Pecks his seed and sprays his water / And enjoys his lively song."

(b) "Young filly / . . . / Leap not capriciously. / Wait, I'll make you / Be submissive beneath me: / I'll direct your gallop in a measured circle / On a shortened bridle"; "Is Russia strong? War and death, / And rebellion, and the pressure of storms / Raving outside, have shaken her—/ Yet look: she still stands! And around her the unrest has abated"; cf. the 'indestructible cliff', in (22).

(32) more or less harmonious ambivalent balance between freedom and bondage: ". . . this dualistic assembly: / Here a fiery onslaught, and there a stern rebuff, / The bold springs of a new civic consciousness / . . . You've seen . . . / An alliance of mind and the Furies, / Law erected by terrible freedom . . ."; ". . . the cold glitter of fortune / Has not changed your free spirit. / You are always the same for honor and for friends"; here belong also situations of 'showing through railings' in (7c) and the ambivalent images of 'granite' in *The Bronze Horseman,* as well as the situations in (4).

Examples in (30)–(32) exhibit numerous affinities, COMBINATIONS, and borderline cases with the situations of the physical and psychological zones. In most cases the ratio is simple:

$$\frac{\text{'movement'}}{\text{'immobility'}} = \frac{\text{'freedom'}}{\text{'imprisonment'}} = \frac{\text{'passion'}}{\text{'impassivity'}}$$

However, sometimes the correlation is inverted: 'freedom' is associated with 'immobility' and 'impassivity', whereas 'bondage' is associated with 'passions'; cf. the 'sweet fetters' in (31) and 'freedom as the unchangeability of the soul' in (32). Thus the typical motif of the 'yoke of passions'—burdensome or beneficent—arises; cf. (33):

(33) positive release from the yoke of passions or positive control over passions; superior or detached rest, invulnerable indifference and calm: "Having left their [the passions'] riotous power, . . . / Blessed is he who . . . / . . . has finally broken with them . . . / Who has cooled love with separation . . . / When the flame of passions dies down, / And we find their willfulness / And their gusts funny . . . , / Restrained not without effort . . . "; cf. also numerous examples in (35a), (37), (43), (44).

(34) positive submission to passions ensuring tranquility and even invulnerability: "Blessed a hundredfold he who is devoted to faith, / Who, having calmed cold reason, / Rests in the heart's languor . . . / But pitiful is he who foresees everything, / Whose head does not spin . . ."; "Since then, with soul aflame, / He did not look at women . . . / Since then he did not raise / The steel lattice from his face . . . / 'Lumen coelum; sancta rosa!' / He shouted loudest of them all / And the awe of him / Haunted the Muslims everywhere."

In (34) the paradoxical disagreement between social, physical, and psychological manifestations of the two main poles is pushed to the

extreme: the 'cold intellect' needs 'calm' (whereas usually in Pushkin it is 'passions' that require 'subduing'); 'fever' calms, 'passion' grants 'invulnerability', whereas usually the source of 'invulnerability' is the 'hardness' of a 'rock' or 'submission' of a docile 'horse' to the 'bridle'—cf. (31b); and finally, "passion' is symbolized by 'steel lattice' on the face of the *poor knight!* Such a "reversed" cross-combination of CONCRETIZATIONS of 'changeability/unchangeability' is yet another manifestation of Pushkin's ambivalence.

5. Motifs of the Psychological Zone

Here the central theme appears in the form of the opposition *'passion, involvement, immoderation / impassivity, noninvolvement, moderation'*.

I will first concentrate on Pushkin's peculiar *'interest for and positive attitude toward impassivity'*, although his texts also contain the less original motifs of 'positive passion', as well as situations like (28), situated midway between the psychological and social zones. Let us begin with situation

(35) (a) positive or negative impassivity, sublime or innocent calm; (b) calm beyond the grave; cf. (9), (10):
(a) "Here is the proper, dreary city, / Here speeches are ice, the hearts are granite; / Here there is no nice frivolity . . . "; cf. (24); "I was confused by the severe beauty / Of her head, her calm lips and glances, / And her words full of holiness"; ". . . my Madonna, / Purest model of the purest charm."
(b) "Blessed are those who have fallen in battle: / Now they have entered Eden / And sunk in a delightful ease / That nothing can poison."

The links connecting (35b) with 'death as one way to the desired rest', 'love for death-like beauty', 'sweet resignation' (see (29), (36b), (37c)) seem evident, as well as the typological analogies with the physical motif of 'immobility'. As for analogues to the situations of 'replacement, shift, switch' in the previous zones (see (12), (14), (15), (27)), they are represented here by COMBINATIONS *in succession* of 'passion' and 'impassivity', cf.:

(36) (a) sudden transitions from impassivity to passion; (b) cooling down or sweet resignation from passions; (c) (positive or negative) memories of past passions:

(a) " . . . My days dragged quietly along / Without divinity, without inspiration, / Without tears, or life, or love. / Then my spirit awoke. / And once more you appeared, . . . / And my heart beats intoxicated. . . "; cf. (5b).

(b) "But all has passed—the blood in my heart has grown cold . . . / My sportive temper has lost its stamp, / My soul grows dumb from hour to hour; / It no longer feels anything; thus the light leaf of the grove / Is petrified in Caucasian springs"; "But meeting her, embarrassed, you / Suddenly halt involuntarily, / Caught in a reverence of prayer / Before the shrine of beauty"; cf. (5a), (8a).

(c) "With anguish and yearning I rush thither, / Intoxicated by recollection . . . / And I feel again; tears are born again in my eyes; / My soul seethes and sinks down"; "For naught I roused that feeling . . . / So that was whom I loved with soul aflame / With such heavy tension / . . . / Where those torments, where that love? / . . . / For the sweet memory of unreturnable days / I can find neither tears nor reproaches."

Simultaneous COMBINATIONS of 'passion' and 'impassivity' fall into two groups, differing as to the feature 'distribution of the poles among autonomous persons / no such distribution' (see §1.3); cf. (37) and (38) respectively.

(37) (a) passionate love for a cold or reserved woman; (b) impassivity against the background of passion or in circumstances predisposing to passion; (c) love for a deathlike beauty, rendezvous beyond or across the grave:

(a) "When I enclose in my embraces your slender waist, / Unspeaking, . . . / You listen, despondent, to me without participation or attention"; cf. the emotional attitudes in the pairs 'Don Juan–Dona Anna' in the *Stone Guest* and 'Onegin–Tat'jana' in *Evgenii Onegin;* "Oh, how much dearer you are, my restrained one! / . . . / Tender, you give yourself up to me without intoxication, / Modestly cold. . . ."

(b) "An indifferent spectator of merriment, / Silently I will yawn"; "They came together. Wave and stone / Verse and prose, ice and flame / Are not so different from each other / . . . / He listened to Lensky with a smile / . . . / His chilling comments / He tried to restrain on his lips" . . . and further on: "Restrained not without effort, / We . . . "; see (7b).

(c) "There is no breathing from her lips, but how / Piercing is the cool osculation without breathing, . . . "; see (27) in Chap. 10; cf. similar motifs in (24); "Appear, beloved shade, / . . . / Pale, cold, as a winter's day, / Contorted by a last torment / . . . / I want to say that I still love, / That I'm still yours: hither, hither!'"; cf. also 'apparitions and conversations from beyond the grave' in (25).

(38) (a) impassive love (not requiring requital); (b) deliberate or compulsory restraining of passions; (c) rational self-moderation (or rejection of moderation); (d) other ambiguous states:

(a) "I'm yours as ever, I love you all over again / Without either hopes or desires"; "You blossomed—with reverence / Now I bow down to you. / I trail after you with heart and eyes / With an involuntary trembling. / And like an old nanny am proud / Of your reputation and you; see also (7b, c).

(b) cf. 'resignation' in (36b), 'innocent passion and reservedness' of the poor knight in (34), and also: "At first she broke down and wept, / All but divorced her husband / . . . / Got used to it, became contented. / Habit is granted us from above— / It's a substitute for happiness"; "Learn to control yourself"; "I control my day, the mind is fond of order; / I am learning to maintain the attention of lengthy thoughts."

(c) "From in your youth you cleverly diversified / Your long clear age, / Sought the possible, made moderate mischief; / Pastimes and ranks came to you one after another"; "Young man! Feast modestly, and Bacchus' noisy liquid / Mix with a sober stream of water and wise conversation"; cf. the contrary attitude: "Boy! pour more . . . / I want to drink like a wild Scythian / . . . / I am glad to drown reason."

(d) "I'm sad and cheerful. My melancholy is bright"; "You were able to unite with a coldness of heart / The magic fire of captivating eyes"; cf. also: "in sad voluptuousness"; "love with piety demurely to combine" (7c); "half-tormenting joy"; "with sad joy" (43b); "loved . . . with such heavy tension" (36c); "with what heavy endearment / I enjoy . . ."; and similar ambivalent "mixed" feelings.

In terms of material, the main subdivision of the psychological zone is into the motifs that deal with '*love passion*', discussed above, and those that deal with '*poetic creativity*' as a special kind of emotion. Worthy of note is the complete homology between the two series of motifs; compare the situations (39)–(42) below, that repeat the main patterns of the motifs (36)–(38) and the pattern of 'superior peace':

(39) sudden coming of poetic inspiration to the poet or sudden ceasing of creativity (cf. (36)): "Until Apollo summons the poet / To his sacred sacrifice, / He is pettily immersed / In the vain world's cares / . . . . But as soon as the divine word / Touches his sensitive ear, / The poet's soul shakes itself, / Like an eagle waking . . . "; cf. the same in "I remember the wondrous moment . . ." (36a) and in "The prophet"; ". . . to my lyre / I entrusted the pampered sounds / Of frenzy, laziness and passions. / But even then despite myself / I interrupted the cunning string's chime, / Whenever your majestic voice / Startled me suddenly"; cf. (36b).
(40) the poet in front of the cold loved one or an indifferent crowd (cf. (37)): ". . . Why should the poet / Trouble his heart's heavy sleep? . . . / Like a goddess she has no need / Of the outpouring of earthly ecstasies . . ."; "He sang— but cold and arrogant / The uninitiated throng all round / Listened to him without understanding."

(41) pure ambitionless inspiration not requiring the attention of others (cf. (38a) 'impassive love'): "He loves his song, for pleasure he sings, / Without further designs; he knows neither fame, / Nor fear, nor hopes . . . / Like him, without response, I sing, soothed / And love to think up secret verses."

Structurally similar are also those motifs which, in the domains of 'love' and 'poetry', implement the pattern of 'superior peace'. In 'love' it takes the form of

(42) superior indifference to the beloved's coldness motivated by (*a*) purely inward reasons; (*b*) a viewpoint from the future:
    (a) ". . . As God grant to you to be loved by another"; cf. also (33)
    (b) "I pray: do not approach / Near the body of your Jenny; / Touch not her dead lips, / Watch her from afar . . . / And when the infection has passed / Visit my poor dust. / But Jenny will not abandon / Edmond even in heaven"; see also (30)–(32) in Chap. 3.

In the domain of 'poetic creativity' we find the same:

(43) the poet's superior indifference to the opinion of the crowd motivated by (*a*) inward reasons; (*b*) the view from the future:
    (a) "You are tsar: live on your own, . . . / You are content? Then let the mob revile your work . . . / And in its childish playfulness rock your tripod"; the same at the end of "The monument": ". . . Accept both praise and slander with indifference".
    (b) "Mourn, dear ones, my lot in silence; / Beware of arousing suspicion by your tears / . . . / When the storm passes, in a superstitious crowd / Gather sometimes to read my faithful scroll"; "Sad am I: no friend is with me / . . . / I drink alone . . . / Which of us in old age, then, will have / To celebrate our lycée's day all on his own? / Unhappy friend! . . . / Let him at least with sad joy / Spend then this day at the cup, / As now I, your disgraced recluse, / Have spent it without grief or cares"; "Accept, then, my thanks, / Worshiper of the peaceful Aonian maids, / O you, whose memory will preserve / My flying creations; / Whose well-meaning hand / Will pat the old man's laurels!" (the poet "pats" condescendingly the future reader on the shoulder, who in turn pats the poet).

In fact, the borderline between the personal and artistic spheres is not inviolate. In the fragment about the Lycée's anniversary, in (43b), the wise and imaginative speaker of the poem not only attains 'superior peace' himself but also raises his friend above his loneliness and troubles: he thus acts like those gods, saints, and tsars who, in other Pushkin poems, raise the poet himself (or his hero) into their proximity and above his troubles. This motif of 'proximity to a wise friend who observes the world from the superior position of detached non-involvement' is halfway between man's personal ('friendship') and creative ('wisdom, creativity') spheres. It underlies the two following fragments whose similarity is especially striking because they are addressed to such different people as the conservative old Prince Jusupov (44a) and the outlawed freethinker Chaadaev (44b):

(44) (a) "Everything has changed . . . / All, all have passed by and away. Their opinions, chatter, passions / Are forgotten for others. Look: around you / All seethes anew, destroying the past / . . . / Only you are the same / . . . / I listen to you: your free conversation / Is filled with youthfulness . . . / You, without joining in the world's excitement, / Sometimes mockingly gaze at them through the window."

(b) "The voice of slander by then could no longer hurt me / . . . / Should I grieve . . . / When I could be proud of your friendship? / I thank the gods . . . / I will see the study / Where you are always wise and sometimes dreamer / And impassive observer of the flippant crowd."

6. On the Status of Invariant Motifs

The nature and mode of existence of invariant motifs is a theoretical problem that has wider significance than just the psychological zone or even Pushkin's PW as a whole. As has been said, the core of the psychological zone in Pushkin is the interest in various blends and interactions of 'passion' and 'impassivity'. Let us stress once more that it is this principle and not the lifelike "surface" motivations, varying from one situation to another, that determine the meaning of the psychological situations. The same holds true for the existence and unity of every individual Minv; e.g. (38a) 'impassive love' ("without . . . hopes or desires"), is based on all its manifestations having a common thematic denominator which can be traced back to still more abstract invariants of the given PW, not on complete identity of all surface properties of the motif's manifestations. Still less relevant for the status of an Minv are the motivations that are only implicit in the surface structure of an individual text.

Discussing certain manifestations of 'impassive love', critics keep debating with much ingeniousness the problem "sincerity or pretense?" (Blagoj 1931: 215–19; Akhmatova 1977; Shklovsky 1969). The "reality" of this and certain other M̄inv (e.g., (28b) 'love at the price of death') can also be questioned—in view of their being but trite cliches of romantic rhetoric. Well, does "pretense" invalidate the "deep reality" of such motifs? To be sure, in some cases the situation of 'impassive love' is more or less clearly motivated by the 'strategy of seduction' (e.g., in *The Stone Guest*). But in other cases the same situation may result from 'true hopelessness of love' (in Chap. 1 of *The Negro of Peter the Great*); 'peculiarities of (cold) temperament' ("No, I do not value the riotous joys . . ."); 'external circumstances' (e.g., separation, as in "Upon the hills of Georgia . . ."); 'ethical principles' (Tat'jana in Chap. 8 of *Evgenij Onegin*); 'sublime inaccessibility of the object of love' (e.g., of the Holy Virgin in "There lived in the world a poor knight . . ."); 'altruistic considerations' (the song of Mary in *The Feast at the Time of Plague*, (see (42b)); 'shallowness of the feeling' ("Approaching Ižory . . ."); and so on.

That "pretense" pertains only to the surface structure can be seen also from the fact that its direction is sometimes reversed. Thus, in "I loved you . . ." the lyrical hero pretends not to love any longer not only before the 'cold woman' ('altruistic considerations and/or ethical principles'), but before himself (with the hidden purpose of 'self-consolation'); Ibragim (*The Negro of Peter the Great*) in a letter to the lover he abandons 'pretends that he continues to love her in order to sugar the pill'; in several light verse dedications (e.g., in "No, no I should not . . ." and "Once, I remember with fondness, . . ." (see (38a)) the pretense consists in the poet's passing off a mere 'album-genre compliment' for 'hopeless passion'.

I have so far tried to refute what might be called a "naively ideological" objection to treating 'impassive love' as a single invariant motif. Let us now take up the opposite objection, the "sophisticatedly formalist" one. Namely, that the poet is interested, rather than in the feelings he depicts, in the very element of pretense, which creates rich possibilities for the artistic play of ambiguities; cf. in particular the remarks of Shklovsky (1969: 223) on litotes and the "letting slip" in "I loved you. . . ." see p. 179). There are two ways to respond to this: first, that the motif of 'love without desire' itself often figures as a fully "real" state, and, second, that it is connected by a series of gradual transitions with other, also "real" (i.e., involving no "pretense") states, namely, 'passions cooled down', 'passion in front of coldness', and so on. On the other hand, it is true that the principle of 'ambivalence', as well as considerations of expressiveness, naturally call for COMBINATION of the poles (in particular, of 'passion' and 'impassivity') and that that COMBINATION, in its turn, predisposes to using, among others, the motif of 'pretense'—both on the plane of expressiveness and on that of "real-life" motivations. The approach based on the concept of invariant motif can, therefore, claim to be a kind of golden mean between the "naively ideological" and the "sophisticatedly formalist" extremes.

7. On Code-Sphere Motifs

I cannot at the moment produce a systematic description of Pushkin's code-sphere $\bar{M}inv$ and will, therefore, limit myself to several brief considerations.

One characteristic motif is the paradoxical counterpoint of 'passion' (or 'fast movement') as depicted in the referential sphere with 'impassivity' created by code-sphere means. Let us consider the two concluding lines of "Upon the hills of Georgia. . . ."

(45) I serdce vnov' gorit i ljubit—ottogo,   And the heart again burns and
     Čto ne ljubit' ono me možet.   loves—because
                                      It is incapable of not loving.

Here the contrast consists in the fact that:

1. on the plane of reference, (45) deals with 'love, passion' ('the heart burns, it can't help loving'), but
2. on the plane of expression, it is a dry, tautological, even a slightly boring dissertation ("loves—because . . . is incapable of not loving"), interrupted every now and then by pauses: in the first of the two lines the syntactic structure is such that pauses occur between all the words; the series of pauses culminates in the one after *ottogo* 'because'.

Technically, the pauses are "thrust upon" the verse jointly by the following code-sphere factors:

1. The fully accented iambic pentameter predisposes one to slow reading and pauses.
2. The straight word order without inversions calls for the same.
3. *Ottogo* is followed by verse boundary.
4. *Ottogo* is preceded by a dash that marks the end of the main clause.
5. *Gorit* 'burns' is followed by a caesura.

6. *Serdce* 'heart' and *vnov'* 'again' are syntactically unrelated, so that a separating pause is required.

7. In the reading that links the modifier *vnov'* 'again' to the coordinated predicate *gorit i ljubit* 'burns and loves' (and such a reading is only natural, since the two verbs are not only coordinated but synonymous as well), a pause is necessary between *vnov'* and *gorit*, for otherwise *vnov'* would refer to *gorit* alone.[3]

Several code-sphere invariants are discussed in Chapter 9 in connection with the role they play in the structure of a particular Pushkin poem. Among them are the 'showing of "direct" syntactic constructions through "oblique and heavy" ones' (see §2.5); the 'counterpoint of insistent passion in the referential sphere with increasingly casual mention of it in the code sphere' (see §2.2); the 'counterpoint of passionate involvement or movement in the referential sphere with detached point of view in the code sphere' (see Chap. 9, §2.2, and Chap. 3, §3). A systematic description of Pushkin's code-sphere invariants remains, however, one of the unsolved—and challenging—tasks confronting Russian poetics.[4]

9

Invariants and the Structure of a Text: Pushkin's "I loved you . . ."

Ja vas ljubil: ljubov' ešče, byt' možet,
V duše moej ugasla ne sovsem;
No pust' ona vas bol'še ne trevožit;
Ja ne xoču pečalit' vas ničem.

I loved you: love still, perhaps,
In my soul has died out not
   completely;
But let it not disturb you any more;
I do not want to sadden you by
   anything.

Ja vas ljubil bezmolvno, beznadežno,
To robost'ju, to revnost'ju tomim;
Ja vas ljubil tak iskrenno, tak nežno,
Kak daj vam bog ljubimoj byt' drugim.

I loved you speechlessly, hopelessly,
Now by shyness, now by jealousy
   tormented;
I loved you so sincerely, so tenderly,
As God grant to you to be loved by
   another.

This lyric is one of the indisputable masterpieces of Russian poetry. The enigmatic simplicity of the apparently calm eight lines that tell and overcome the drama of an unhappy love are a challenge for scholars. D. N. Ovsjaniko-Kulikovskij (1923: 29) cited it as an instance of "trope-less" poetry. Jakobson (1981) analyzed it as an "example of the monopoly of grammatical devices." Shklovsky (1969: 223) put Jakobson's title in ironic quotes and offered his own solution: the poem *is* based on a trope—a litote: "the lyrical hero downplays his grief and love, but lets the truth slip out." Slonimskij (1959: 118–20) drew attention to "a syntactic perturbation" in the last line "under the impact of an emotional outburst." This observation is referred to by

Earlier versions of this chapter appeared as [1976d(2), 1977c, and 1978e].

Jakobson and at the same time is close to Shklovsky's idea of "letting slip," "blurting." In general, most of the points made—sometimes polemically—about the poem seem to be compatible within a single comprehensive analysis; such an analysis is, however, missing. What should such a description be like? I believe that it must explicitly show *what is said and how it is said in the poem, and in what sense it is Pushkinian*. In the language of PE, an ideal description derives the text from its theme in terms of expressive devices and of the poet's invariants.[1]

1. Overall Structure

1.1. *Thematic and Artistic Design*

1.1.1. *Theme.* The local theme of the poem is the "eternal" one of

(1) unhappy love.

In "translating" theme (1) into the language of Pushkin's poetic world, a cluster of invariant motifs is drawn in:

(2) passion in the face of impassivity; the cooling of love; suppression of passion; passionless love ("without hopes or desires"); memory of past feelings.[2]

One possible COMBINATION of Θ*loc* (1) with Θ*inv* (2) produces the following integral theme of the poem.

(3) Θ*int:* restrained memory, in the spirit of superior peace and love without desire, of a cooled passion (and, perhaps, beneath it all a declaration of a continuing passion) for a cold (or necessarily restrained) woman.

An important feature of the thematic complex (3) is its 'ambivalent and indeterminate quality'. One is struck by the very uncertainty of the circumstances of the romance between the two figures. First, such lack of concreteness in the local theme is characteristic of abstract lyricism, which aims primarily to make manifest the author's poetic world.[3] Second, this is the reverse side of Pushkin's "vertiginous laconism" (Akhmatova 1977: 161). Finally, the very fact of this indeterminacy and its bearing on the key components of the theme (a declaration or only a recollection? love has died or is it still alive? coldness or self-restraint or necessity?) help emphasize the ambivalent central motif ('passionless love'). This 'ambivalent indeterminacy' is sustained and developed in the text in a variety of ways.

Thus, the COMBINATION 'declaration plus recollections' is used to carry the theme of 'passionless love' through two temporal planes. Everything that is said of this past 'love' (being tongue-tied, jealousy, alleged cooling of the embers, etc.) is also conveyed by the structure of the discourse embodying the present state of the hero and of his 'love' (by the obliqueness of the confession, by the self-denial for the sake of "another," and by the hint of jealousy in the last line). The problem "has it cooled or not?" is developed into a miniature plot: first we are told that 'love' has passed, then doubt is cast on this ("not completely"), then we are given to understand that this is not the cause of the 'impassivity' anyway ("I do not want to sadden you").

On the other hand, the indeterminacy of the heroine's behavior is not dramatized, which conveys

(4) the lyrical hero's reverential and distant attitude to the heroine.

Among the other manifestations of this passionless veneration are the polite plural *vy* 'you', noted by Shklovsky (1969: 222), and the consistent use of only the oblique cases of this pronoun, noted by Jakobson (1961: 405). The emotional stance (4) is a CONCRETIZATION of

(5) altruistic suppression of love's claims,

a motif introduced as a psychologically based COMBINATION of the thematic components 'love without desire' and 'superior peace' in (3). In motif (5) this COMBINATION is not built on a compromise but on the ultimate development of the poles of the theme: 'a denial of one's claims out of a desire for the good of the loved one' is at once the greatest possible manifestation of 'love' and a 'renunciation of love', a conscious 'necessity' and a demonstration of 'freedom and superiority'. It is typical, too, that in the poem's plot the cause ('love') and the consequence ('renunciation of claims') do not replace one another in time but coexist simultaneously, creating the impression, so appropriate to the theme of 'an ambivalent mixture of two states', of an extended presence in the magnetic field of both poles, of "sacrificial fire," "quietly smoldering heat," "sad voluptuousness" (typical Pushkin images; cf. Chap. 8, (38), esp.(d)).

1.1.2. *The deep design.* The theme of 'love being tamed, suppressed' determines both the tone of the poem—unassertive, restrained, muted—and, by the same token, the basic creative problem which is being resolved—how to combine the moderate tone with a degree of expressiveness (the latter being dictated both by the general artistic requirements and by the inner contrastiveness of a theme which includes such a "hot" component as 'passion'). The elements which make up the poem are chosen not in the extreme or most vivid forms but at their most moderate; the effects are diffused; a point which is "vivid" in one respect remains muted in another. Incidentally, this is one reason why so great a role is played by the minutest structural details, the "poetry of grammar."

This overall muted tone makes itself felt, for instance, in what we might call the "oblique" mode of exposition. The predominant tense is not the present but the past, which tinges everything being described with unreality. There are numerous negative or noncategorical forms and expressions ("let it not disturb you"; "I do not want . . . by anything"; "still, perhaps"; "not completely"; etc.). In addition, there are passives, nominalizations, and other heavy constructions ("by jealousy tormented," "to be loved by another"). Also working in this direction are the detached plural "you" in oblique cases and the various manifestations of 'uncertainty' mentioned earlier, as well as the poem's often-remarked lack of imagery, avoidance, as it were, of all rhetoric. Last but not least, is the muting effect played by the "averaging" normality of the verse structure.

If there is any deviation from the "norm" in the rhyme scheme it is toward a greater muting and monotony. In the eight lines there are not four but only three rhyming vowels, which form a transition from /o/ through /e/ to /i/. In all the rhymes, moreover, there is a play of repetition and alternation of the consonants /ž/ and /m/. This consistency of the rhyming syllables creates overall a flowing transition through the lines:

(6) /ož/ — /em/ — /ož/ — /em/ — /ež/ — /im/ — /ež/ — /im/.

However, creating a muted effect is not the sole function of this transition—it also plays an important compositional role.

1.2. *Deep Structure: the Composition*

Through its rhyme scheme and its syntax (particularly the periods) and its thematic parallelism (in each stanza the hero first tells the story of his love and then announces his renunciation of it for the heroine's sake), the poem is clearly divided into two equal parts, with an intensification from stanza 1 to stanza 2: the intensity of each of the poles of the dual situation 'love / suppression', the CONTRAST between them, and the closeness of their intertwining increase toward the end. This intensification in a sense weakens the similarity of the two stanzas, which is also undermined by the interweaving of rhymes (see (6)), culminating in a new and particularly sharp rhyme on /i/ (line 6). The anaphoric "I loved you", too, both links stanzas 1 and 2 and destroys the symmetry between them—by producing an overall scheme 4 + (2 + 2). Hence the two stanzas tend to be united into a single construction which intensifies toward the end, a kind of eight-line verse. How is this intensification devised?[4]

On the *plot-and-theme* level, the intensification of 'love' is motivated by the hero's permitting himself, under the guise of 'memories', to talk quite freely about his passion (which has died down?). In a sense, his "present" 'amorous claims' are intensified too: note the 'hint of jealous interest' which forces itself through the eighth line, counter to the total restraint and objectivity of the fourth. In parallel with this the 'suppression-submission' also intensifies: a mere renunciation of his claims on the heroine ("let it not disturb you any more"; "I do not want to sadden you") becomes a readiness to give her up to "another."

On the plane of *mode of exposition* the intensification of 'love' works as follows. In stanza 1 the leitmotif phrase "I loved you" breaks against a pause already in midline and is then whittled away in denials and provisos; in the first line of stanza 2 it syntactically takes charge of the whole line, yet reaches the end of the line shrouded, as it were, by two negations ("speechlessly" and "hopelessly"); on its third appearance it at last bursts through the curtain of denial into open affirmation: line 7 is the only fully assertive line in the whole poem. The *rhythmic-intonational* intensity also grows as the poem progresses; from stanza 1 to stanza 2 there is a simultaneous heightening of both integration and fragmentation of the sentences (as a simple comparison of the punctuation shows). But parallel with this the corresponding symptoms of 'submission'—the manifestations of "obliqueness"—gain in power, for it is in the second stanza (line 6 of the poem) that the passive and dependent constructions appear. The highest point in 'obliqueness' is reached in the eighth line, which combines subordination, a passive, and a heavy complex object construction.

The accentuation of the poles of the theme leads, naturally, to an intensification of the CONTRAST between them. Simultaneously, as we have said, there is increasing interpenetration (i.e., COMBINATION) of the poles. If at the end of stanza 1 the COMBINATION of 'love' and 'suppression of love' into (5), 'renunciation because of love', is offered *sotto voce* ("I do not want to sadden you by anything"), by the end of stanza 2 this paradox is uttered loud and clear: the speaker's love is described in terms of a comparison (a trope, almost!) with the supposed love of "another." And the last line at once incorporates both 'love's claims' and a 'renunciation' of them.

A rather special vehicle for this greater and greater weaving together of both poles of the theme is the 4 + (2 + 2) compositional scheme (marked by the anaphoric "I loved you"). In principle the range of expressive possibilities offered by this scheme includes such effects as 'intensification' (resulting from an increase in rhythmic frequency), 'anticlimax' (resulting from rhythmic fragmentation), and 'deepening', sometimes a lyrical 'self-absorption' (this is the interpretation, on the content plane, of an 'intensification without expansion').[5] Here it is clearly this last possibility which is realized, harmonizing well with the assertion of (5), 'sacrificial love without claims'.

An important role in the overall compositional intensification from stanza 1 to 2 is played by the redistribution of the plot-theme material. In stanza 1 there are three temporal planes, ensuring a gradual transition from 'passion' to 'submission, restraint': the 'past' ("loved"), the 'present' ("has died out not completely"), and the 'future' ("let it not disturb you any more"). Half of the stanza is allotted to the first two stages, the other half to the third. In stanza 2 the intermediate present stage is left out, and its place—and part of that of the third stage (line 7)—is taken by the first. This shift involves many consequences.

First, the shift makes the growth of 'passion' not merely quantitative (three lines instead of two) but qualitative as well: its assertion and development occur in the very place (line 3 of the stanza) where, according to the pattern established in the first stanza, one might have expected a 'bridling of that love'. This effect helps to sustain the sensation, noted earlier, of a 'breakthrough' in line 7.

Second, an additional intensification of both the CONTRAST and COMBINATION of the poles is due to their extreme manifestations ('past passion' and 'future submission') now clashing directly: they occur as immediate neighbors in the text and even as members of a single syntactic and rhetorical construction (the comparison "so . . . , as . . .").

Finally, the combination of this redistribution of the material with the 4 + (2 + 2) scheme produces a further important compositional effect, which also strengthens the COMBINATION of the poles of the theme. What happens is that out of the final two lines one (the seventh) is devoted to the 'history of love', and the other (the eighth) to a 'program of submission'. In other words, we are presented here with a condensed form of the relationship obtaining between the initial and final episodes within each stanza. Thus the seventh and eighth lines form a kind of résumé of the whole poem. Since line 8 also COMBINES both poles of the theme, the composition of the poem as a whole emerges as a series of COMBINATIONS, one inside the other and condensing more and more toward the end. Indeed, the motifs of 'passion' and 'impassiveness' run throughout the poem, but they are presented more powerfully in stanza 2, which in turn has the second clause as its résumé, and within this clause, again, it is the final line that best fuses the two poles.

2. Details of the Surface Structure

2.1. *Stanza 1: Rhythm and Intonation*

The first quatrain is constructed around a conflict between the expressive presentation of dramatic events and the orientation toward restraint. The basic division in the quatrain coincides with the boundary between the distichs. It is revealed by the only conjunction, the adversative *No* 'But', and is supported by the mirror symmetry of the anaphorically similar enclosing lines (1: *Ja vas* . . . / 4: *Ja* . . . *vas* . . .). If we take the distichs as wholes, the first one (devoted to 'love') is built on an intense musical development, while the second (devoted to 'taming') slows down and muffles the upsurge. But this conflict between upsurge and slowing down runs through each of the distichs as well.

The intonational development in the first half of the stanza begins with the immediate picking out of a very short, hemistich-size leitmotif (*Ja vas ljubil*).[6] Then comes an energetic crescendo built on a cumulative principle: the first hemistich, the second hemistich, and the second line form the figure $(0.5 + 0.5) + 1$ (see Fig. 9.1). But the second term is fractured: $\approx 0.5 + (0.25 + 0.25)$. In this particular context this fragmented pattern (see above, on the $4 + (2 + 2)$ pattern) mainly realizes its potential for creating tension, since (*a*) syntactically, the second hemistich is an incomplete fragment, striving for completion (the second line), so that intonationally we have a rise; (*b*) rhythmically, this is the second link in the unmistakably active cumulative pattern $(0.5 + 0.5) + 1$. All-in-all we get the pattern $(0.5 +$

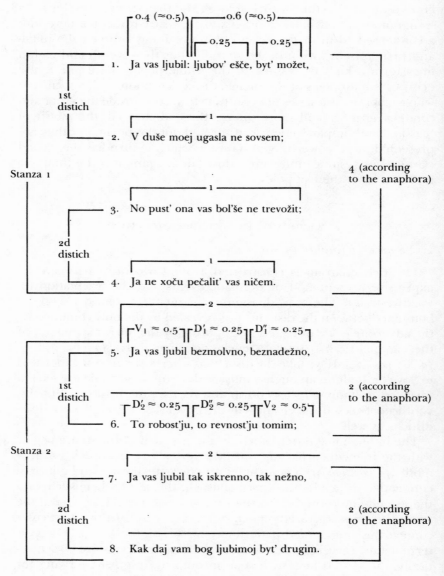

Figure 9.1. "I loved you . . . ": Formal articulations

[0.25 + 0.25]) + 1, that is, an extremely dynamic transition from a fraction (0.5) to a further fragmentation (0.25 + 0.25), and then to the whole (1).

The intense movement seems to overwhelm the pauses: the caesura is bridged by a semantic and phonetic link (. . . *ljubil: ljubov'* . . .), while the rhythmic pause at the end of the line is smothered by the syntactic wholeness of the clause. The resulting effect is of 'the lingering of a seemingly fading impulse'.[7] This effect may be regarded as a kind of rhythmic-intonational equivalent of the thematic element 'love lingers, continuing from the past into the present', that is, what the first distich is talking about.

However, the intense intonational development is muffled by the overall languor and obliqueness of the exposition and above all by the maze of qualifications, denials, and denials of denials ("still, perhaps, . . . has died out not completely") in which the movement of the intonation gets stuck, as it were (see Jakobson 1981). As far as rhythm and intonation are concerned, this manifests itself, for instance, in the means by which the second hemistich's "dynamizing" fragmentation is devised:

1. Lexically, the fragmentation is created with the aid of those un-categorical seminegative and parenthetic expressions ("still" and "perhaps"), which slow down the movement.[8]

2. Formally, the division is not as precise as it could be: syntactically the parts of the second hemistich (*ljubov' ešče / byt' možet,* or, divided differently, *ljubov' / ešče byt' možet*) are not homogeneous.[9] The articulation is based on "weaker" factors: the separation signified by the parenthesis; the fact that there is no subordinating link between parts either (they each refer separately to the verb *ugasla* 'faded'); the correlation of the stressed vowels in the first hemistich and the parts of the second: i — [o —o] (which is like the construction 'similar members, subordinated to a main one' and hence corresponds to the pattern 0.5 + [0.25 + 0.25]).

3. If we also bear in mind that the second hemistich is both metrically (three feet) and rhythmically (two fully stressed feet) much heavier than the first (two feet, only one stressed), then we will understand how the movement in the second hemistich is relatively slower and less confident.

In the second distich the rhythmic development is cut short: instead of the possible and natural continuation of the crescendo (0.5 + 0.5 +

1 + 2), there is a stabilization (0.5 + 0.5 + 1 + 1 + 1): each of the two last lines is a separate sentence. It is true that somewhere in the background there is a sense of wholeness: on a deep level the conjunction *No* 'But' may be understood as relating to the whole distich and the connection between the third and fourth sentences (= lines) as an unconjoined-subordinating (causal) one. Yet on the surface level this connection is still coordinative (a semicolon); the coordination is also supported by the parallelism of the clauses (homogeneity, we should remember, contributes to articulation). Thus the rhythmic-intonational growth halts in midstanza. This static symmetry is not broken until stanza 2.[10]

And yet in one respect the forthcoming burst of 'passion' (see §2.4, below) is anticipated even here. On the crest of the upward intonation curve of the first two lines, into the third (normally the culminating) line the most powerful word in the whole verse is 'tossed in': *pust'* 'let'. This exclamation is the most direct utterance by the speaker in the whole stanza, and the only imperative. Moreover, in its pattern of stresses the beginning of the third line most sharply deviates from the pattern established by the first line and resumed in the fourth: ⌣´⌣(´) instead of ⌣(´)⌣´; this deviation is prepared for by the intermediate pattern ⌣´⌣´ in the second line.

Still, this exclamation is not intensified into a shout but is muffled into a short, weak sigh. Functionally, it is an imperative but it is formally neither direct speech nor an exclamation (say, *Farewell!*) but a third-person imperative used with the form of the indicative mood. It is pronounced with a falling intonation and is placed at the beginning of the third line, so that the fall begins almost from the very start of the second half of the stanza.

In the fourth and final line complete calm is achieved, underscored by the indicative mood and the double negative.

2.2. *Stanza 1: Points of View*

The most intense point in the first stanza is line 3, where on the *plot* level 'passion' is overcome by 'submission', while an intense *rhythmic-intonational* growth breaks against a barrier and is replaced by a fall. Mimicking the collapsing effect in these two planes, the *mode of exposition* seems to extinguish the very intensity of this change.

The *point of view* in line 3 is organized in such a way that attention is focused there not on the dramatic part of what is taking place—'the hero's suppression of his desires, his despair and self-denial'—but on the relatively calm 'putting an end to discomfort for the heroine'. By referring to his own 'love' in the third person and by observing as if from afar its negative and somehow insignificant impact on the heroine ("disturb"), the hero seems to be suggesting to her that she should "brush aside" his love.[11] This external view of his own "I" has already been established in the second sentence (= second part of line 1 and the whole of line 2), where the hero regards his own emotion in a detached and alienated way, making cautious, "scientifically objective" comments ("perhaps")—just as if he had no direct connection with it. Formally, this is expressed by the parentheses, whose grammatical function is to separate the speaker from the content of his utterance. This division of the "I" (into 'feeler' and 'speaker') begins surreptitiously even in the first sentence (= first part of line 1), due to the latent duality of point of view which characterizes the past tense.[12]

The detached point of view is maintained by the way 'love', which is mentioned so insistently in each sentence, is signified *lexically*. The wording gradually becomes more and more oblique and detached, negligent almost: "loved"—"love"—"it"—literally "[by] nothing", that is, a personal verb—an abstract noun—a third-person pronoun—a negative inanimate pronoun.

Thus, Stanza 1 is built around the pattern of 'superior peace':

(7) Down below is an "I" suffering from unhappy love; above it is a cold or restrained heroine; higher still is the "speaking I," which sets about trying to resolve the conflict between the first two characters: "let it not disturb you."[13]

2.3. *Line 6: The Culmination of Intensity*

The third quarter of a whole is the natural point for the culmination. As I have pointed out, on the level of *theme and plot* the 'story of the love' is here told in more detail, with all its contradictions and deviations. On the *rhythmic-syntactic* level here at last we reach the full breadth of tone to which the melodic line in stanza 1 has been tending (with its clauses of 0.5, 1.5, 1, 1 lines in length, but never of 2 lines). The unity of this clause, which takes up half the stanza, is accentuated by the chiasmus: on the outside, the iambic verb forms with stressed /í/ describing the hero's 'love' (*ljubíl, tomím*), and between them, pairs of equivalent three- or four-syllable dependents with stressed /ó/ and /é/ describing various 'braking' factors (*bezmólvno, beznadéžno, / to robóst'ju, to révnost'ju*). This produces a double fusing effect—both a "join" and a "link."[14] At the same time the mirrorlike similarity of the lines and the equivalence of the attributes within each of them tend to increase the effect of fracture (six phrasal units). The resulting symmetric arc creates a sense of spaciousness and, at the same time, of a faster breathing tempo—a sense of intense and unbroken movement from the beginning to the end of the sentence.

Lines 5 and 6 display an increase in intensity not only as compared with the first stanza: there is a pronounced intensification within the sentence itself. On the *plot* level there is a development from the more or less neutral "loved" to its clash with the static and unmistakably negative adverbs (with "speechlessly" involving only external manifestations of the 'hindrances' to 'love' and then "hopelessly" extending them inward to the hero's soul and ahead to his whole future) and from there to dramatic emotional drives. Of these two, "shyness" suggests only an indecisive striving toward the heroine, while "jealousy" is far more active, making claims to some kind of—albeit imaginary and "negative"—rights over her. From "shyness" to "jealousy," then, there is a growth not only in the activeness and drama of the emotions but in that very 'egoism of claims' which has to be held in check and which is mentioned explicitly here for the first time.

Activization takes place on other levels of the text, too. *Syntactically,* the adverbs of manner ("speechlessly" and "hopelessly") are replaced by agentive instrumentals; *rhythmically and intonationally,* there is a piling on of equivalent forms[15] and an intensifying switch from the normal word sequence in line 5 to the inversion in line 6, involving also a switch from a fragmenting construction (where the head word "loved" seems to split into two equivalent qualifiers) to the more active summative construction (where "by shyness" and "by jealousy" add up, as it were, to "tormented"; cf. note 6). *Phonetically,* the fifth and especially the sixth lines are among the peaks of the poem. Alongside the precise patterning of vowels (see above), there is a clear play on the consonants (three /b/, two prestress /r/, three prevocalic /t/); play on /r/ and /t/ (as well as the "sharp" rhyme on /í/ mentioned earlier) appears in line 6 for the first time in the entire poem.

A particularly vivid effect in line 6 is created by the interplay of several linguistic means, which underpins the drama in the story line. The powerful phonetic, rhythmic, and syntactic similarity between *róbost'ju* 'by shyness' and *révnost'ju* 'by jealousy' highlights the distinction between the stressed /ó/ and /é/, which turns out to be virtually the only external expression of the semantic distinction between the two words. The fact of this distinction is accentuated by the semantics of the construction *to . . . to . . .* ('now one thing, now the other') and the word *tomim* 'tormented' (≃ the ebb and flow of feeling, intermittent states). In its turn, the syllable *to-* (or rather [ta-]) in *tomim* acquires a semantics of its own, being subliminally perceived as containing the seme 'alternation of states'. This is then underpinned by the phonetic series [ta . . . ó—ta . . . é—ta . . . . í], where all three stressed vowels are different and happen to be those very three different vowels upon which the rhyme scheme of the poem is built.[16] Indeed, if torment is a switch from one state to another and then a return to the first state, and so on, then we see something analogous to this on the phonetic level too: different states—/ó/-/é/-/í/; similar states—/t/-/t/-/t/; r .´. . st'ju—r .´. st'ju; /m/-/m/ (in *tomim*). What is more, the final word, one might say, repeats in condensed form the phonetic "alternations" which had initially been taking place in terms of whole adverbial phrases (recall the parallel "summing up" of *to robost'ju, to revnost'ju* into *tomim* on the rhythmic-syntactic plane; see above).

2.4. *Line 7: Restrained Assertion*

If the sixth line is the peak of emotional tension, line 7 is the most affirmative one in the poem. This 'burst of assertive positiveness' (see above, §1.2) is supported by a variety of means: by its position in the third line of the quatrain, which is a normal culmination point and which, moreover, is an 'extra' one about 'love' (breaking the analogy with the first stanza: now 'love' continues as the topic where in the third line of the previous stanza 'submission' had taken over—"But let it not disturb you any more"); by the anaphoric repetition of the leitmotif ("I loved you") and by the pressure of "positive" matching adverbs ("so sincerely, so tenderly"). However, the assertion of 'love' is evidently not made with the maximum power; it is not a triumphal (even if doomed to a subsequent defeat) upsurge but rather a heartfelt sigh of nostalgia; not so much a 'breakthrough' as a 'showing-through' (cf. Chap. 8, formula 7 and elsewhere). How is this restrained effect achieved?

In terms of *plot*, 'love' is played here in its kindest and most 'conflict-free' key ("sincerely," "tenderly")—as distinct from the restless (and sometimes even dark—"by jealousy") passions in the preceding lines and in harmony with the forthcoming 'renunciation of claims'.

Moreover, while breaking through the veil of negativity and across the boundary between distichs, 'love' in line 7 still does not break through from the past into the present.

Compositionally, the seventh line is in the fourth quarter of the poem—the natural zone for a closing fall. The sentence as a whole is committed to 'renunciation', and this commitment extends into the positive seventh line, assisted also by the inertia of the division of the verse into halves as established in stanza 1 (two lines about 'love', two about 'submission'). The breaking of this inertia (see above) is weakened by the fact that the first three lines of stanza 2 are not united in a single wave whose crest might have been the seventh line: the boundary between the sentences (= distichs) is emphasized by the anaphora so that line 7 forms a separate, shorter wave which begins afresh from a low point.[17]

At the same time there is a slowing down of *rhythm and intonation* in comparison with the previous distich.

1. The inversion ("Now by shyness, now by jealousy tormented": the agents are in the instrumental before a passive), which gave the sixth line and the whole distich its dynamism, gives way to a calm direct word order.

2. Extrametrical stresses appear, making the line heavier; and, of course, the fact that they fall precisely on the words which emphatically stress 'love' (*tak . . . tak . . .* 'so . . . so . . .') is just one more code-sphere COMBINATION, however minute, of 'passion' and 'restraint'.

3. The accumulation of parallel constituents (apparently entirely analogous with line 5) is intonationally weakened in advance by the fact that it is not going to be continued in the following line.

4. From the first and longer of the parallel constituents (*tak iskrenno*) to the second, shorter one (*tak nežno*) a rhythmic fall takes place: $(\acute{\smile})\acute{\smile}\smile/(\acute{\smile})\acute{\smile}\smile$; the fall also takes place within each of the micromotifs: from the stressed syllables, including the extrametrical ones, to the unstressed ones. In both these respects the seventh line contrasts with the syntactically similar fifth (. . . *bezmolvno, beznadežno*), where there is a lengthening toward the end: $\smile\acute{\smile}\smile/-\smile\acute{\smile}\smile$ (cf. note 15).

On the *phonetic* level, the rhyme is less intense compared with the previous one, being a feminine rhyme built upon the already familiar medium-high vowel [é] (cf. the *sovsem-ničem* rhyme in lines 2 and 4), which occupies the middle position in the rhyme sequence of the whole poem (o-e-i).

2.5. *Line 8: Final COMBINATION*

The closing line is a sort of "total" line for the whole poem, and it draws together in a focal point all the motifs which have been running through the text on various levels and in various sections. In terms of *plot and theme* these are 'love', 'jealousy', and 'renunciation'; in terms of *mode of exposition* they are the categories of obliqueness and explicitness, negation and assertion; in the *rhythmic-intonational* terms, the stress patterns which characterize the different lines; *phonetically,* the reversal of the sequence [bí-bó-bi-ó] from the first line to [bó-bí-bɪ-í], echoing the *syntactic* reversal of the active "loved" to the passive "be loved," the *lexical* replacement of the "I" by "another," and the replacement of the "expected" rhyme *ljubim* 'loved [by]' by "another" rhyme—the word *drugim* 'another' (see Chap. 12, §3).

The play with direct and oblique *modes of exposition* is particularly intriguing. The final admissions of 'love' (for the heroine) and 'jealousy' (toward "another", who literally appears at the very last moment, Jakobson 1981) are wrapped up—in keeping with the motif of 'altruistic submission'—in a 'thick veil of obliqueness': a subordinate clause, a full passive (with object in the nominative case and agent in the instrumental), and a dry, almost bureaucratic construction of the accusative-cum-infinitive type ("grant to you to be"). This deliberate bunching of heavy constructions is carefully prepared. The subordinate clause in the last line—the only one in the whole poem—is anticipated (ED PRESAGE) by:

1. the implicit subordinate relation between the third and fourth lines in the end of stanza 1 ("But let it not disturb you any more; / [for] I do not want to sadden you by anything"); and
2. the participle construction, i.e., a subordinate clause in miniature, in the sixth line (. . . *tomim* '. . . tormented').

The passive in line 8 is prepared for by:

3. the passive participle construction (see item 2);
4. the instrumentals of instrument and of agent in the fourth and sixth lines respectively (*ničem* 'by anything'; *robost'ju* . . . *revnost'ju* 'by shyness . . . by jealousy');
5. the symmetrical reflection (on many levels) of the active *ljubil*

'loved' (at the beginning of the fifth line) in the passive *tomim* 'tormented' (at the end of the sixth), which facilitates the passivization of *ljubil* into *ljubimoj*.

At the same time the 'heaviness' of the resulting construction is, as it were, played down by the phraseologism *daj . . . bog* 'God grant' that governs it, which, thanks to its idiomatic character, is perceived as a natural and ordinary—ready-made—whole.

But all this 'indirectness' does not remain impenetrable. As is required by the principle of 'passion showing through impassivity', the 'indirectness' is literally broken by a "direct" form—the imperative *daj* 'grant', which is ungrammatical in a Russian subordinate clause.[18] This *daj* shows a marked increase in 'directness' as compared with its counterpart in stanza 1—*pust'* 'let': it coincides morphologically with the "real"—second person—imperative (while *pust'* is clearly a third-person form) and involves the heroine as its primary object (*daj vam* '[God] grant to you'). Yet, even *daj* is not as absolutely "direct" as it may seem. Strictly speaking, it is still a third-person (irreally optative, Švedova 1970: 579) form, whose subject is other than the heroine (very much like in line 3).

To conclude, many of the features of the last line depend on various properties of the expression *daj [vam] bog* 'God grant to you'—its oblique imperativeness, its unreal affirmativeness, its idiomatic tone, its syntactic government, the stress on both monosyllables, and, of course, its (imaginary) address to God. It is so much the key to many crucial aspects of the aesthetic structure of the poem that it becomes "indispensable"[19]—an image which can stand for practically the whole poem. The other equally crucial component is the leitmotif phrase "I love you," which even in its first occurrence contains a protoform of both poles of the theme 'passion, impassivity', and on its subsequent occurrences accumulates the effects of their further elaboration. In the closing distich the two major motifs meet.

10

Comparing Poetic Worlds

1. Contrastive Poetics and the Concept of "Poetic World"

The theoretical framework of PE outlined in earlier chapters and in particular the concepts of poetic world (PW), invariant and local theme (Θinv, Θloc), invariant motif ($Minv$), invariant derivation, and grafting of $\bar{M}inv$ onto Θloc in the derivation of an author's individual text $T(A)$ have been designed as a metalanguage for the accurate description ("portrayal") of individual literary texts and groups of texts. The affinities and contrasts between different poetic systems— for instance, the shared local themes—might seem marginal to PE interests. And yet, the indicated zone of overlap between the two fields of inquiry—the immanent and the contrastive description—is neither occasional nor the only one possible. Contrastive poetics is interested in stating the texts' similarities and differences, as well as in setting up typologically relevant classes and categories. It sets itself the task of observing difference in similarity and similarity in difference, for "one and the same thing" in different authors is, in fact, not "the same." PE concepts appear to be relevant to problems of this kind in a variety of ways.

1. Methodologically, as a metalanguage for the description of text and PW structures, they constitute a set of bases for the comparison of such structures.
2. Ontologically they actually presuppose interstructural comparisons: in stating that certain motifs are characteristic of an author, PE implies their discriminatory power. A list of Victor Hugo's $\bar{M}inv$ inev-

This chapter is a revised version of [1980b] and a part of [1977b].

itably poses the question whether the same motifs occur in Byron, Verlaine, and others. A responsible answer can consist only in compiling the other lists and systematically comparing them with the first one.

3. Ontologically again, the notion of local theme implies the existence of a common stock of such themes. It is the different realization of one and the same Θloc in different authors that provides the raison d'être of the notions of Θinv, $Minv$, and PW and a convenient starting point for contrastive description.

Thus, the application of PE concepts to the tasks of contrastive poetics appears natural and promises to be mutually rewarding.

One advantage of relying on invariant motifs is that the comparison is then conducted in terms of categories relevant for the compared objects. Instead of wondering how the authors under consideration treat such a priori categories as 'time', 'class struggle', 'love', 'spring', one can address oneself directly to the invariant motifs of the corresponding PWs. A linguistic analogy: to ignore the hierarchies of $\overline{M}inv$ is like comparing the expression of 'time' in Russian, English, and Chinese without taking into account the presence or absence, in the corresponding grammars, of the very category of 'tense' and of its language-specific articulations.

To be sure, such emphasis on the relevant features of corresponding systems does not dispose of the problem of universal bases for comparison: at best it will have to be faced one step further along. Perhaps this problem becomes even more acute, for only now is the very existence of such universals called into question. An analogy with the notorious "linguistic relativity" (the "Sapir-Whorf hypothesis") suggests itself. Moreover, in the literary domain the existence of "mutually incommunicable" systems seems even more probable.

I do not believe, however, that either demonstration or refutation of such statements can be achieved by theoretical arguments. I propose, therefore, to proceed, in the spirit of cautious optimism, with empirical comparisons, certain that many valuable insights await us in these pursuits even if we must eventually run into an epistemological impasse. As for the universals, I intend to fall back, provisionally, on commonsense categories, corrected, clarified, and redefined, where possible, by the practical experience of carrying out actual comparisons.

Contrastive description can be performed on three major levels of abstraction—those of entire poetic worlds, of individual invariant motifs and of concrete texts. Comparison of entire PWs is of greater typological interest, but is inevitably very complicated and abstract; where it happens to be vivid and tangible, it boils down in practice to a comparison of individual motifs. This latter (as well as the direct comparison of texts) is, of course, much more palpable; but the theoretical value of these comparisons depends completely on their ability to state the role played by the compared motifs (respectively, text fragments) in the corresponding PWs. As a result, the three types of comparative study are usually combined in actual research. They also share the following essential characteristic: their respective objects— an entire PW, an M*inv* and a T(A)—are, all three, *messages*. For a text this is obvious; an invariant motif is a portion of the author's favorite messages; and a poetic world is the complete set of the messages that are included by the author, in one or another combination, into any text and in this sense "built into" his code.

2. Comparison of Entire Poetic Worlds

Comparison of entire hierarchical systems is, naturally, very abstract and often amounts to setting up of typological classes. Typological comparison of PWs is based on "structural" and "contentual" characteristics, some of which I briefly discuss in §§2.1 and 2.2.

2.1. *"Structural" Parameters*

1. *"Unity."* A PW is highly "unified" if the hierarchy of $\bar{\text{M}}inv$ is crowned with just one Θinv. Recall that the concept of the "central theme" was introduced (in Chap. 3, §4) rather informally and in such a way that "unity" was effectively taken for granted in any given PW. This, however, restricts unduly the notion of PW by confining it to its most "normal" and pronounced case. Indeed, PWs are naturally represented by structures like that shown in Figure 10.1. In the simplest case the most general, top-echelon invariant motifs exhibit considerable thematic similarity, that is, they have a fairly specific common denominator—the Θinv. Pasternak's PW appears to be an example.[1] But there is no reason for excluding the theoretically possible alternative case: the "top" motifs, obtained by extracting common denominators from lower echelons of the invariant derivation, may well turn out to be the ultimate level of abstraction, failing to provide the hierarchy with a single apex. Empirically this seems to be corroborated by

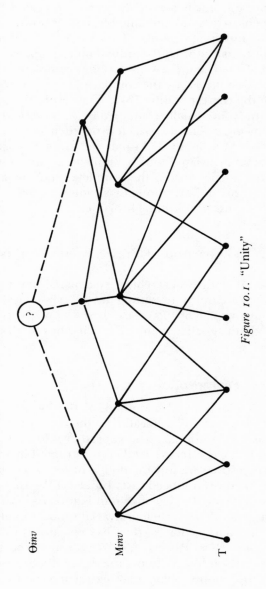

Figure 10.1. "Unity"

Akhmatova's PW; cf. Shcheglov's special remarks on this point [1979a: 28ff.]. Such PWs can be said to "lack unity."

2. *"Cohesion."* If "unity" has to do with the PW structure's convergence at the top, "cohesion" is defined by convergence at the bottom. A PW is the more "cohesive" the greater the number of abstract $\bar{M}inv$ represented in every concrete motif and every actual text. "Cohesion" is lower if some $\bar{M}inv$ find their expression in one group of the author's texts, some in another. Compare the poets whose oeuvres clearly divide into periods (genres, works) centering around different motifs and even themes; for example, Pasternak (see Nilsson 1978). The properties of "unity" and "cohesion" are mutually independent: the most abstract $\bar{M}inv$ can well converge into a single Θinv at the top and completely diverge at the bottom (Fig. 10.2) or vice versa (Fig. 10.3); also theoretically possible is a PW which is neither "united" nor "cohesive"; the "normal" case we started with (Fig. 10.1) combines "unity" with "cohesion."

3. *"Richness."* Let us call "rich" a "normal" PW implied by the initial definition and Figure 10.1, that is, one where most of the themes and motifs intensely vary and combine with one another on the way down to texts. A PW can also be characterized by "paucity"—that of variation and/or of combination. There is a correlation between "paucity" of combinations and "lack of cohesion" (see Fig. 10.2).

4. *"Depth"* of a PW is the greater the more levels there are between the most abstract one, that of themes, and the most concrete one, that of real texts; for example, Figure 10.1 is "deeper" than Figure 10.2. In a "deep" PW, the abstract ideas are fully "dissolved" in vivid "real"

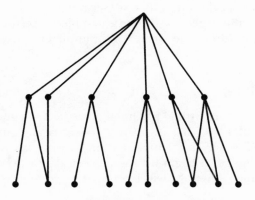

Figure 10.2. "Unity" without "cohesion"

199

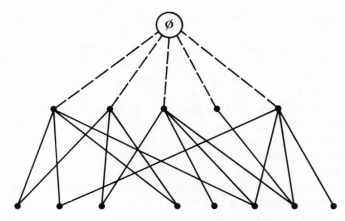

Figure 10.3. "Cohesion" without "unity"

objects, situations, and so on. On the contrary, in a "shallow" PW ideas will "show through" the transparent guise of imagery. There is considerable logical overlapping between "shallowness" and "transparency" (see below).

5. *"Coverage"* (of texts by PW) is the better the higher the ratio of elements and characteristics of the real texts that are accounted for by the set of M̄*inv.* "Coverage" is low if the invariant motifs have explanatory power only for a small part of what is there in the texts, that is, if they occur in them rarely, and much has to be accounted for by local themes of individual texts. "Low coverage" in no way implies a negative evaluation: rather, it corresponds to the "objective" type of poetic vision in which local themes (e.g., described objects, events, persons, etc.) are not submerged by the lyrical subject. Accordingly, "coverage" is better when the reality is completely overshadowed by invariants.[2]

2.2 *Contentual Parameters*

In discussing "structural" parameters we had to concentrate solely on the form of PWs, that is, on the geometrical figures cut by the hierarchies. Now we shift our attention to what is contained in the nodes of the figures. I begin with some very abstract characteristics of this content and only in §3 will I proceed to those portraying it in all concreteness.

6. *"Monovalence/ambivalence."* A PW is "monovalent" if its central

Θinv is unambiguous in the evaluation of its components, for example, 'X is good, non-X is bad'. Pasternak's PW furnishes an example: Θ*inv* = 'the unity and magnificence of the universe are good'. An "ambivalent" PW derives from a Θ*inv* with opposites evaluated similarly: 'X and non-X are both good [bad, questionable]'; compare the PW of Pushkin (see Chap. 8) and that of Mandel'štam, built around Θ*inv* = 'stability and instability, the simple, rough, basic and the whimsical, refined, nonbasic, are both good and bad'.

A PW can also be eclectic in this respect. Thus, most of Bulat Okudžava's invariant motifs go back to a monovalent Θ*inv* = 'the pure positive ideal might overcome the hard negative reality'. But some M̄*inv* are ambivalent, for example: 'the used, worn clothes and shoes', 'the natural, but hard and irrational fate', 'love that ensnares and binds one, making life hard'. These M̄*inv* indeed approve of both the 'ideal' pole ('genuiness', 'disregard of appearances', 'soul', 'love') and, with a characteristically Russian masochism, 'life's hardships' ('poverty', 'difficulties', 'brevity of life', 'loss of freedom').

7. *"Reference/code."* This parameter is defined by the ratio of motifs belonging to the two principal spheres of the "reality" *about which* and *in terms of which* literature speaks. A PW is purely "reference-oriented" if its Θ*inv* and most of its M̄*inv* are concerned with "life" and realized as events, characters, and so on. "Code-orientation" means that either the central theme or many of the top-echelon M̄*inv* or both are Class II themes, that is, messages concerned with problems of natural and poetic language, literary convention, and so on. According to Čudakov (1972), Chekhov's PW is at least 50 percent "code-oriented": the central Θ*inv* = 'in life fortuity is all-important [a Class I, reference-type theme]; in narration, insignificant accessories are important, not the conventional plot (*fabula*) [a Class II, code-type theme]'. A PW is completely "code-oriented" if the author's artistic *élan* concentrates on a reform of style and language so that his texts display no ideological invariance whatsoever.

8. *"Thematic type"* depends on the specific purport of the most general M̄*inv*. In "referential" PWs the typical categories are: philosophical, ethical, social, psychological, spatial, and so in; in "code" PWs, concern with and innovations in rhyming, rhythm, syntax, narrative, and so on. Most PWs include motifs of various thematic types, the difference residing in the place specific types occupy in the overall hierarchy. For instance, tropes are common property of most poets, but in Pasternak metaphor and metonymy play the essential thematic role of 'bringing together' all that is 'different' in the world and in the

language. At the same time, whereas for another, socially, politically, and so on, oriented author the ideological distinctions between Christ, Peter the Great, Lenin, Pushkin, Mejerxol'd, and the lyrical "I" would be of paramount importance, for Pasternak all these personalities are "synonymous" manifestations of 'genius', that is, of an M*inv* combining 'unity' with 'magnificence'.

9. *"Transparency"* means that the abstract categories (e.g., philosophical, ethical) that constitute the central theme, are present, more or less undisguised, at the surface levels of the hierarchy. Compare Okudžava, whose texts abound in words and images like "pure," "honest," "hope," "sublime," "difficult," "hard", and so on, which name with almost terminological precision the corresponding M̄*inv*. "Transparency" usually involves (and Okudžava is not an exception) "shallowness." In a "nontransparent" PW the theme is encoded in a completely different medium, changing "beyond recognition." Pasternak's PW provides instances of both principles:

1. Words and images like "heaps," "piles," "lots"; "as if having reached the highest phase"; "the same," "again," "close by"; and so on, which are direct, "transparent" manifestations of the two central themes ('magnificence' and 'unity'), abound in the texts.

2. But also numerous are motifs like 'over-poweredness', 'clutching', 'mixing', 'compressing', 'penetration through a window', and so on, which embody the same themes in a veiled, "organic" way.

3. Motif-for-Motif Comparison of PWs

Here we leave the ground of typology and turn to concrete comparison of individual PWs. Predictably, it is concerned with stating the presence/absence in these of common or at least similar invariant motifs (M̄*inv, com*). There seem to be four major types of motif-for-motif correlation.

A. An invariant motif of an author is *absent* in the other's PW.

B. The similar motifs differ already in the definitions of their content, that is, the distinctions can be formulated as direct *intersystemic* contrasts in terms of a universal metalanguage.

C. The common motifs differ only in their *intrasystemic* connections, "horizontal" and/or "vertical,": in the respective PWs they belong to different synthematic sets or come under different generalizations or both.

D. The common motifs, otherwise similar, differ in the *position* they occupy in the two PWs. The most current case is when in one PW a given M*inv,com* is situated "at the top and center," whereas in another it plays but a subordinate peripheral role.

I will briefly illustrate the four cases, A–D.

3.1. *Case A: No Similar* M̄inv

Pushkin's motif of 'superior peace, detachment, uninvolvement' and Mandel'štam's motif of 'teasing' have no parallels in Pasternak.

Okudžava's M̄*inv* 'entreaty, praying', 'hope', 'once there is X, immediately there is an important Y', and so on, are rare in Pasternak's texts. Uncharacteristic of Okudžava, on the other hand, are such Pasternakian motifs as 'penetration through a window', '"distributed" contact of A with B, C with D, . . .' (see [1982a]), 'physical objects running into abstract entities', and so on.

The absence in both of the above of counterpart motifs stems from a fundamental thematic difference between the PWs. But, in fact, two PWs can be built around perfectly synonymous Θ*inv* and yet differ in a particular motif. Compare, for instance, the version of Pasternak's PW outlined in Lotman 1978 (and discussed in Chap. 3, §5) with my version (Chap. 3, §2; Chap. 7): in the former the theme of 'unity' lacks the various physical manifestations present in the latter. One can imagine the opposite as well—a poet who glorifies 'magnificence and unity' in many "physical" ways, but just fails to invent 'shifts of co-occurrence' and other code-sphere manifestations of 'unity'.

3.2. *Case B: Differences in Content*

In Pasternak the 'window' (looked through from inside) embodies the unconditional 'unity of the internal and external world' (see Chap. 7). The articulation of space into 'home' and 'the outside' is purely rhetorical and only helps stress their 'contact'. In the PW of Conan Doyle, 'window' is also an invariant, but there it 'separates' the cozy room from the chaos and fear that are bound to invade the room and the plot together with Holmes's client, who is first seen through the window of the Baker Street flat. The 'window' is also recurrent in Okudžava, but the formulation is again different: 'the window is a guiding light seen by a wayfarer from the road'. The perspective 'from the outside' distinguishes Okudžava's 'window' from the two former ones; its essential 'openness' makes it similar to Pasternak's 'window', while the 'need for help in a troubled world' is mindful of Conan Doyle. But on the whole, the three 'windows' are different.

Seen in a wider perspective, the 'window' is an instance of 'border'. In Pasternak, 'borders' are always successfully transcended, overcome, obliterated. In Mandel'štam, on the contrary, the 'border' proves unattainable, uncrossable or only crossable by an 'illusory, mental gesture'.

Prominent in Mandel'štam's PW are the geometrical motifs of 'curved, winding, ornamental, capricious patterns' and similar ' "non-basic," whimsical, refined, "play-acting," teasingly arrogant, and so on, emotional states and postures'. They are opposed to 'simple, basic, elementary, "rough," straight, and so on, physical characteristics and emotional states'. The opposition is ambivalent: the poet seems to favor and question both poles. Pasternak, on the other hand, unambiguously likes all things 'simple, straight, basic, devoid of ornaments and caprices' (manifestations of Θinv 'magnificence').

Invariant in Okudžava is the negatively evaluated $Minv$ 'lack of forces, time, means, food, and so on', which embodies 'life's hardship'. In the Pasternakian world there is a similar but unambiguously positive motif—'overpoweredness, something being beyond one's forces', expressing 'magnificence of existence'. Mandel'štam's PW includes a motif that is apparently similar to this 'powerlessness', namely the various 'sick states' like 'fragility, hoarseness, choking, etc.' But the ambivalence of Mandel'štam's 'attraction to / rejection of everything pathological, sick, overrefined, nonbasic' distinguishes his treatment of this common motif from both Okudžava and Pasternak. The 'powerlessness à la Mandel'štam' has a partial parallel in Pushkin's ambivalent 'love for sickly or deathlike beauty and death as a way to desired rest'. Pushkin's PW includes also a 'powerlessness à la Pasternak': 'rapid switches from life to death' and 'tempestuous outbursts of life on the brink or against the background of death'. Evidently, the common motifs are treated differently in every one of these four poetic worlds.

3.3. *Case C: Intrasystemic Differences in Content*

Frequent both in Ovid and Pushkin are positively evaluated images of 'water turning into ice'. Moreover, no difference transpires even after a primary abstraction, which results again in a common invariant: 'the transformation of the liquid into the solid'. But at the next step of abstraction the paths of the two motifs part.

Ovid's is a 'stable, balanced world of normal, "model" objects'. Once upset, the balance can be restored through a 'metamorphosis' (say, of a human into a tree, a snake, a frog, etc.). 'Metamorphoses' consist of elementary 'transformation types', which can occur in the physical sphere (e.g., 'the straight → the curved'), the functional sphere (e.g., 'dwelling in cities → dwelling in swamps'), and so on. It is at this level that the transformation 'the liquid → the solid' finds its place.

Now, in Pushkin's world the same transformation reads clearly as a manifestation of 'changeability/unchangeability'. The set of $\bar{M}inv$ embodying this Θinv can be represented as the applications of various 'types of combination of the poles' to various 'types of material'. Among the 'types of combination' there are (besides 'transformation'): 'confrontation', 'hybrid formations', 'showing through', and so on; while the 'material manifestations' of Θinv include (besides 'liquidity/hardness') various, emotional, social, etc., as well as other physical oppositions (e.g., 'movement/immobility', 'heat/cold', etc.). The motif we are interested in is the product of 'transformation' (as a 'type of combination') applied to 'liquidity/hardness' (as a 'material manifestation').

Thus, two identical (and similarly evaluated) situations belong, in two respective PWs, to different synonymous sets and yield different generalizations. Thus, in the long run, they have different meanings.

Fet and Pasternak have a common positive motif of 'a shaking shadow or reflection'. In both PWs it lies at the intersection of two other positive $\bar{M}inv$: 'shaking, trembling' and 'reflection, shadow, projection'. In other words, at this level of abstraction, too, the two PWs do not differ. A difference emerges only at the next level—that of themes manifested by the apparently same motifs. In Pasternak 'shadow' and 'reflection' are varieties of 'contact' and near-synonyms of 'clutching', 'leaving a trace', 'embracing', and so on, while 'shaking, trembling' is a variety of 'intense movement' ('magnificence'). In Fet's PW the "same" motifs are manifestations of 'elusive, unsteady, momentary subjective states'.

3.4. *Case D: Intrasystemic Differences in Position*

As I have noted, intrasystemic differences in position occur if the central theme of one PW plays but a marginal role in the other, that is, if the second PW includes the first one within it. For example, the 'positively evaluated magnificent contact' is Pasternak's Θinv. In the PW of Cvetaeva there is also a group of 'positive contacts' whose many varieties ('contiguity', 'touching', 'penetration', 'heading for', etc.) are the same as in Pasternak. But in Cvetaeva all these are but a part of a wider—tragic—picture of the universe, which includes also 'negatively evaluated false contacts', 'absence of genuine contacts', and so on. As a result, in spite of the striking similarity, the role of the $\mathrm{M}inv,com$ 'positive contact' in the entire framework of the two PWs is different.

It is worth noting that the distinctions between the four cases A–D are relative: one might well argue that the intrasystemic differences (cases C, D) could be incorporated in the very formulations of the corresponding motifs, so that these cases would coincide with case B. And yet the three grades of distinction seem to reflect a certain intuitively felt reality and thus should stand.

4. Motif-for-Motif Comparison of Individual Texts

A strategy for such comparison is prompted by the genre of literary parodies whose principle lies in the question, How would a given author develop a given well-known theme? In a successful parody of this type the theme emerges clothed in the garb of a variety of the author's favorite situations, images, phrases, and constructions. Contrastive description of real texts from different PWs could envision every such text as a "parody" of its author, that is, as an exercise in a "typically his" solution of the "common local theme" ($\Theta loc,com$). An essay in contrastive description along these lines is offered in [1980c]. I will briefly outline the strategy of the comparison and some theoretical conclusions.

The strategy is, roughly speaking, to compare the texts' derivations, constructed according to the "grafting" principle (1) (cf. Chap. 3 §5):

(1) $(\Theta loc + (\Theta inv \rightarrow \bar{\mathrm{M}}inv)) \rightarrow \mathrm{T}$
It is implemented in six steps.
1. Texts by different authors on a *common local theme* are chosen; in this case, two poems by Pasternak and two by Okudžava, abbreviated as: Past 1, Past 2; Ok 1, Ok 2.[3] Their $\Theta loc,com$ is formulated:

(2) the hero is visited by his beloved (a traditional Θloc; cf. Pushkin's famous love lyric "I remember the wondrous moment . . .").

2. Those invariant motifs which are similar in the two PWs and common to the texts under comparison are identified:

(3) the beloved incarnates for the hero the sublime and he passively admires her
(4) the hero's home is modest to the point of poverty—a background and symbol of the hero's inner, spiritual, etc., treasures.

3. The combination of $\Theta loc,com$, (2), with these $\bar{M}inv,com$ yields the *common theme* of the four texts:

(5) Θcom (Past 1,2, Ok 1,2): the hero is visited, in his modest surroundings, by his beloved, the incarnation of the sublime.

After this the themes of the texts start diverging; first they branch into the two PWs, then they diverge within each of these.

4. *The common theme of each pair* of poems (the Pasternak pair and the Okudžava pair) is formulated as a COMBINATION of Θcom = (5) with invariant themes and motifs from the respective PWs. The Pasternak PW contributes to the eventual Θcom (Past 1,2) the themes of 'unity' and 'magnificence' in general, and, more specifically, two of their manifestations that blend naturally with the "proposed" common theme (5):

(6) penetration from the outside into the inner space of home through a window or door
(7) insistence on the essentials (the "gist") and rejection of the unnecessary, false (the "trash").

This yields:

(8) Θcom (Past 1,2): magnificence of existence and intense contacts: the beloved (the essence, opposite of trash) penetrates through the door (world-home contact) into the hero's modest room.

Okudžava's PW "reads" into (5) its own central theme:

(9) Θinv (Ok): a qualified, uncertain, "modal," minor-key overcoming of life's everyday and fundamental hardship,

with its two manifestations that suit the occasion:

(10) humble worship of the ideal
(11) opening the door as a symbol of kindness, hospitality, mutual assistance.

This results in

(12) Θcom (Ok 1,2): "modal" overcoming of life's hardship: the hero opens the door (kindness, help) and worships his beloved (the ideal) visiting his squalid room.

Worth noting is the similarity and difference of the motifs introduced by each of the PWs: the 'door' with the two different messages it conveys ('penetration, contact' *vs.* 'kindness, help') and the two different comments on the 'sublime' ('gist, not trash' *vs.* 'object for worship'); compare §3, case B.

5. *The specific themes* ($\Theta spec$) of individual poems are formulated, distinguishing, thematically, Past 1 from Past 2 and Ok 1 from Ok 2.

(13) $\Theta spec$ (Past 1): "spring" mood—unlimited joy of love.

All the components of (13)—'spring', 'unlimitedness', 'joy' and 'love' are invariant motifs in Pasternak, so (13) can be said to represent a special "angle" of his poetic universe.

(14) $\Theta spec$ (Past 2): "winter" mood—sad loneliness.

These minor-key motifs are alien to Pasternak's PW (in fact, they rather remind one of Okudžava), so their combination with and reinterpretation in the light of his $\overline{\text{M}}inv$ is an interesting problem for both artistic solution and contrastive description (see [1980c]). To turn to Okudžava's two poems,:

(15) $\Theta spec$ (Ok 1): an active set toward mediation between the ideal and reality
(16) $\Theta spec$ (Ok 2): awareness of the impossibility of mediation between the ideal and reality.

These two themes represent two of several possible gradations of the '"modality," uncertainty, and so on', that is part of Okudžava's central $\Theta inv = (9)$.

6. The *integral themes* (Θint) of individual poems are formulated, for example:

(17) Θint (Past 1) = Θcom (Past 1,2) + $\Theta spec$ (Past 1).

Every *individual poem* is then considered as an *embodiment of its* integral theme, that is, as the result of the gradual "grafting" onto this theme of the poet's more concrete invariant motifs. For every $Minv$ one states whether, in what form, and with what differences it is represented: (*a*) in the other poem by the author; (*b*) in his other texts in general; (*c*) in the two poems by the other author; (*d*) in his texts in general.

The *theoretical interest* of such parallel description focuses on three issues.

1. *Similar themes are realized differently in texts by different authors—* under the impact of different PWs. Indeed, many details clearly distinguish the two Pasternak poems from Okudžava's, for example:

(18) Past 1,2:
    (a) plants, snow, day, etc. (as if) inside the house (contacts, unity);
    (b) quick motion of snow and heroine; trembling of curtain; catching hold of heroine; chirping, singing (of birds, door); metaphorical spasms of hunger (intense states, magnificence);
    (c) blowing dust off a book as off life; simplicity, lack of caprice in heroine's dress; future entering with heroine (essence, magnificence, no trash).

(19) Ok 1,2:
    (a) praying, kneeling, "goddess," "Your Majesty Woman" (worship, the ideal);
    (b) "must," "ought," "believe," "enchantedness," "did you really?" (modality, unreality);
    (c) "everyday," "worn," "old," "the dark," "squalid," "badly lit," etc. (hardships of life).

2. *Similar motifs and details in poems by different authors mean different things* (see Table 10.1).

3. *Texts by the same author on different specific themes are similar*—more so than texts by different authors on similar specific themes. For instance, Pasternak's sad "winter" poem has more in common with his joyous "spring" one than with the sad poems of Okudžava. In fact,

Thematic Invariance

Table 10.1. Similar motifs—different meanings

| Common motifs | Details → Motifs → Themes | |
	Pasternak	Okudžava
(20) entering the room, door, oscillation	heroine's invasion makes curtain tremble → penetration through window or door, trembling → home/world contact, intensity → unity, magnificence	hero opens door, heroine and swaying shadows of both on threshold → hospitality, the very beginning, uncertainty → ideal, overcoming, modality
(21) kissing	hero touches, grabs heroine, kisses her, flowers → touching, catching hold, overpowering, kissing, man/nature contact → unity, magnificence	hero kisses heroine's windbeaten hands and old shoes → worship, humility, modesty, worn objects → "modality," ideal, hardship
(22) sad loneliness	repeated states of dejection → repetition → plurality, past/present contact → magnificence, unity	low key, the blues → silence, modesty, genuineness → hardship, modality, ideal
(23) heroine's simple clothes	dress without fancy extras, like snowflakes → gist, not falseness, contact with nature → magnificence, unity	light overcoat → lack of warmth, poverty, modesty → hardship, modality, ideal

every one of the invariant motifs that distinguish Past 1,2 from Ok 1,2 (see (18), (19)) is represented in each text by the corresponding poet, for example:

(24) (a) nature inside the house: orange-tree, oak color, violets, snowdrop—metaphorically or physically inside the house or on the heroes (Past 1); snow, hoarfrost, snowflakes, day, dusk—metaphorically or physically inside the house or on the heroine (Past 2);

(b) gist, not trash, contact with great entities: blowing dust off a book as off life (Past 1); heroine entering like future in a simple dress without extras and straightforwardly similar to snowflakes (Past 2).

(25) (a) worship: praying, kneeling down, "goddess" (Ok 1); "Your Majesty Woman" (Ok 2);

(b) threshold: shadows swaying on the threshold (Ok 1); "why stop at the threshold?" (Ok 2).

5. Motif-for-Motif Comparison and the Problem of Intertext

So far our $\bar{\text{M}}inv$-based comparison was motivated by purely typological reasons. Can it be applied to intertexts, that is, to pairs of texts by different authors of which one (T2) refers—explicitly or implicitly—to the other (T1)? Let us consider Pasternak's T2 (from *Tema* "Theme") and Pushkin's T1 (from *Kak sladostno javlenie ee* . . . "How delightful is her appearance . . .").

(26) T2:   . . . I gul, i polyxan'e
Okačennoj lunoj, kak iz loxani,
Pučiny. Šum i čad i štorm vzasos.
Svetlo, kak dnëm. Ix ozarjaet pena
[. . .]
. . . Pesok krugom zaljapan
Syrymi pocelujami meduz.
On češui ne znaet na sirenax,
I možet li poverit' v rybij xvost
Tot, kto xot' raz s ix čašeček kolennyx
Pil, bivšijsja, kak ob led, otblesk zvëzd?

. . . And the rumble and the blazing
Of the gulf, drenched by the moon as if from a washtub.
Noise and fumes and gale kissing aloud.
It is light, like in the daytime. They are illuminated by the foam [. . .]
. . . The sand all around is besmeared
By the wet kisses of medusas.
He [Pushkin] knows no scales on sirens,
And can he believe in a fish tail,
The one who at least once drank from their knee-caps [lit., knee-cups]
The gleam of stars beating against the ice?

(27) T1: Kak sladostno javlenie ee
Iz tixix voln pri svete noči lunnoj!
U strojnyx nog, kak pena belyx, volny
Laskajutsja, slivajas' i žurča.
Eë glaza to merknut, to blistajut,
Kak ne nebe mercajuščie zvëzdy
[. . .]
. . . skol'
Pronzitel'no six vlažnyx sinix ust
Proxladnoe lobzan'e bez dyxan'ja
—Tomitel'no i sladko'; v letnij znoj

How delightful is her appearance
From the silent waves in the light of a moonlit night!
Near [her] slender legs, white as foam, waves
Caress, flowing and rippling.
Her eyes now grow dark, now are sparkling,
Like stars flickering in the sky [. . .]
. . . How
Piercing is the cool osculation without breathing

Xolodnyj mëd ne stol'ko sladok
   žažde [. . .]
Mgnovennyj xlad, kak užas,
   probegaet
Mne golovu, i serdce gromko
   b'jëtsja,
Tomitel'no ljubov'ju zamiraja.
I v ètot mig ja rad ostavit' žizn'—
Xoču stonat' i pit' ee lobzan'e. . . .

Of these moist blue lips
—[It is] agonizing and sweet; in a
   summer heat
Cold mead is not this sweet to
   [one's] thirst [. . .]
Instant cold, like terror, runs across
My head, and [my] heart pounds
   loudly,
As if dying of agonizing love.
And in this moment I am glad to
   leave life—
I wish to moan and to drink her
   osculations. . . .

The two texts share several remarkably concrete motifs:

(28) bright moonlit night on a beach; waves, stars; a tryst with a woman
appearing from the waters; insistence on her human, not mermaid, nature
(legs in T1, knees in T2—instead of a mermaid's or siren's tail); kisses compared to drinks.

The fact of an intertextual reference, once T2 is confronted with T1,
seems evident,[4] especially since T2 is a fragment of the opening poem
of the "Theme with variations" cycle, which unambiguously refers to
Pushkin. Differences in the treatment of the common motifs, (28), are
striking, but clearly accountable for in terms of the two respective
PWs. In T1 the components of (28) serve to express Pushkinian

(29) ambivalent combinations of passion and impassivity, heat and cold, life
and death (see Chap. 8).

Note:

(30) (a) brightness of night,
      (b) love tryst with a beloved who is either dead or at least belongs to the
other world (cf. in particular: her [live] legs that are [deadly] white like the
[cold] foam; her eyes, intermittently shinning and dark; her kisses that are
without breath);
      (c) cold mead drunk in summer heat;
      (d) heart beating loudly because of coldness;
      (e) love and gladness manifested through readiness to leave life.

Turning to T2, we see that it is permeated with varieties of the
Pasternakian

(31) unity and magnificence of existence.

'Unity' is expressed by several varieties of 'contact', for example:

(32) (a) touching, projection of light, leaving a trace, loving contact, kissing (involving waves and the shore, cf. in particular *zaljapan* 'besmeared');

(b) meeting of extremes: night and day; the magnificent and the ordinary (sirens—fish scales and tail; moon—washtub; kisses—besmearing; drinking the stars—drinking from cups); the material and the abstract (something drinkable and similar to struggling fish—the reflected gleam of stars; medusas—kisses);

(c) phonetic and lexical similarities: *ób led* 'against the ice'—*ótblesk* 'gleam'; *čašečki* 'knee caps' as both "knee-cups" and "cups for drinking."

'Magnificence' is manifested through its varieties

(33) (a) various intense states involved in the storm (noise, fumes, gale, etc.) and in passionate (metaphorical) kissing (see ex. 32(a));

(b) swaying, swinging (the struggling of fish against the ice);

(c) intensity and universality inherent in the meeting of extremes (see ex. 32(b)).

In "appropriating" Pushkin's poem, Pasternak treats it rather freely.[5] Some of T1's components are completely omitted from T2, for example, 'death', 'impassivity', 'cold'. Others are transformed; for instance, 'passion' is extended to include the whole scene: the quiet night (cf. "from the silent waves" in T1) is turned into a stormy one ("noise and fumes and gale" in T2); 'passionate kisses' now bring together not only the lovers (and the waves, cf. "waves caress, flowing and rippling" in T1), but also the lyrical hero and the waves, the hero and the stars, the waves and the beach (cf. "medusas" seen as 'traces of sea's kisses on the sand' in T2); in addition, "kisses" now indicate the degree of 'magnificent saturation of the whole landscape with energy' (cf. "Noise and fumes and gale kissing aloud"). Last, but not least, T2 includes a number of completely new—Pasternakian—motifs (see (32), (33)). In their context even those motifs from T1 that are preserved in T2 (see (28)) are pressed into the service of Pasternak's PW.

Description of intertexts can therefore be seen as a modification of "normal" motif-for-motif comparison (see §4). Texts T1 and T2 share a common local theme (≃ 'tryst with a mermaid'), responsible—at least in part[6]--for the shared motifs (28). These motifs—and the two texts as wholes—are assigned different derivations in terms of the two respective PWs.[7] Now, what is specific of intertext is that the "old" derivation is "edited" into the "new" one and they both, together with the fact of "editing", form the integral derivation of T2. Pasternak's new reading of a Pushkin poem is a Class II thematic element that must be reflected in the theme of T2—as its Θ*spec* component.

(34) Θ*spec* (T2): appropriation of T1.[8]

The intertextual, inter-PW replacement of one set of motifs with the other is but a way of implementing this special type of theme.

PART FOUR

EXPRESSIVE DEVICES

11

How to Show Things with Words: On the Iconic Representation of Themes by Expression-Plane Means

In his Notes to *Don Juan* (Canto I: XI), Byron relates the story of a poetic combat between two English poets. Challenged with

(1) *I, John Sylvester,*
   Lay with your sister,

the other countered:

(2) *I, Ben Jonson, lay with your wife.*

"Sylvester answered,—'That is not rhyme'.—'No', said Ben Jonson: 'but it is *true*'."

Ben Jonson here pushes to the extreme the realistic principle of "naked truth" that has no place for any sort of fiction, to say nothing of such useless ornaments as rhyme. Of course, art has never followed these ultradocumentalist precepts. It has been quite willing to use, for the expression of its themes, fictional characters and events, and a wide variety of metrical, compositional, and other patterns. Moreover, rhyme, meter, and other semantically irrelevant adornments often directly represent certain elements of the theme. It is this CON-CRETIZATION of thematic elements by units of the code sphere that will constitute the subject of this chapter. This type of CONCR is in fact

This chapter is an abridged version of [1978d].

remarkably widespread and even underlies the patently antiliterary text (2). Ben Jonson's witticism owes its bite to a minus-device (Lotman 1977), that is, the renunciation of an accepted formal constraint (in this case, rhyme, and more specifically, *the* rhyme 'son', prompted by the analogy with "sister"). Minus-devices rely heavily on the conventionality of artistic form and are valid only in confrontation with such conventionality (in this case, with the rhymed text (1)). Minus-devices use conventions—by violating them—in order to CONCRETIZE the theme of 'truth, reality, authenticity (and not conventionality, fiction)'; cf. Ben Jonson's own comments on (2).

A related theme is developed by somewhat similar code-sphere means in:

(3) There once was a lady of Spain,
    Who said: "Let us do it again
    And again and again
    And again and again
    And again and again and again."

In spite of—or, rather, in subtle CONCORD with—the fact that the heroine is fictional and anonymous and the narration circumlocutional (unlike in (2)!), the code-sphere aspect of the limerick (3) creates a fairly detailed, if mischievously noncommittal, picture of the theme.

1. The thematic element 'regular reiteration', directly expressed in the referential sphere by the word *again* (or the phrase *again and again*), is "enacted" by the regular and multiple repetition of this word in the text.[1]

2. The INCREASE in the number of occurrences of the word *again* with each new line (0-1-2-2-3) reads clearly as an iconic representation of 'increase, climax'.

3. Another essential element of the theme is represented by the fact that the last three lines, and therefore all the three rhyme slots (that call for new lexical material), are filled exclusively with one and the same word—*again*—providing an iconic CONCRETIZATION of Θ 'only X and nothing but X'.[2]

4. The poetic form of limerick is treated in such a way that only the most elementary constraints are observed: the 5-line *a a b b a* pattern with longer lines 1,2,5 and shorter lines 3,4. The rules that provide for any originality are violated: the two series of rhymes (*a* and *b*)

should be phonetically different, but are identical; the rhyming words should be different, but are the same. This play with convention (of the minus-device type) conveys iconically a rather subtle message: 'it is original to be banal and stick to fundamentals'.[3]

5. A similar effect is also produced, on the level of plot and characterization, by the contrast between the conventionally specific and even exotic protagonist (*a lady of Spain*) and her pointedly trivial behavior (it is so trivial, in fact, that it can be dismissed with an *it*).

6. This "it," as well as the complete absence in text (3) of any more specific reference to the implied 'lovemaking', conveys, iconically again, the 'unmentionability' of the subject.

7. This, together with items 4 and 5 above makes the limerick an instance of 'ostensibly "plain" and artless, but in fact very rich and sophisticated, structure' with the characteristic emphasis on the code sphere ("poetry of grammar" in Jakobson's classic formulation).

Taken all together, the iconic CONCRETIZATIONS add up to something like the following message:

(4) An original and subtly playful claim that, trivial and conventionally unmentionable as it is, lovemaking, with its regularity, multiplicity and culminating gusto, is a fundamental, in fact, the sole important thing.

The way this theme, (4),[4] is embodied in text (3) is somehow at once more arbitrary, dependent on "artificial" play with convention, and more graphic than in the case of an ordinary plot; it is more subtle and subliminal and yet more striking. How can we account for this?

The greater *arbitrariness* of code-sphere CONCRETIZATIONS consists in the following: the interpretation of the text "unexpectedly" takes into account those properties of the signifier, which, under the normal convention of language and plot, are considered irrelevant for the signified. Generally speaking, the content plane should be absolutely unaffected by the phonetic, rhythmic, and other patterns formed by the constituents of the text—apart from the morphological, syntactic, intersentential and, finally, narrative conventions specified by the "primary" linguistic-and-literary code. For the perception and thematic interpretation of these patterns, an *additional* convention has to be introduced.

On the other hand, the same arbitrariness of linguistic code is responsible for the "actual and indisputable" presence of the signifiers in the text, whereas the signified meanings are there only conditionally, on a sort of contingent basis—as the content plane of the former, that is, by virtue of convention. The fact is that the meaning of the word *again* is only symbolized in text (3), while the same meaning when enacted by the repetitions of the word, is manifested iconically and therefore quite graphically and palpably. Roughly speaking, the Spanish lady and her intentions are fictional, whereas the repetition of the word *again* is a fact.

A paradox thus arises: the additional conventionality of code-sphere CONCRETIZATIONS consists in supplementing the arbitrary symbolic relation between the signifier and the signified with a "natural" iconic one. And the fact that the code-sphere CONCR proves more "absolute" and unconditional follows from the fundamental conventionality, that is, arbitrariness, of language. This double paradox seems, however, to be one of the essential properties of the literary code.[5]

The code-sphere CONCRs are, on the one hand, more striking, and original than "normal," referential CONCRs—since establishing iconic similarity between thematic elements and units of expression plane is a difficult and spectacular artistic feat. On the other hand, these CONCRs are "swallowed" by the reader almost imperceptibly, subliminally, as something that goes without saying: by virtue of the automatism of the practical language, their connection with the theme is not perceived explicitly—they are, after all, purely "formal" and "meaningless." We have to do here with an extreme instance of a fundamental principle of all art—the refusal to name ideas directly that leads to their embodiment in a material that is more palpable and, at the same time, more "remote" and resistant. A first-order convention (that of plot narration) projects ideas onto objects and situations of the referential sphere (see Chap. 2). The second-order convention we are concerned with involves the code sphere with its greater arbitrariness as well as its greater "naturalness": it authorizes the projection of ideas onto the still less yielding material of phonetics, syntax, meter and composition.

The difficulty of such projection results in a comparative scarcity of the themes for which it is possible. Sometimes only a part of a thematic complex can be projected onto the code sphere; for instance, in the limerick, (3), this is the case of the various statements concerning "it," but not of the "it" itself. In addition, the code CONCR is usually in need of a parallel referential CONCR, which

1. prompts the correct interpretation, e.g., in (3) the repetition (a code-sphere phenomenon) takes place in the context of the thematic

element 'multiple' (denoted in the referential sphere by the word *again*—actually *the* repeated word) and reads accordingly

2. helps connect the disparate thematic elements (iconically expressed through code CONCRs) into a coherent statement, e.g., in (3), the code-sphere manifestations 1–7 cohere into a meaningful message about life only if the referential sphere is taken into account.

As the set of themes that admit of code-sphere CONCR is rather limited, it may be possible to calculate it formally. Theoretically speaking, these should be all and only those thematic elements that are common to the two spheres; that is, such as 'beginning' and 'end'; 'more' and 'less'; 'principal' and 'secondary'; 'boundary'; 'observing'; and 'violating'; etc. (see [1976a: 31; 1977a: 15]). Still, it would seem advisable to start with empirical accumulation of the relevant data. As a step in this direction I propose to discuss three groups of examples.

1. Lengthening/Shortening of Segments

1.1. Let us begin with a fairly obvious case (from Mayakovsky's *Oblako v štanax* ["The cloud in trousers"]):

(5) Vošla ty   Entered you
     rezkaja, kak "nate!"   Snappish as "here y'are!"
     muča perčatki zamš,   Torturing [your] kid gloves,
     Skazala: Said:
     "Znaete—   "You know—
     Ja vyxožu zamuž."   I am getting married."

Here the first members of both rhyming pairs are, in the segments after the stress, one syllable shorter than the second: *náte/znáete; zámš/zámuž*. Now, Mayakovsky's rhymes in general tend to punning exactness, an effect achieved by stretching and adjusting the different sound complexes while superimposing them on each other (cf. the typical rhymes *razžal usta* 'opened the lips' / *požalujsta* 'please'; *let do sta rasti* '[supposed to] grow for [about] a hundred years' / *[nam bez] starosti* '[we, without getting] old', and so on). In such cases the "equating" principle results in the clarification of the reduced unstressed vowels by means of scansion (*požaluj-sta, sta-rosti*). In (5), on the contrary, equating requires the extra syllable to be skipped in the second members of the rhymes: since there is no way of stretching *nate* into *[z]naete, znaete* has to shrink to *zna^{e}te*. In this way the difference of rhyming endings encodes an abrupt, that is, snappish (cf. *rezkaja* 'snappish' in the second line of (5)) enunciation of the words in question (*znaete, zamuž*). As a result, the 'abruptness, snappishness', which is called in (5) by name, is CONCRETIZED iconically by code-sphere means.

Moreover, a code CONCR is provided for a still larger segment of the direct message of the text, namely, for the simile drawn between the heroine's abruptness and the abrupt word *nate!*: first the simile is spelled out for the reader (in the second line) and then it is realized literally by the code-sphere equation of the heroine's statement (*znaete* 'you know') with the abruptness of *nate*.

The overall construction is made more convincing (if less original) by the fact that the words *znaete* and *zamuž* are part of a character's direct, oral speech and, therefore, admit of reduction and play with the manner of pronunciation more easily than would the "objective," authorial speech.

Thus,

(6) abruptness <ins>CONCR</ins> "shrunk rhyme," skipping a syllable in the ending of the second member of the pair.

1.2. Pushkin's *Obval* ("Avalanche") is written in six-line stanzas consisting of iambic tetrameters and dimeters. In all the stanzas but one the dimeters comprise two words; in the second stanza, however, these short lines are composed of one word each:

(7) Ottol' sorvalsja raz obval,
I s tjažkim groxotom upal,
I vsju tesninu meždu skal
Zagorodil,
I Tereka moguščij val
Ostanovil.

From there once there broke loose an avalanche,
And it fell down with heavy rattle,
And the entire tight place between the cliffs
[It] blocked,
And the mighty flow of Terek
[It] stopped.

The theme of 'a mound of snow so big that it blocks the entire space and stops all movement' is twice CONCRETIZED in the code sphere. Two whole lines are occupied each by a single long word that concludes the sentence so that any further syntactic development is blocked: the sentence cannot be continued in the following lines, nor can there be any syntactic links within the line, that is,

(8) (a) taking up the entire space <ins>CONCR</ins> a single word occupying the whole line

(b) stopping the movement <u>CONCR</u> the last word of a sentence being the only word in the line.[6]

1.3. Note Pushkin's *Carskosel'skaja statuja* ("A statue in Carskoe Selo"):

(9) Urnu s vodoj uroniv, ob utes ee deva razbila.
Deva pečal'no sidit, prazdnyj derža čerepok.
Čudo! ne sjaknet voda, izlivajas' iz urny razbitoj,
Deva, nad večnoj struej, večno pečal'na sidit.

Having dropped an urn with water, a maiden broke it against a rock.
The maiden is ruefully sitting, holding a useless crock.
A miracle! the water does not run dry, pouring forth from the broken urn,
The maiden, over the eternal jet, sits, eternally rueful.

Central to the poem is COMBINATION of 'the momentary' with 'the eternal' and of 'movement' with 'rest'.[7] The first line, in particular, depicts 'momentary movement'. I will concentrate on its code-sphere CONCRETIZATION in the first hemistich.

1. Two two-syllable words are followed by one three-syllable word which is syntactically the most important; phonetically, the third word includes certain features of the two preceding words (see item 4, below). As a result, the sequence 2 + 2 + 3 constitutes a *summing* pattern (ideally, [2 + 2] + 4), capable of conveying 'intense increase' and 'completed development' (Mazel' and Cukkerman 1967: 397–441).[8]

2. On the rhythmical level first comes the most static trochaic motif ($\acute{\smile}$, a downbeat pattern, an impulse which then fades away); this is followed by a more dynamic iambic one ($\smile\acute{\,}$, an upsurge of activity), which is further "stretched" into a still more intense anapaest ($\smile\smile\acute{\,}$). The stressed syllable is, as it were, made to relinquish its initial position of rest (in the first word) and to shift first to the second place (in the second word) and finally to the third, thus describing a trajectory.[9]

3. This gradual rhythmical dynamization is accompanied by the lexical sequence: "a static object ("urn")—a liquid ("[with] water")— a verb of motion ("dropped")."

4. On the phonetic level there is a parallel vowel shift to the front from *u* via *o* to the intense *i;* the outline of the shift is summarized in the third word [uraníf]; this is even more evident in spelling: *ú-u/o-ó/u-o-í*. The consonants are also partly summarized: *uroniv* contains *r-n* from *urnu* and a labial fricative from *vodoj*.[10] The summariz-

ing lends phonetic support to the summing pattern of item 1, while the presence and the direction of the vowel shift upholds the trajectory of items 2 and 3.

5. At the same time, the continuity of the phonetic material (in the three words, especially the first and the third) seems to indicate that we are dealing with the *same urn*, formerly static and solid but now transformed into pure movement. This, by the way, is another reason for treating the stressed syllable that describes a trajectory (see item 2) as a one and the same entity.[11]

6. 'Completion' (mentioned in passing in item 1) is expressed, in the referential sphere, by the meaning of the verb ("to drop") as well as by the fact that in the verb of the main clause (to which the gerund *uroniv* 'having dropped' points syntactically) the movement does not continue: instead, the main verb, *razbila* 'broke', states the result. Rhythmically, the 'completion' is CONCRETIZED through the stressed syllable's attaining, as a result of displacements, a final position (a property which is, admittedly, the rule for initial hemistichs of the elegiac distich). Syntactically, *uroniv* is followed by a stop (the comma at the end of the gerund phrase); metrically, by a caesura.

All these factors COMBINE to produce a fairly accurate code-sphere equivalent of the 'falling (of an urn)':

(10) an object relinquishes its immobility and describes a trajectory; the movement intensifies as it approaches completion.

The main constituents of this overall code CONCR are:

(11) (a) dynamization, increase and completion CONCR the summing pattern CONCR [2+ 2] + 3, in which 3 is rendered heavier in several respects (e.g., it phonetically summarizes [2 + 2]);
(b) dynamization, trajectory, completion CONCR displacement of the stressed syllable from the first place in the word to the second and then the third and last place;
(c) trajectory CONCR the vowel shift to the front (*u-o-i*);
(d) identity of the (moving) object CONCR phonetic similarity of words.

1.4. The theme of the poem *À mes amis* ("To my friends") by Evariste Parny may be formulated approximately as

(12) exhortation to enjoy life in defiance of all obstacles.

Of special interest is the third stanza:

(13) Un jour il nous faudra courber   One day we will have to bend
      Sous la main du temps qui nous   Under the hand of time pressing us,
         presse,   But let us be joyous in youth,
      Mais jouissons dans la jeunesse,   And let us withhold from old age
      Et dérobons a la vieillesse   All that can be withheld from it.
      Tout ce qu'on peut lui dérober.

This stanza is crucial in several respects: it is the last; it is one line
longer than the two preceding ones (an INCREASE, also functioning as
the change that marks the end); it contains a striking paronomasia
(*jouissons–jeunesse*), highlighting the theme of 'youth and enjoyment'.
I will concentrate on the rhyming and stanzaic pattern as a means of
iconic code CONCR.[12]

In the first and second stanzas the rhyming pattern is *a b b a;* in the
third, *a b b b a*. In other words, from the outset the appearance of the
last rhyme is maximally postponed; in the last stanza it is delayed still
longer by the addition of an extra penultimate line. The effect is one
of 'postponement of the end (of the stanza, the poem)', which echoes
the idea of 'taking as much as possible away from old age and death'
as expressed in the penultimate, that is, "extra" (!) line. Therefore,

(14) (a) postponing the end CONCR *a b b a* type of rhyme;
      (b)*a b b a* rhyme scheme that postpones the end AUGM 5-line *a b b b a* last
      stanza after a succession of *a b b a* quatrains.

Rule (14a) is also exemplified by a stanza from Pasternak's *Poezdka*
("A ride").

(15) Na vsex parax nesëtsja poezd   The train is running at full speed,
      Kolësa vertit parovoz.   The locomotive is turning the wheels.
      I les krugom smolist i xvoist,   The wood around is resinous and
      I čto-to vperedi ešče est',   coniferous,
      I sklon berezami poros.   And there is yet something ahead,
                                               And the slope is grown with birch-
                                                  trees.

Here, too, it is in the last of the two internal lines (rhyming in *b b*), that
is, the "extra" one, that 'postponing the end' is expressed in the referential sphere: *I čto-to vperedi ešče est'* 'And there is yet something
ahead'.[13]

1.5. Our next example also has to do with the 'approach of death'. Bulat Okudžava's poem *Pervyj gvozd'* "The first nail" (describing the ritual of 'consecrating' a newly built house by drinking) concludes as follows:

(16) Pervyj gvozd' v pervoj svae ržaveet,   The first nail in the first pile is
      my p'ëm,   getting rusty, we are drinking,
      on ržaveet, my p'ëm, on ržaveet.   It is getting rusty, we are drinking, it
                                   is getting rusty.

The poem's theme COMBINES Okudžava'a invariant motifs 'the beginning, the first' and 'the brevity of life, the inexorable march of time'. The COMB is based on an 'increase of hopelessness' (also an invariant, see [1979e]). The 'march of time' is CONCRETIZED through the repetition of manifestations of 'life' (*my p'ëm* 'we are drinking') and of 'approaching old age and death' (*ržaveet* 'is getting rusty'), which alternate regularly, as equals. In the first line 'life' literally has the last word: *p'ëm* occupies the prominent final position. But this line is not the last: it functions as the RECOIL stage of a SUDDEN TURN. As the 'march of time' is taken in its entirety—prolonged until the very end of the poem—it is 'death' that has the last word. In the referential sphere this is supported by the self-evident fact that all that exists (life, buildings, nails, . . .) is transitory, in particular, by the fact that 'rusting' is a longer and more relentless process than 'drinking'. As a result, (16) expresses iconically a fairly complex thematic-expressive message:

(17) in spite of the regularity of the alternation of X and Y, and even of the odds being temporarily in favor of X (life), the course of Z (time) results in Y (death) (NB: the elements 'life', 'death', and 'time' are supplied by the referential sphere).

The principal constituent rules of the overall rule (17) → (16) are as follows:

(18) (a) regular process <u>CONCR</u> alternation: X-Y-X- . . . ;
     (b) odds in favor of X <u>CONCR</u> the last link in the chain of alternations is X;
     (c) taking the whole scope of the process into consideration <u>CONCR</u> prolonging the chain of alternations up to the end of a longer segment (a stanza, an entire poem);
     (d) Y in spite of AntiY <u>CONCR</u> S-TURN <u>CONCR</u> sequence 'line ending in AntiY—line, ending in Y'.

2. Reaching across Boundaries

From cases of mere 'lengthening, stretching' of a segment, I will now proceed to those of its encroachments on the territory of the following one. The themes which can be expressed iconically thereby are more or less predictable. The violation of a boundary is associated with 'breakthrough', 'sweeping increase', and so on; the establishment of new boundaries, with 'containment', 'statics', 'rest'. The interpretation is given further subtle nuances by the more immediate referential and code-sphere context.

2.1. In Pushkin's lyric "I loved you . . .," developing the ambivalent opposition 'passion/restraint' (see Chap. 9), the assertion of 'passion' reaches its peak in the seventh line:

(19) *Ja vas ljubil tak iskrenno, tak nežno* "I loved you so sincerely, so tenderly."

As I have pointed out (see Chap. 9, §1.2), this line is the only one in the entire poem that is completely affirmative: in the first line the leitmotif assertion is stopped short by the midline caesura; in the fifth, it manages to reach the end of the line but only so under the cover of negatives (*bezmolvno* 'without words', *beznadežno* 'without hope'). This "horizontal" 'breakthrough of affirmation' is COMBINED with another code-sphere 'breakthrough', this time "vertical." The poem consists of two quatrains forming a number of parallelisms. The first stanza introduces a pattern of clear-cut thematic division: two lines about 'former passion' and two lines about 'future restraint'. In the second stanza, however, the theme of 'former passion' spills over the boundary between the two periods, thus producing an "extra" line about 'love', the seventh (see Chap. 9, §1.2).

(20) breakthrough CONCR→ shifting a thematic boundary forward across a formal one as compared with their coincidence in the preceding stanzas.

It is worth noting that although this example is very much like example (13), the presence of an "extra" line in the two cases receives different interpretations, cf. rules (20) and (14b), which, by the way, reflect the necessary measure of similarity: 'postponement [of death]' is, in a sense a 'breakthrough [for life]').

2.2. In the first stanza of the same Pushkin poem the 'continuation of love from the past into the present' is also expressed by the interplay of meter and syntax. The sentence in which this theme is

CONCRETIZED in the referential sphere ("love still, perhaps, / In my soul has died out not completely") begins in the second half of the first line, spreads over the boundary between the lines and occupies the whole of the second (see Chap. 9, §2.1).[14] Thus

(21) continuation CONCR sentence crossing the boundary between lines.

Rule (21) also underlies the compositional pattern of the first part (four stanzas) of Pasternak's lyric *Zamestitel'nica* "Proxy").

(22) Ja živu s tvoej kartočkoj, s toj, čto
  xoxočet,
 U kotoroj sustavy v zapjjast'jax
  xrustjat,
 Toj, čto pal'cy lomaet i brosit' ne
  xočet,
 U kotoroj gostjat i gostjat i grustjat.

 Čto ot treska kolod, ot bravady
  Rakoči,
 Ot stekljašek v gostinoj, ot stekla i
  gostej
 Po pianino v ogne probežitsja i
  vskočit -
 Ot rozetok, kostjašek, i roz, i kostej.

 Čtob pričesku oslabiv, i čajnyj i šalyj,
 Začažennyj buton zakolov za kušak,
 Proval'sirovat' k slave, šutja, polušalok
 Zakusivši, kak muku, i ele dyša.

 Čtoby, komkaja korku rukoj,
  mandarina
 Xolodjaščie dol'ki glotat', toropjas'
 V opojasannyj ljustroj, pozadi, za
  gardinoj,
 Zal, isparinoj val'sa zapaxšij opjat'.

I live with your snapshot, with the
 one that laughs boisterously,
Whose joints crackle in the wrists,
The one that is breaking its fingers
 and does not want to throw
 them,
With which people visit and visit and
 are sad.

Which from the crackle of card
 packs, from Racocsi's bravado,
From the pieces of glass in the
 drawing room, from the glass
 and the guests,
Along the piano, in flames, will run
 and jump up—
From the rosettes, the bone keys, and
 the roses, and the dice.

In order to, having loosened the
 hairdo and having a tea-rose,
 crazy,
Fumed bud pinned inside a sash,
Waltz towards glory, jokingly, having
 taken a bit of the shawl
Between the teeth, like a torment,
 and hardly breathing.

In order to, hands crumpling the
 peel, the tangerine's
Chilling lobules to swallow, hurrying
Into the hall, encircled by a
 chandelier, behind a curtain,
[Hall,] that is once again smelling of
 the waltz's perspiration.[15]

A central component of the theme is

(23) increasing dynamism, rushing forward.

In the referential sphere this is expressed by a gradual acceleration of the depicted states ('laugh', 'crackle', 'running jump', 'waltzing', 'hurrying') and emphasized, in the last two lines, by crossing a certain 'boundary': ". . . Into the hall encircled [lit. "girdled"] by a chandelier, behind a curtain, . . ."

This expressive pattern is echoed in the code sphere. First of all, the 'aim of the movement' (*zal* 'hall') is accorded the *final place* in the sequence. Syntactically, all four stanzas form a single period (= 'rushing'), divided by stanzaic boundaries, which are marked by periods (= 'boundaries'). The latter are, however, overcome by the syntactic continuity of the text: periods are merely emphatic, for they separate clauses of a single complex sentence: 'I live with . . . whose . . . the one that . . . with which . . . //Which . . . will . . . jump . . . //In order to . . . //In order to . . .' (= 'crossing the boundaries').

Within individual stanzas the 'crossing of boundaries' takes the form of close syntactic links reaching over line breaks, for example, "a tea-rose, crazy, / Fumed bud"; in some cases the effect is enhanced by inversion, for example, "tangerine's / Chilling lobules to swallow" instead of the normal word order "to swallow the chilling lobules of a tangerine."

An exact code-sphere counterpart of 'rushing across the boundary' is present in the penultimate line. An extra syllable, unprovided for by the meter (anapaestic tetrameter), is introduced between the second and the third stressed syllables: *ljustroj, [po]zadi*. This makes for a pause which is also prompted by the syntax (comma). As a result, a new 'boundary' appears in addition to and right between the 'girdling chandelier' and the 'curtain':

(24) rushing across a separating boundary CONCR→ a syntactic entity transcending the boundaries between clauses, stanzas, lines, caesurae.

2.3. Another rule of the same kind as (21), (24) underlies a code-sphere CONCR in the two following Pasternak fragments:

(25) (a) Lodka kolotitsja v sonnoj grudi.   A boat is beating in a somnolent
          Ivy navisli, celujut v ključicy,   breast.

V lokti, v uključiny—o, pogodi,
Èto ved' možet so vsjakim slučit'sja!

Willows hang over, kiss on the
   collar bones,
On the elbows, on the rowlocks—o,
   wait,
This really can happen to anyone!

(b) Net vremeni u vdoxnoven'ja.
   Boloto,
Zemlja li, il' more, il' luža,—
Mne zdes' snoviden'e javilos', i sčěty
Svedu s nim sejčas že i tut že.

Inspiration is short of time. Swamp,
Ground, or sea, or a puddle,—
It is here that a dream has visited
   me, and the scores
With it I will settle right now and
   right here.

In both cases the message concerns a powerful force ('ecstasy of love'; 'creative inspiration') that acts blindly and indiscriminately upon everything within its reach. In the code sphere this is rendered by an enumeration which crosses the line boundary. Two specific characteristics of this 'crossing' should be noted:

1. The lines in which the enumeration begins (second in (25a); first in (25b)) contain only one term and it is only after the line break that the fact of enumeration becomes known.
2. The end of the enumeration does not coincide with the end of a larger unit: in (25a) the enumeration ends in the middle of a line; in (25b) although the enumeration ends at the end of the line, the sentence continues (or, rather, it just begins, the enumeration being an elliptical conditional clause).

These two properties make the enumeration 'chaotic, *impromptu,* unfinished'. In the referential sphere this is expressed by the general import of the sentence and also: in (25a), by the 'confusion' of parts of the human body (*ključicy* 'collar bones', *lokti* 'elbows') and those of the boat (*uključiny* 'rowlocks'); in (25b), by emphatic and diverse—"no matter which"—conjunctors (comma, *li, il'*). To sum up:

(26) (a) = (21);
   (b) many $\xrightarrow{\text{CONCR}}$ enumeration;
   (c) chaos, disorder $\xrightarrow{\text{CONCR}}$ enumeration begins with the last word of a line and its end does not coincide with major boundaries.

2.4. 'Breaking through boundaries' is often accompanied by phonetic similarity, which CONCRETIZES iconically the identity of objects (cf. §1.3, item 5; rule (11d); and note 11). For instance, in "I loved you . . ." (see Chap. 9), whose theme includes 'continuation of love', this construction occurs in the very first line. The boundary is marked by the end of the sentence and, therefore, a falling intonation, and the switch of tense (*ljubil* 'loved' / *byt' možet* 'may be'). This boundary is then crossed in the referential sphere by the statement that love continues and in the code sphere by the lexical and phonetic similarity of the words *ljubil* 'loved' / *ljubov'* 'love' which straddle the boundary. This makes for an effect of 'relay', reinforced by the relation between the two intonational patterns—the falling (i.e., spent), in *ljubil* and the rising (i.e., incipient and forward-aiming), in *ljubov'*.

However, in accordance with the general 'muffling of passion' in the poem, the 'relay' is far from active. A more clear-cut and energetic 'relay' is found in the lines:

(27) Stoit Istomina; ona,	There is Istomina standing; she,
Odnoj nogoj kasajas' pola, . . .	Touching the floor with one foot, . . .

followed by a description of the ballerina's pirouettes and leaps. The referential identity of the words on both sides of the semicolon is obvious (*Istomina* and *ona* 'she' refer to the same person); it is echoed in the code sphere by their phonetic similarity [ó-i-na/a-ná].

The 'relay crossing of the border' is supported by a number of devices. The transition from the end of a sentence to the beginning of a new one resembles, on the whole, the preceding example, with the difference that the preboundary phase occupies a much greater part of the line, while the new impulse is reduced to a two-syllable word. As a result, both the '*stop*' and the new '*impulse*' are stressed. The 'stop' is expressed, in the referential sphere, by the posture (*stoit* 'stands') and this is in turn reinforced, in the code sphere, by a paronymy (*stoit* ≃ *Istomina*); the 'impulse' is strengthened by the fact that a short subject (*ona*) is allotted all the intensity of the high intonational beginning of a new sentence. The shortness of this intense *ona* is emphasized by the end of the line and a comma, which separates it from the gerund construction in the following line. In the referential sphere *ona* 'she' is the subject of a series of motion verbs (toward which it is syntactically directed). Rhythmically, *ona* is a rising (i.e., dynamic) iambic motif ($\smile'$), which contrasts with the falling (i.e., "braking") *Istomina* ($\smile'\smile$).[16] Thus,

(28) relay of a spent movement and the spreading of it across a boundary
CONCR phonetic similarity of words on both sides of the boundary, the first of

them having a falling rhythmic-intonational pattern, and the second, a rising one.[17]

2.5. Let us now turn to a rule that is opposite to (21), (24) and the like:

(29) reserve, restraint, "braking" <u>CONCR</u> pauses.

This iconic CONCRETIZATION of 'restraint' is widely spread; compare, for instance, the penultimate line of Pushkin's "Upon the hills of Georgia . . . ," discussed in detail in Chap. 8, §7. I will now consider a more specific use of 'pause'.

2.6. The third line of the poem *Carskosel'skaja statuja* (see ex. (9)) mentions in so many words the 'miracle' of the girl's metamorphosis into a statue:

(30) *Čudo! ne sjaknet voda, izlivajas' iz urny razbitoj.* "A miracle! the water does not run dry, pouring forth from the broken urn."

The 'miracle' is also projected into the code sphere, and the resulting code CONCR is superimposed on the very word *čudo* 'miracle'. The 'miracle' is described in the third (i.e., the culminating) line of the quatrain (the fourth assuming the role of a final still). The word *čudo* is stressed by the exclamatory intonation, making it the poem's single emotional outburst set against a pronouncedly calm epic background. Syntactically, the word forms a separate sentence, set off by the line break on the left and the exclamation mark and the pause on the right, the pause being the only one in the whole poem situated at this point (after the first foot). Since the usual caesura (after the third foot) is also present, the line falls into three (instead of the usual two) autonomous syntagms and becomes the most "weighty" in the whole poem. The third line COMBINES this "weight" with emotional intensity (incidentally, it is the only line in the poem that does not end with a period). Thus,

(31) miraculous, strange, unusual <u>CONCR</u> a special (e.g., culminating) line; departure from a norm or inertia characteristic of the text (e.g., an extra pause).[18]

This rule has much in common with the notion of "rhythmic italics" as introduced by Taranovsky (1976: 142), the difference being that, in addition to mere expressiveness, (31) involves a code-sphere CONCR of a thematic element.

The specific form the 'departure from norm' assumes in (30)—namely, that it manifests itself as an 'extra pause'—seems to be determined by rule (32):

(32) miracle <u>CONCR</u> suspension (of the laws of nature; of the activities of the dumbfounded observer) <u>CONCR</u> a pause.

Reference to an observer's reaction is quite legitimate, since it is implied that the remark *Čudo!* 'A miracle!' belongs to one.

3. Transfer to the Frame

3.1. The opposition between the "frame" of a text (e.g., the frame story featuring the narrator and his listeners) and the "content proper" (the inner, or framed story, told by the narrator) is one of the most general categories of the code sphere. The iconic potential of 'transfer to the frame' comprises several characteristics inherent in this code-sphere pattern.

1. First of all, the relation between its two components resembles the relation between the extratextual reality and the text itself: the frame connotes 'reality, unconditionality, something taken for granted', while the framed story (i.e., the "text proper") connotes 'arbitrariness, invention, fiction,' etc.).

2. In eliminating the boundary between the two components the 'transfer' lends itself to interpretations involving 'destruction, death, obliteration, annihilation'.

3. In encompassing, together with the "content," the "container" itself (i.e., "all there is" in the text), it can embody the theme of 'completeness, universality, finality'.

4. Finally, the very switch to the opposite is a particular case of SUDDEN TURN. In addition to purely expressive effects, this construction helps convey the thematic element of 'unexpectedness, novelty, originality,' which is in fact inherent already in the opposition 'taken for granted/fictional' (see item 1, above).

Thus, the rule would be as follows:

(33) transition: (*a*) from the fictional to the real and/or (*b*) from the existing to the annihilated and/or (*c*) from the partial to the complete and/or (*d*) from the obvious to the original <u>CONCR</u> transfer to the frame.

3.2. All these effects seem to be present in the plot of the Babylonian "Pessimistic dialogue between Master and Servant" (see Pritchard 1969: 437–38).

(34) In each of its dozen episodes, the master orders the slave to make preparations for certain actions (to go to the court, to help a friend, etc.), listens to his arguments that the intended actions are futile, and revokes the orders. In the final episode the master, convinced of life's futility, decides to die and gives corresponding orders, including, among other things, the death of the slave even before that of his master.

Referentially, the plot (34) is a dramatic switch from disparate and illusory life-pursuits to the ultimate truth of complete abnegation of life, especially for the slave: after having taken for granted his peripheral and thus immune role of a discussant and instrument of his master's intended actions, he is suddenly involved "for real" by the last and deadly one—as its object. In the code sphere this is echoed by 'transfer to the frame': the action, which was confined to the inner story ('the master's worldly pursuits'), in the end engulfs and destroys the frame ('the dialogue between the master and the slave'), that is, *all* the characters of either story.

If in the "Dialogue" the referential sphere claims, roughly speaking, the entire iconic potential of the 'transfer to the frame', in other cases it can bring out only some of the thematic elements listed in rule (33).

3.3. Mandel'štam's poem *Ja p'ju za voennye astry* . . . ("I drink to the military asters . . .") (see Mandel'štam 1967, 1: 165–66) is written in the form of a toast—to objects and values treasured by but inaccessible to the speaker ("St. Petersburg days," "Paris paintings," "Champs Elysées," "Rolls-Royce," "Alpine cream," etc.). In the last couplet:

(35) Ja p'ju, no ešče ne pridumal, iz dvux
    vybiraju odno:
Veseloe asti-spumante il' papskogo
    zamka vino . . .

I drink, but I have not yet thought
    up [i.e., decided or invented], out
    of the two I choose one:
The joyous "Asti-Spumante" or the
    wine of "Château des Papes" . . .

it turns out, however, that the wine, a *sine qua non* of 'drinking a toast', is itself out of the speaker's reach—just as the objects mentioned *in* the toast are.

The theme and plot of the poem involve 'loss of everything' (and, ambivalently, insistence on 'symbolic possession of everything'). It is, therefore, the thematic elements 'completeness' and 'annihilation' (see (33 b,c)) that come to the fore in the iconic interplay of the referential story and the code-sphere 'transfer to the frame'. The 'annihilation' of the frame ('the toast') is so much the more 'complete' and spectacular, because its reality has been taken for granted while what is inside it ('the listed objects') have been presented from the start as values, that is, merely ideas. (In other words, rules (33 b,c) are supported and reinforced by (33 a,d).)[19]

3.4. A different component, (33a), of the overall rule—'truth, reality' as opposed to 'fiction, illusion'—is highlighted in the Somali tale "A Soothsayer Tested" (see Chap. 4). The inner story is about the soothsayer's interaction with the chief of his tribe; it is framed by the soothsayer's exchanges with the snake. In the end it unexpectedly (see (33d)) turns out that these exchanges are subject to the same laws as those between the soothsayer and the chief. Thus a status of 'revelation' is conferred on the plot's denouement. In the code sphere this effect is iconically supported by the corresponding components of (33), and also by an additional refinement of the 'transfer to the frame':

(36) truth $\xrightarrow{\text{CONCR}}$ similarity between the outer story and the already known content of the inner story.

In "A Soothsayer Tested" this "similarity rule" operates in conjunction with the more usual "contiguity rule," on which, for instance, the plot of the "Dialogue," (34) is based (in both cases the inner and outer stories share a character: the slave; the soothsayer). The 'transfer to the frame by contiguity' tends to emphasize the *realness*, tangibility, earnestness of the 'truth', while 'transfer by similarity' is more concerned with 'truth's *accuracy*'. Consider the 'transfer to the frame by (almost) pure similarity' in Hamlet's "mousetrap": the enacted play resembles the hypothesis he is testing for accuracy, but none of the actors takes part in the subsequent action. The contiguous impact is confined to the King and Queen's leaving the audience (*Hamlet*, III, 2).

4. Conclusion

The examples of 'transfer to the frame', which expresses the 'truth' of artistic invention, bring us back, in a sense, to those examined at the beginning of the chapter and with them I will round off my series of illustrations.

In analyzing the examples I tried throughout to outline the corresponding rules of code-sphere CONCRETIZATION, and it is in these that the theoretical purport of the discussion resides. The complete set of such rules, together with a similar catalogue of referential sphere CONCRs, would form the "lexicon" component of the PE model of literary competence; this "lexicon, or dictionary, of reality" is indispensable for the functioning of the other major component of the model, a "grammar" made up of expressive devices (see Glossary).

The compilation of such a dictionary would of course be a superhuman task. To a certain extent it might be facilitated by an eventual generalization of the rules. First, it would be sufficient to state the primary correspondences (of the type: 'boundary" → 'pause'; 'something taken for granted' → 'frame'; etc.);) from these one could derive more complex ones (like rules (20) and (21)), which I have preferred to write out in full as separate items. Second, even these primary correspondences are, in principle, reducible to still more elementary data, namely, to the definitions of code-sphere units: thus, the definition of 'pause' should of necessity include the property of 'being a boundary'. Yet, such generalization of the rules will hardly exempt scholars from the preliminary task of empirically listing the rules of iconic code CONCRETIZATION of thematic elements.

12

On the Preparation of the Final Rhyming Word: PRESAGE and RECOIL in Rhyming

The theoretical apparatus of this chapter has been called forth by a strictly descriptive problem—the artistic riddle presented by the last word of a Pushkin lyric. My hypothesis was that this rhyme, along with many others, owed its effect to the way it was prepared for throughout the entire stanza and thus emphasized as an unexpected and natural closure. Once seen as a *preparation of a result,*[1] the structure warranted recourse to concepts devised for similar plot techniques. In terms of poetics of expressiveness, the relevant devices are PRESAGE and RECOIL, that is, respectively a "direct" and a "reverse" PREPARATION (see Glossary).

1. PRESAGES

1.1. *Some Concepts*

It has been noted that the word concluding a poem, a stanza, a couplet, or an important line often "clicks neatly into place."

(1) We cannot fight for love, as men may *do* (R1);
   We should be *woo'd* (PreR2), and were not made to *woo* (R2).

This chapter is a considerably modified version of [1979d]. A number of Russian examples have been replaced by English counterparts and the exposition has been changed. For more Russian material and some of the theoretical points omitted here, see [1979d].

(2) Jesus Christ, *Superstar* (R1),
   Do you think *you're* (PreR2) what they say *you are?* (R2)

(3) From the bonny bells of heather
   They brewed a drink *lang-syne* (R1)
   Was sweeter far than *honey* (PreR2),
   Was stronger far than *wine*. (R2)

(4) . . . The play's the *thing* (R1)
   Wherein I'll *c*atch (Pre$_1$R2) the *c*onscience (Pre$_2$R2) of the *k*ing. (R2)

The "punch word" R2 (the second term of the rhyming pair: *woo, you are, wine, king*) is either guessed by the reader in advance, or in a shock of recognition he at least "guesses backward." Tracing back the path that led up to R2, the reader perceives he was prompted to anticipate it not only by R1 (the first term of the rhyming pair, i.e., the word that R2 must rhyme with: *do, Superstar, lang-syne, thing*), but also by some other word(s), which I call PreR2. Such "guesswork," whether prospective or retrospective, conscious or unconscious, successful or frustrated, constitutes a legitimate object of modeling, as it reflects the way a well-staged "denouement" R2 crowns the infrastructure of "clues" planted in the preceding text.

   In (1) and (2), however different the sources, the pattern is the same: PreR2 (*woo'd; you're*) is the same lexical unit as R2 (*to woo; you are*). In (3) the similarity is a semantic one (PreR2: *honey;* R2: *wine*), while in (4) the double PRESAGE (Pre$_1$R2: *catch;* Pre$_2$R2: *conscience;* R2: *king*) is phonetic [k.].

   The three codes—lexical, semantic, and phonetic—do not exhaust all the possibilities: syntactic, morphological, stylistic, and other similarities can also serve as PRESAGES. Nor are these codes mutually independent: very roughly speaking, "word = meaning + sound." Still, empirically, they constitute the most important articulations of the material that is molded into "predictive" patterns.

   The overall effect of a PRESAGE (in terms of 'direction', 'explicitness', 'accuracy', etc.) is determined by the material (code), the pattern, and their interplay. Among the codes, for instance, there is a distinct hierarchy of 'explicitness', with lexical PRESAGES as the most obvious and phonetic as the least obvious. As for the patterns, their major types naturally apply to all codes. *Quantitatively*, the similarity between PreR2 and R2 can be characterized by:

   1. "richness," e.g., the common semantic denominator of *honey* and

wine in (3) is quite modest ('a treat'), while the common lexical de-nominator of PreR2 and R2 in (2) is comparatively rich (two words: *you* and *are*)

    2. "coverage" of R2 by the sum total of R1 and PreR2, e.g., in (4) [k-] from *catch* and *conscience* plus [-íŋ] from *thing* together predict *king* completely, although [k-] as such is not a rich PRESAGE

    3. "number" of PreR2, cf. the double PreR2 in (4) *vs.* the single in (1), (2), (3).

Qualitatively, the relation between PreR2 and R2 can be on the whole "positive, straightforward" (e.g., *honey* and *wine* in (3) are near syn-onyms, the three occurrences of [k-] in (4) are homophonous) or "negative, contrastive" (e.g., *woo'd* and *to woo* in (1) are clearly opposed both grammatically and semantically). *Structurally* relevant features include:

    1. "absolute distance" in the text between PreR2 and R2 (e.g., short in (1), (2), (4); longer in (3));
    2. "relative distance": after R1, i.e., in the zone of active anticipation of R2, (e.g., (1) − (4)) or before R1 (e.g., in (12) and (13));
    3. "position": weak, somewhere inside the line (e.g., in (1), (2), (4)), or strong, at the end of a line, often in a rhyme (e.g., in (3));
    4. "complexity": a minimal pattern, consisting only of R1, PreR2, R2 (see (1), (2)), or a proportion (i.e. a ratio) between at least two pairs of terms (e.g., in (3): *sweeter : honey = stronger : wine*).[2]

    The major pattern types outlined here neither form a complete set (there are many subtler and more specific subtypes), nor are they mutually independent. (There are numerous interdependencies be-tween types; for example, proportions presuppose multiple PreR2.) But the contribution of each type to the overall effect of the PRESAGE is usually clear: for instance, greater similarity, shorter distance, and proportions enhance explicitness, while negativity increases paradox. I said "increases," not "creates," because a touch of paradox (i.e., RECOIL) is by definition inherent in any PRESAGE, whose effect lies in a PreX, i.e., something that *is not* X, being *similar to* and *preparing* the final X. In our case the element of RECOIL consists in the very fact that the "punch word" is prepared not only where and in the way this is specified by the rules of rhyming (i.e., not only by R1), but also in a *different place* (PreR₂), *another code* (e.g., semantic), or a *different (nega-tive) mode.* Often PreR2 and R1 prepare *different parts of the word* R2, cf. [k-] ≠ [-íŋ] in (4).

The listing of all possible material and pattern types, all their inter-dependencies and interrelations, and resulting overall effects is beyond the scope of this chapter. I will illustrate the introduced concepts and some other points by considering a limited number of samples of rhymed verse (English, Russian, French, and Latin).

1.2. *Semantic Presages*

Consider examples (5)–(15):

(5)   ... *home* (R1)
To the *glory* that was *Greece* (PreR2),
To the *grandeur* that was *Rome* (R2).

(6) In politics if thou would mix
    And mean thy fortunes *be* (R1),
    Bear this in mind—be *deaf and blind* (PreR2),
    Let great folks *hear and see* (R2).

(7)   ... kto xočet!   ... who wants!
    Čerstvejet s každym dnëm surovyj   More and more insensitive becomes
      mir (R1).   the cruel *world*.
    Porok gremit, sverkaet i groxočet.   Vice blasts, blazes and thunders
    On *bog* (PreR2) zemli! On—*mirovoj*   It is the *god* of the earth! It is the
      kumir (R2)!   world's *idol!*

(8)   ... *dies* ($R_1$1).
    We two will love, till in our *eyes* ($R_2$1)
    This heart's *Hell* (PreR2) seem *Paradise* (R2).

(9)   ... *befell* (R1).
    Parting is all we know of *heaven* (PreR2)
    And all we need of *hell* (R2).

(10) Podxodjat noči v sombrero sinix,   Nights come close in blue sombreros,
    Sozved'ja vzorov pojut *zvezde* (R1),   Constellations of glances sing to the
    Pojut *v peščerax*, pojut *v pustynjax*,   *star*,
    Pojut *na more* (PreR2), pojut   Sing *in caves*, sing *in deserts*,
      vezde (R2).   Sing *by the sea*, sing *everywhere*.

(11) The mute *bird* sitting on the stone,
    The dark *moss* dripping from the *wall* (R1),
    The garden *walk* with weeds o'ergrown (PreR2),
    I love them—how I love them *all* (R2).

(12) Death and life were not
    Till man made up the *whole* (Pre_1R2),

Made lock, stock and *barrel* (R1)
Out of his bitter soul,
Aye, *sun and moon and star* (Pre_2R_2) *all* (R2).

(13) I am the *truth,* but you will *not believe me* (Pre_1R_2),
   I am the *city* where you will not *stay* (R1) (Pre_2R_2),
   I am your *wife,* your *child,* but you will *leave me* (Pre_3R_2),
   I am that *God* to whom you will *not pray* (R2).

(14) The sand slips,
   The last he *hears* (R1)
   From the world's *lips* (PreR2)
   Is the sand in his *ears* (R2).

(15)   . . . Sgubit'   . . . To destroy
   Sebja legko, i svet nebes *ne videt'* (R1).   Oneself is easy, and the light of the
   Čto ž èto: zlo staraetsja *ljubit'* (PreR2)   skies *not to see.*
   Ili ljubov' mečtaet *nenavidet'* (R2)?   What's it: evil trying to *love*
                                                   Or love dreaming of *hate?*

Example (5) is a replica of (3) in several respects; among others, in the inexactness of the synonymy (*Greece/Rome*). In contrast, the next two are feats of semantic precision. Number (6) is very rich: ideal similarity covers three words (*deaf and blind / hear and see*). Example (7) is a graphic example of the kind of "addition" our PRESAGES are based on: [mír] + 'god' = Russ. *kumír* 'idol'; the punch word is found at the intersection of two searchlights, a phonetic and a semantic one.[3]

Numbers (8) and (9) exemplify negative, that is, antonymous, relations between PreR2 and R2. In (9), as in most cases, PreR2 is in the strong position at the end; the weaker position of PreR2 in (8) is compensated by the shortness of absolute distance. As for relative distance, all eleven examples (5)–(15) place PreR2 within the zone of active anticipation of R2.

Examples (10)–(12) share a remarkable pattern: in all three (*a*) the meaning of the punch word R2 contains the universal quantifier 'all, every'; (*b*) in the preceding lines this idea is conveyed not by a word but by an iconic enumerative construction, covering "the entire universe."[4] (In fact, in (12) the PRESAGE includes a quantifier word—*the whole*—as well.)

Examples (13) and (15) illustrate semantic proportions (cf. (3)), which in both cases are quite explicit. In (13) there are four (!) parallel figures; in (15) just a minimum of two.[5] Remarkably, in each separate figure and between PreR2 and R2 the relationship is negative, but the parallelism *between* figures is positive (the proportion is not inverted).

In fact, more or less pronounced proportions are present in many other examples: compare *know/need* in (9); *zemli* 'of the earth' / *mirovoj* 'the world's' in (7); *be/let* in (6) and *glory/grandeur* in (5).

Finally, in (11), (12), and (13) we come across PRESAGES that start before R1 (cf. especially *whole* in (12)), although they do not stop there but continue into the active zone of anticipation.

Example (14) would have been a banal "dictionary" rhyme (see note 5), were it not for the bold image (*hears . . . sand*) supported by a PRESAGE "addition" ([híəz] + 'hears' + 'lips' = *ears*), in which R1 takes part both phonetically and semantically.

1.3. *Phonetic* PRESAGES

Consider examples (16)–(26):

(16) Kogda na tëmnyj gorod sxodit
    V gluxuju noč' glubokij *son* (R1),
    Kogda metel', kružas', *zavodit* (PreR2)
    Na kolokol'njax *perezvon* (R2), . . .

When on the dark city descends
On a deaf night a profound *sleep,*
When the snowstorm, swirling, *starts*
On the bell-towers a *ringing,* . . .

(17) Dans les plaines de l'air *vole* (PreR2)
    avec *l'aquilon* (R1),
    Avec le doux rayon de l'astre de
    mystère
    Glisse à travers les bois dans l'ombre
    du *vallon* (R2).

On the plain of air *fly* with the
    aquilon,
With the sweet ray of the mysterious
    luminary
Slide across the woods in the shade of
    the *valley.*

(18) And silence sounds no worse than *cheers* (R1)
    After *earth* (PreR2) has stopped the *ears* (R2).

(19) But most thro midnight streets I *hear* (PreR2)
    How the youthful Harlot's *curse* (R1)
    Blasts the newborn infant's tear,
    And blights with plagues the Marriage *hearse* (R2).

(20) *Idi* (PreR2) i gljadi—ne žizn', a *lilija*
    (R1).
    Idillija (R2).

Go and look: it is a *lily* of a life.
Idyll.

(21) Son leleja, liloveet *zapad* (PreR2) *dnja*
    (R1),
    Snova serdce dlja rassudka *zapadnja*
    (R2).

Cherishing the sleep, scarlet becomes
    the *west of the day,*
Again the heart is for the reason a
    trap.

(22) For he is *nothing* (PreR2),
    He is *less* (R1)

Than Echo answering
"*Nothingness*" (R2)!

(23) The boast of heraldry, the pomp of power,
    And all that beauty, all that wealth e'er *gave* (R1),
    Awaits alike the inevitable hour;
    The paths of *glory* (PreR2) lead but to the *grave* (R2).

(24) Nakoplen vekom gor'kij *opyt*,   The century has accumulated a bitter
    Prjamoj opasen *razgovor* (R1):   *experience,*
    Naoborot pročtite *ropot* (PreR2)   Dangerous is a straightforward *talk:*
    I oboznačitsja *topor* (R2).   Read backwards [the word] *grumbling*
                            And you will see the contours of an
                              axe.

(25) O feare me not, thou pretty *mayde*
    And doe not fly from *mee* (R1);
    I am the kindest man, he *said* (PreR2),
    That ever eye did *see* (R2).

(26)   . . . *summer*
Sleepy with the flow of *streams* (R1),
Far I hear the steady *drummer* (Pre$_1$R2)
Drumming (Pre$_2$R2) like a noise in *dreams* (R2).

In (16) *perezvon* results, if not completely, from [z-vó] + [-ón]; in (17) [v-l-] + [-lõ] = [valõ]. Incidentally, (17), as well as (19)–(22), are examples of PreR2 preceding R1. Examples of rich and complete phonetic PRESAGES abound: compare such sequences of words at the ends of lines as: *swim—sweet singing—*dim*—swift sails winging—swinging* (Shelley); *passe* 'passes'—*sang* 'blood'—*pas lasse* 'not tired'—*passant* 'passer-by' (M. Desbordes-Valmore); *jazve* 'ulcers'—*velik* 'big'—*razve* 'whether'—*jazyk* (Severjanin). Sometimes the PRESAGE is richer and more complete than meets the ear (see (18) and (19), where *earth* and *hear* are sort of "eye-prerhymes," anticipating the spelling of, respectively, *ears* and *hearse*).

Pushed to the extreme, exact phonetic PRESAGES produce punning rhymes, as in (20)–(22). The English example, (22)—unlike the two Russian ones—is impure: *nothingness* is related to PreR2 not just phonetically, but lexically as well.

Number (23) COMBINES, within one and the same word, phonetic and semantic foreshadowing: *glory* is loosely antonymous to *grave* and supplies the *-r-* that is missing in *gave*. The pattern is somewhat similar to example (5) (*home—grandeur—Rome*), but there is a significant difference. Semantically, example (23) is contrastive and this is echoed by a sort of phonetic contrast—an inversion: in *glory* the *-r* follows, while in *grave* it precedes the stressed vowel. The same effect of coupling semantic and phonetic paradoxes is much more pronounced (in fact, laid bare) in (24), yielding the palindrome (i.e., inverted pun) *ropot* 'grumbling'/*topor* 'axe'.[6]

The last two examples display phonetic proportions (completely similar to the semantic ones in (13), (15)): in (25), for instance, [méid] : [mí:] = [séid] : [sí:]. The proportion in (26) is less exact (*sʌ́* . . .: *strí:* ≃ *drʌ́* . . . : *drí:.* . .), but the richness, completeness, and multipleness of the PRESAGE compensate.

1.4. Lexical PRESAGES

The formula "semantic + phonetic = lexical" (see §1.1) is, of course, an oversimplification. We have seen how the two COMBINE without producing the same word (see (21), (24)). On the other hand, lexical identity does not strictly presuppose phonetic similarity, for example, in cases of suppletion (cf. (27), (28)).

(27) Le même cours des planètes   The same course of the planets
        Règle nos jours et nos *nuits* (R1).   Governs our days and our *nights*.
        On m'a vu ce que *vous êtes* (Pre₁R2),   I was seen [to be] what *you are*,
        Vous serez (Pre₂R2) ce que *je suis* (R2).   *You will be* what *I am*.

(28) Puppets passing from a *scene* (R₁1)
        What but mockery can they *mean* (R₂1)
        Where I am (PreR2)—*where thou hast been?* (R2)

(29) She died, and left to *me* (R1)
        This heath, this calm and quiet *scene;*
        The memory of what has *been* (PreR2),
        And never more will *be* (R2).

The structure of the first two examples is quite similar (leaving aside for the time being the lexical proportion in (27)). In both cases the phonetic difference between tense forms is exploited as a contrast that supports the semantic opposition (cf. (1), (23), (24)). To be sure, suppletive forms are an extreme case of a divorce between semantics and phonetics in a lexeme. Usually, the phonetic (and morphological) difference is less pronounced, but even then it can be coupled with semantic contrast. Compare example (29), with its *been*/*be* (where (28) had *am*/*been*), and also

(30)   I ja ušël. . . . V duše temno . . .
  A ty vse ždëš', kak *Jaroslavna* (R1).
  To bylo, možet byt', *davno* (PreR2),
  No možet byt', sovsem *nedavno* (R2).

And I left. . . . It is dark in my
 soul . . .
But you keep waiting, like *Jaroslavna.*
This happened, maybe, *long ago,*
But may be quite *recently* [lit., *not long ago*].

Here the antonymy of PreR2 and R2 is underpinned phonetically by a stress shift (*davnó/nedávno*); compare also (36).[7]

 Phonetic (morphological, etc.) differences do not necessarily echo semantic contrasts; often they just make the similarity less complete and obtrusive; see:

(31)   All else is gone from those great eyes,
  The soul has *fled* (R1).
  When faith is lost, when honour *dies* (PreR2),
  The man is *dead* (R2)!

and also

(32)   Ne vidno ptic. Pokorno čaxnet
  Les, opustevšij i *bol'nój* (R1).
  Gribý (PreR2) sošli, no krepko paxnet
  V ovragax syrost'ju *gribnój* (R2).

No birds are seen. Submissively
 rotting
Is the forest, empty and *sick.*
Mushrooms are over, but there is a
 strong smell,
In the ravines, of *mushroomy*
 dampness.

In (32) the semantic relation between PreR2 and R2 is, in fact, negative, but it hardly correlates with the phonetic difference.

 The following examples display an increasing use of lexical proportions:

(33)   How can I call the lone *night good* (PreR2),
  Though thy sweet wishes wing its *flight* (R1)?
  Be it not said, thought, understood—
  Then it will be—*good night* (R2).

(34)   Dame souris trotte
  Noire (PreR2) dans le gris du
   soir (R1).
  Dame souris trotte
  Grise dans le *noir* (R2).

Lady mouse is trotting,
Black in the grey of the *evening,*
Lady mouse is trotting
Grey in the *blackness.*

(35) All my faults perchance thou *knowest,*
All my madness none can *know* (R1).
All my hopes, where'er thou *goest* (PreR2),
Wither, yet with thee they *go* (R2).

(36) Ce qu'Amour viaut, doi je *amer*   What love wills I must *love*
    (PreR1)   And she must me friend *call,*
Et moi doit ele ami *clamer* (PreR2)   Yes, indeed, for I *love* her,
Oil voir, por ce que je l'*aim* (R1)   And I *call* her my enemy.
Et je m'anemie la *claim* (R2).

(37) I vesel zvučnyj les, i veter mež *berëz*   And cheerful is the noisy forest, and
Už veet laskovo, i belye *berëzy* (R1)   the wind between the *birches*
Ronjajut tixij dožd' svoix almaznyx   Already winnows tenderly, and the
  slëz (PreR2)   white *birches*
I ulybajutsja skvoz' *slëzy* (R2).   Drop a soft rain of their diamond
                                                   tears
                                              And smile through the *tears.*

(38) Naprasno vy togda pribegnete k   In vain will you then resort to
  zloslov'ju—   scandal—
Ono vam ne pomožet *vnov'* (R1)   It will not help *again*
I vy ne smoete vsej vašej čërnoj   And you will not wash off with all
  krov'ju (PreR2)   your black *blood*
Poèta pravednuju krov' (R2).   The poet's righteous *blood.*

In (33) and (34) the proportions deal with antitheses, and this is supported by the inverted order of terms (positional contrast). In (35)–(37) all four related terms occur in the rhymed position resulting in a very obvious *figura etymologica.* The structure of (37) is devoid of contrasts; in (35) the first two lines couple phonetic and grammatical differences with a semantic opposition (*knowest / none can know*), but the pattern is lost in the next two lines. In (36) the shift is in the opposite direction: from a quasisynonymy ("love / call friend") to a contrast ("love / call enemy"), supported by a shift in sound ([ér]/[ájm]) and in stress (on the suffix / on the root) (cf. (30)). In (38) the proportion is less precise, but the phonetic difference ([-óv'ju]/[-óv']) is like that in example (35), lines 1 and 2, and is coupled with a semantic contrast ("*your base* blood / *the poet's noble* blood").

Probably the most intense and obvious type of lexical PRESAGE results from COMBINATION of proportions with multiple PreR2; see (39) and (40), where the device is laid bare:

(39) *Pense* (Pre₁R2) un peu quels *pensers*   *Think* a little what *thoughts* you *thought*
    (Pre₂R2) tu *pensais* (Pre₃R2) en   in childhood
    enfance (R1)   And what *thoughts* later from age to

Et quels *pensers* (Pre$_4$R2) depuis d'age
  en age tu as:
En *pensant* (Pre$_5$R2) ces *pensers*
  (Pre$_6$R2), *pensif* (Pre$_7$R2) tu
  penseras (Pre$_8$R2)
Que pour *penser* (Pre$_9$R2) à Dieu, tout
  est vain ce qu'on *pense* (R2).

age you have had:
In *thinking* these *thoughts, thoughtful,*
  you *will think*
That for *thinking* about God, all is
  vain that one *thinks.*

(40) *Ližet* (Pre$_1$R2) nogu, *ližet* (Pre$_2$R2)
    ruku,
   Ližet (Pre$_3$R2) v pojas, *ližet* (Pre$_4$R2)
    niže (R1).
   Kak kutenok *ližet* (Pre$_5$R2) suku,
   Kak kotenok košku *ližet* (R2).

Licks the foot, *licks* the hand,
Licks in the waist, licks *lower down,*
Like a pup *licks* a bitch,
Like a kitten *licks* a cat.

In both cases the polyptoton is rounded off with a contrast, semantic in (39) ('thinking of God *vs.* of all else'), positional in (40) (Subject—*licks*—Object / Subject—Object—*licks*).

2. RECOILS

2.1. RECOILS in PRESAGES

PRESAGE by definition contains an element of RECOIL (see §1.1), which is naturally reinforced when the structure displays contrasts. So far I have concentrated exclusively on the anticipatory relations between PreR2 and R2. As a matter of fact, PreR2 is sometimes also similar to R1—with interesting RECOIL implications. The "classical" pattern, diagrammed in (41), locates the punch-word X at the intersection of two unrelated PreXs: the *obligatory* PreX = R1 and *another* PreX = PreR2. An additional link between R1 and PreR2, diagrammed in (42) (usually phonetic, i.e., an "internal rhyme," e.g., the common [u:] in *do—woo* in ex. (1), or [−n] in *lang-syne—honey* in ex. (3)) results in an uninterrupted thread running through all three terms that highlights the unity of the structure and its twists (i.e., RECOILS).

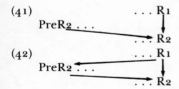

(41)
          . . . R1
PreR2 . . .
          . . . R2

(42)
          . . . R1
PreR2 . . .
          . . . R2

I will not dwell on the subtle effects of various interrelations between the similarities that link PreR2 to R1 and to R2. The most important overall effect is this: a link between R1 and PreR2 creates the impression that that is all there is to it, making a further "leg" (PreR2 → R2) improbable, i.e., unexpected, a SUDDEN TURN; thus it functions as a RECOIL.[8] The unexpectedness is the more striking the greater the difference between the two links. For example, in (1) the sound [u:] runs through all three terms, but an additional source of surprise is tapped when the *lexical* similarity is revealed on the "leg" between PreR2 and R2 (*woo'd/woo*); in (16) all three terms (in fact, all four rhymes) share [o], but only the last two have [z–vó]; in (17) all three have [l] and [o], and PreR2 is linked to R1 by paronomastic alliteration (*vole avec l'aquilon*); but then it turns out quite unexpectedly that *vole* predicts also the [v–] in *vallon*. The effect is, on the contrary, rather monotonous and straightforward when PreR2 has no "surplus foreshadowing" in store, for example, in sequences like *rozovéet* 'is rosy' (R1)—*véet* 'blows' (PreR2; in the middle of the line)—*govéet* 'fasts' (R2) (Kuzmin).

All such RECOILS, embedded in PRESAGES, add piquancy and unexpectedness but never destroy the effect of prediction, foreshadowing. In the following section I consider a totally different RECOIL technique.

2.2. *One Type of Lexical RECOIL*

This very particular pattern is singled out here for its relevance to the problem awaiting us in §3. Consider (43)–(48):

(43) Well, a chap must do somethin', I always tell *chaps* (R1),
For if a chap didn't a *chap* (AntiR2) would *collapse* (R2).

(44) For all things change: the darkness *changes* (R1),
The wandering spirits *change* (AntiR2) their *ranges* (R2), . . .

(45) The airless secret I strangle not to *share* (R1)
With all others as others *share* (AntiR2) the *air* (R2).

(46) I vzmaxnuv svoej levoj *nogoju* (R1),   And, having raised his left *leg*,
On pritopnul *nogoju* (AntiR2) *drugoju*   He stamped with his *other leg*.
(R2).

(47) Nouveau venu, qui cherches Rome en   Newcomer, [you] who are looking for
Rome (R1)   Rome in *Rome*

Et rien de Rome en Rome n'aperçois,	And nothing of Rome in Rome perceive,
Ces vieux palais, ces vieux arcs que tu vois,	These old palaces, these old arcs that you see,
Et ces vieux murs, c'est ce que *Rome* (AntiR2) on *nomme* (R2).	And these old walls, that's what *Rome* they *call*.

(48)	Meum est propositum in taberna *mori* (R1)	My plan is in the tavern *to die*
	Ut sint vina proxima *morientis* (AntiR2) *ori* (R2).	So that wines be close to the *moribund's* lips.

In all these cases,

1. AntiR2 is between R1 and R2;
2. AntiR2 is lexically similar to R1;
3. AntiR2 does not "prepare" R2: the similarity decreases, not increases, along the second "leg" of the route;
4. AntiR2 is not in the final position.

The overall effect is that of *one entity* (R1) *relinquishing its strong position for a weaker position* (where it appears as AntiR2), *while the next strong position, "vacated" by it, is occupied by a different entity* (R2).
This effect is clear only when

5. Semantically the text contains a RECOIL, i.e., is antithetic. Condition 5 is fulfilled in all of the above examples: compare *if . . . didn't . . . collapse* in (43), *change* in (44), *not* and *others* in (45), the "other leg" in (46), the opposition of 'real Rome' and its 'mere appearances and name' in (47) and, finally, the placing of the wines not merely close to the dying man, but exactly to his lips in (48).[9] Without the support of semantics the pattern can read differently; compare the straightforward (i.e., RECOIL–less) last line in (7)—in spite of the fact that *mirovoj* 'the world's' repeats R1 (*mir* 'world')— with (49), which also has no clear rhetorical opposition, either between *be* and *been* or between *been* and *thee:*

(49) There was a time I need not name,
  Since it will ne'er forgotten *be* (R1),
  When all our feelings were the same
  As still my soul hath *been* (AntiR2) to *thee* (R2).

The same RECOIL pattern and "relinquishing" effect, if somewhat subdued, are there even when the "receding" (RECOILING) word (I will call it PreAntiR2) and R1 are different lexemes, see exx. (50)–(54):

(50) Oh lady! blessed be that *tear* (PreAntiR2)
     It falls for one who cannot *weep* (R1);
     Such precious drops are doubly dear
     To those whose eyes no *tear* (AntiR2) may *steep* (R2).

(51)   . . . *rain* (R1).
     Few things surpass old wine; and they may *preach* (PreAntiR2)
     who please—the more because they *preach* (AntiR2) *in vain* (R2).

(52)   . . . *respect you*
                                            . . . *long* (R1)
                                . . . *suspect you* (PreAntiR2)
     Your smile soon convinced me *suspicion* (AntiR2) was *wrong* (R2).

(53)   . . . pale (R1)
     To rule in a land of *heather* (PreAntiR2)
     And lack the *heather* (AntiR2) *Ale* (R2).

(54) You ask me how Contempt who claims to sleep
     With every woman that has ever *been* (R1)
     Can still maintain that women are skin *deep* (PreAntiR2)?
     They never let him any *deep*er (AntiR2) *in* (R2).

An antithetic twist is evident in the last lines of all five examples.

To sum up, if PRESAGES prepare the final effect by "promoting" a PreR2 from its obscure role to that of R2, the lexical RECOILS we have considered frustrate expectations by "demoting" PreAntiR2 from its strong final position. Schematically these RECOILS are the exact opposite of (41):

(55)   . . . PreAntiR2
           . . . AntiR2   . . . R2

3. Pushkin's SUDDEN TURN

The second (and last) stanza of *Ja vas ljubil* . . . ("I loved you . . .") reads

(56) Ja vas *ljubil* bezmolvno, beznadežno,   I *loved* you speechlessly, hopelessly,
       To robost'ju, to revnost'ju *tomim* (R1)   Now by shyness, now by jealousy
       (Pre$_1$AntiR2);   *tormented;*
       Ja vas *ljubil* (Pre$_2$AntiR2) tak   I *loved* you so sincerely, so tenderly,
       iskrenno, tak nežno,   As God grant to you to be *loved by*
       Kak daj vam bog *ljubimoj* (AntiR2)   *another.*
       byt' *drugim* (R2).

The effect is one of both sophistication and profound simplicity, one of an ingenious *tour de force* and a straightforward truth. I think that, as is often the case with this type of effect, it is due to (*a*) a skillful COMBINATION of contrasting devices that is (*b*) pressed into the service of the theme.

3.1. *The* COMBINATION

The word *ljubil* "[I] loved" is repeated twice—before and after R1 (*tomim* "tormented")—and naturally claims the role of a PreR2 in a PRESAGE-cum-RECOIL pattern; see diagram in (42) and examples in (1), (2), (32), (34), and others, or, to cite Pushkin himself:

(57) Naprasno vospevat' mne vaši imeniny   In vain would I sing your saint's day
       Pri vsem userdii poslušnosti *moej* (R1);   However assiduous be *my* obedience;
       Vy *ne milee* (PreR2) v den' svjatoj   You are *no prettier* on the day of St.
       Ekateriny   Catherine
       Zatem, čto nikogda nel'zja byt' vas   Because one can never be *prettier* than
       milej (R2).   you.

Ljubil in (56) is phonetically ([í]) and prosodically ($\smile\acute{\ }$) similar to *tomim* and positionally opposed to it (just as *milee* 'prettier' is to *moej* 'my' in (57)), and so together they might start a zigzag (as in (42)) leading to the final R2 (cf. R2 *milej* 'prettier' in (57)). Moreover, since *ljubil* and *tomim* are also similar semantically ('passion') and grammatically (verb forms), and form a syntactic parallelism (see Chap. 9, §2.5), *ljubil* is, as it were, mirrored in *tomim,* suggesting a final fusion. Patterned on (57), the fusion would yield:

(58) Ja vas *ljubil* (Pre$_1$R2) bezmolvno,   I *loved* you speechlessly, hopelessly,
       beznadežno,   Now by shyness, now by jealousy
       To robost'ju, to revnost'ju *tomim* (R1);   *tormented;*
       Ja vas *ljubil* (Pre$_2$R2) tak iskrenno, tak   I *loved* you so sincerely, so tenderly,
       nežno,   *As no one was ever *loved.*
       *Kak ne byl nikogda nikto *ljubim* (R2)

The structure of (58) retains the paradox of (56): 'I loved you / no one can love you as much'; cf. Byron's *thou knowest / no one can know* in (35), or Pushkin's own "you are no prettier / one can never be prettier than you" (i.e., you are the prettiest possible). But the pattern employed gives it a superficial, "expectedly unexpected" ring of a mere courteous compliment. The structure of (56) is more complicated. It feigns to use the pattern of (57)–(58), only to set up an expectation and then frustrate it: the final rhyme is *not* the "unexpected" *ljubim*.

But there is even more to it. The form *ljubim* does, after all, appear in the text (*ljubimoj* 'loved by'), only it appears not in a rhyme (as R2) but before it, having conceded the final position to another word—in a typical RECOIL gesture of "demotion" (see diagram in (55)). The resulting structure is schematized in (59) (cf. the notation tacitly introduced in (56)):

(59)

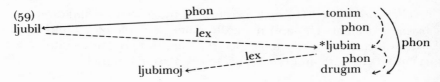

The dotted links (the reconstructed "deep" structure) are the exact sum total of (41) and (55), that is, of PRESAGE and RECOIL.[10]

3.2. *Thematic Relevance*

The spectacular reversal at the very end of the poem is not an artifice for artifice's sake. The way the "banal unexpectedness" of *ljubim* is not just rejected but, in a sense, sacrificed to and "trampled upon" by another, genuinely original rhyme fits in with the text's other structures (see Chap. 9). The "other" word that replaces the predictable rhyme is the word *drugim* 'another' (!). Thus it is original not only in terms of the frustrated expectation, but also semantically, as it conveys the idea of 'contrast, difference', and grammatically, as a noun (and not a verbal form like *tomim* and *ljubim–). All these originalities are well prepared and motivated.

1. It is characteristic of R2 in lexical RECOILS to express—iconically, in fact—the idea of 'difference, change, otherness' (cf. condition 5 in §2.2 and the very word "other" in ex. (46). The pronominal *drugim*

'another' is, moreover, a natural mirror-antithesis to *Ja* 'I', which opens the poem and two lines in (56).

2. Grammatically, the form *drugim,* unexpected as it is within our rhyming pattern, crowns a series of PRESAGES: *ničem* 'by nothing', an Instrumental of inanimate instrument used by animate agent *ja* 'I' in the last line of the preceding stanza; *robost'ju* 'by shyness', *revnost'ju* 'by jealousy', Instrumentals of inanimate agent; *drugim* 'by another', an Instrumental of animate agent.

3. Phonetically, *drugim* is prepared by *d–* in *daj* 'grant', by the velars in *kak* 'as' and *bog* 'God', by *–m* in *ničem* in a similar position (end of quatrain), by *–u–* in *ljubil, ljubimoj.*

4. Finally, and most important, the "self-sacrificial" rhyming gesture echoes the theme of 'restraining the banal passion and egoistic claims on the beloved' and the story of ceding her to the 'other' (see Chap. 9), who appears, as in a classical denouement, literally in the last word of the poem (Jakobson 1981).

Notes

Chapter 1. Eisenstein's Generative Poetics

1. Fairly precise results have been achieved by traditional literary criticism mainly at the "lower" levels of poetic structure such as rhyme, meter, line structure.

2. In the Montagu and Leyda translation (Nizhny 1979), the Russian word *patetičeskij* (lit., "characterized by or creating pathos") is translated as "epic." To be sure, the English "pathetic" would not do, but "ecstatic" seems a closer equivalent than "epic"; moreover, in other texts, Eisenstein, in fact, uses the word "ecstasy" as a synonym for "pathos."

3. In the Montagu and Leyda translation this passage reads: "But only a few would be engaged in taking his sword. . . ." My version is a more exact translation of the Russian original.

4. Montagu and Leyda (Nizhny 1979) have "yawning."

5. In one of his essays Eisenstein uses the word *vyiskivat'* 'to seek for': "*Representation* A and *representation.* B must be so sought for, that their *juxtaposition*—that is, the juxtaposition of *those very elements* and not of alternative ones—shall evoke in the perception and feelings of the spectator the most complete *image of the theme itself.*" (Eisenstein 1975b: 11)

6. The notion of actual elements in a poetic text as realizations of certain functions that are constant for the work in question or even for a whole genre, belongs to Viktor Shklovsky (1929: 125–42). It was most thoroughly developed by Vladimir Propp (1958). This study of functions is entirely in accord with the ideas of Eisenstein considered here [1967a: 374–76]; see also Chap. 2).

7. The problem of describing in formal terms the technique by which the components of a poetic text are made congruent was outlined by Propp (1958), see especially chap. 5, sec. A.

8. Cf. the formulation by L. A. Mazel' (1965: 240, 249–50) of two basic principles of the artistic effect of music: (1) "the principle of multiple and

concentrated effect" according to which "a significant artistic result is usually achieved not through any single device but through several devices directed to the same goal" and (2) "the principle of combination of functions, whereby the essential means, important 'solutions' normally carry several functions at once: for example, two distinct expressive functions, or else one expressive and one formal, purely technical; or, finally, some 'local' function vital for a particular moment in the work and another more general one which has significance for the whole, for connections 'at a distance'."

9. The problem of "reading out" the ideology from the facts, in particular on the basis of a given world view, did not escape the attention of Eisenstein: see ex. (4) and my comments about it and Eisenstein's lecture on the problems of composition (1968: 155–83).

Chapter 2. Deux ex machina

1. Cf. Eisenstein's remarks on how to use the etiquette of removing weapons at a banquet in order to have the hero disarmed by his enemies (Nizhny 1979: 49, and Chap. 1, § 2, ex. (5)).

2. In the Kursk region rich iron beds were found thanks to a magnetic anomaly.

3. *Soprjac' dalekovatye idei*—Lomonosov's felicitous formulation of a poetic principle, as popular in the Russian literary tradition as Coleridge's "reconciliation of opposites" is in the English.

Chapter 3. Thematic Invariance and the Concept of "Poetic World"

1. An explication along these lines was first offered in [1971] and its versions [1975a, b]. Cf. the treatment of the Bernanos world in Greimas 1970 and the tradition of "cluster criticisim," started by Spurgeon (1935).

2. Akhmatova's poem, in a sense, represents this method in Davie and Livingstone 1969, a selection of Pasternak criticism.

3. A more detailed description of Pasternak's PW is offered in Chap. 7.

4. On Pushkin's PW see Chap. 8.

5. More flexible ways of defining PW are offered in Chap. 10.

6. The problems involved in quotation and self-quotation are discussed, in PE terms, in [1976e, 1977b].

7. In fact, one of the striking facts about the process of subtraction, as illustrated in §§ 2 and 3, is the unexpectedly *slow speed* at which concreteness and specificity are lost. Even very abstract common denominators are quite rich and characteristic of the poet in question.

8. Description of changes can also be thought of as static by introducing the concept of the "theme of a period," which would be "invariant" for the

corresponding set of historically related texts but "local" in respect to the overall system of M̄*inv*.

9. In particular, a PW description cannot be accomplished in one go: it involves many feedback shuttles between individual texts and the emerging hierarchy of constructs.

10. Binomials will suffice only as long as we settle for the crude dichotomy of what is specific for the author and the rest. A more sophisticated representation would involve polynomials which add up the local theme, the invariant theme, the themes of the specific period in the author's oeuvre, of the genre, of the literary trend, of the epoch's convention, and of the national culture. Cf. the polynomials implicit in the statement of $\Theta loc,com$, $\Theta inv,com$, $\Theta spec$, and so on in Chap. 10, § 4.

11. Layout of this quotation is my own.

Chapter 4. The Somali Tale "A Soothsayer Tested"

1. I mean the myth's immediate, "open" message, not the hidden archaic oppositions reconstructed for it, e.g., by Lévi-Strauss (1963). Note that in Sophocles' tragedy, fate does triumph in the plot, borrowed from the myth, but as a character Oedipus proves an equal match for it. This is achieved by the tragedy's taking the form of an investigation, instituted and actively conducted by Oedipus and ending in a sentence passed and carried out by Oedipus himself.

2. Such a world view is most clearly stated in Leibniz's "monadology": "Every monad mirrors the universe, not because the universe affects it, but because . . . there is a 'pre-established harmony' between the changes in one monad and those in another, which produces the semblance of interaction," as in different clocks (Russell 1965: 565).

3. Cf. for instance: "Why did he [Bunin] choose terrifying, vulgar, turbid, and troublesome events to develop this theme of gentle breath? . . . A work of art always contains . . . a contradiction, a certain inner incongruity between the material and the form. The more brittle and hostile the material, the more suitable will it be for the author. The form given by the author to this material . . . is intended . . . to overcome [its] properties, to compel the horror to speak the language of gentle breath, and to induce the . . . turbidity of life to breathe and move like the cold spring wind" (Vygotsky 1971: 160).

4. The concept of "artistic discovery," defined as a novel COMBINATION of formerly separate and unrelated functions, was introduced in Mazel' 1966: 20–21, and further developed in Mazel' 1978.

5. The effect of 'meaninglessness" has also a compositional function: by failing to satisfy the reader's interest in the narrative, it makes him suppose hidden reasons. This intellectual suspense is resolved in the end, when the plot relationships turn out to be illusory and the profound truth is revealed.

6. On the effect of 'transfer to the frame', see Chap. 11, § 3.

7. An alternative solution (e.g., 'the protagonist is forced in the time of war to accomplish his plot tasks by military methods') is unacceptable, as it (*a*) presents the relation between 'actions' and 'phenomena' as causal, not "mystical," and (*b*) makes this relation immediately obvious.

8. A COMBINATION of a striking statement with the denouement of the plot is a widespread means of accomplishing SUDDEN TURNS in Somali stories; cf., e.g.: *A man took a foundling but did not feed him. A hyena came, caught the boy in its teeth, and started running away. The man ran after it, hit it with a stick, rescued the boy, and said to him: "True, I never fed you, but did I not now do you a service?" "No," said the boy, "it is just that you cannot stand anybody getting something in their mouth"* (for the Somali text see Moreno 1955). The plot pattern resembles our tale: here again a switch from bad to good behavior is at the same time a continuation of a previous stance (not to let others eat) and this becomes clear through a witty punch line. Incidentally, having the boy (and not the master, hyena, or the narrator) deliver it provides this very original observation with a psychological motivation: it sounds like a natural manifestation of the boy's "undernourishment complex" (= the theme of the story). Let us note that in "A Soothsayer Tested" the final remark does not reverse the course of events in favor of one of the alternatives (is the soothsayer, *resp.* the boy's master, bad or good?) but changes completely the whole perspective, saying, as it were: "In fact, all this does not matter: from the point of view of the world's design both alternatives are equally irrelevant." Evidently, this type of reversal is in complete accord with the theme of 'revelation about the meaning of life'.

Chapter 5. Deriving Poetic Structure: A Somali Proverb

1. See Permjakov 1968, 1979a,b; also see Zavarin and Coote 1979. For a brief exposition of Permjakov's paremiological model and a discussion of its relation to the 'Meaning—Text' model of language and to PE see [1978g].

2. The exposition is based on Permjakov 1968 (rather than on the more sophisticated and comprehensive 1979a version). Translations into English are mine, as are the formulations of the proverb's themes, simplified, but not altered in any significant way, from Permjakov 1968.

3. The deliberately faulty logic used in proving a more or less obvious truth (it certainly is advisable to think twice before speaking, but *not because* there are twice as many ears as mouths) is a subtle effect that cannot be analyzed here. It seems to belong with the "Passing-off" type of comical figures discussed in [1978a], [1980g] and in Chapter 6, cf. especially § 1.2 and note 7 on the "Passing-off" of 'natural death' for 'capital punishment'.

4. Natural apprehension over the arbitrariness of hypothetical formulations and a preference for 'text ↔ text' (rather than 'meaning or theme ↔

text') transformations are widely spread and can be clearly seen for instance in Padučeva 1977: 29ff.

5. This purely rhetorical, i.e., expressive, i.e., theme-preserving double negation is not to be confused with genuine negation, producing an opposite theme. Cf. (1) with Napoleon's *On s'engage et puis on voit* 'One gets involved and then one sees', i.e., 'One should act before thinking'.

6. This is, of course, established not through analysis of the proverb's text and structure, but by directly consulting native speakers (in this case Faadumo Shiikh Cali and Salax Xussein). The more intricate problem of the potential ambiguity of proverbs (and texts in general) cannot be taken up here; at any rate, PE proceeds from the principle "one reading, one description" (see Introduction and [1975b: 17ff.]).

7. The one does not necessarily exclude the other, cf. exx. (1h–j), consisting of paired illustrations with the symmetrical 'thought/action' split in each.

8. The order of steps in a derivation, as we recall (see Introduction), represents purely hierarchical relations in the thematic-expressive structure, making no claims about the order of the actual creative process.

9. About VAR*contr* in service of 'universality' see [1967c, 1977a] Chap. 4, §3, and Chap. 11, note 18. In fact, VAR*contr* sometimes functions as a reduced subtype of VAR*tot* (see Glossary).

10. I.e., CONCRETIZATIONS, since VARIATION is by definition a particular case of CONCRETIZATION; see Glossary.

11. In other words, formula (8) is a purely theoretical construct (dictated by the principle of minimal approximations): no actual text can embody (8) without embodying (9) as well.

12. These constructions are complex combinations of elementary EDs. On SUDDEN TURN see [1976a: 47], [1981a]. "Failure," like other comic figures, is a construction CONCRETIZING a thematic element—'comism'. This element should have been included in the theme, but for simplicity's sake I treat it as a purely expressive effect. On "Failure" and its links with S-TURN, see [1978a: 586–89].

13. Note that the positive version of the theme has been replaced with its negative counterpart for expressive reasons (dictated by S-TURN); cf. the discussion following ex. (2) and note 5.

14. On the role of 'enthusiastic involvement' and 'blindness, inability to understand' in comic "Failure" see [1978a: 587]; the discussion there is based on Bergson 1956 and Koestler 1967.

15. Such 'involving' is one of the expressive effects of ED REDUCTION; see [1976a: 51–52]; cf. Todorov 1968: 127. Note also that one ED (REDUCTION) is used here to implement (= CONCRETIZE) another (CONCORD).

16. COMBINATION is similar to REDUCTION in that it often deletes most of the different properties of the COMBINED objects and preserves only one occurrence of the properties they have in common. Schematically, COMBINA-

TION of ABCDE with ABFGH usually yields something like ABCDEFGH and not like ABABCDEFGH.

17. Note that REDUCTION and COMBINATION work, in a sense, in a direction opposite to that of AUGMENTATION, VARIATION, and CONTRAST. Namely, the former compress the structure expanded by the latter. This interplay of expansion and compression is a universal property of derivations: it reflects the artistic tendency to both maximally unfold the theme, infusing it with telling details and connotations, and to present it in a maximally compact form (cf. Chap. 6, § 4.2). This compression, however, never cancels the expressive results achieved by expansion; cf., for instance, the very scanty formula (7) with (16), which is as short but much richer in concrete detail.

18. On the expressive patterning of code-sphere elements in proverbs, see Jakobson's classic article (1973b).

19. On the 1 + 1 + 2 and 1 + 1 + 1 patterns of symmetry, cf. Chap. 9, § 2.1 and notes 5 and 6.

20. There is even more to the proverb's plot structure. It comes very close to blending a pair of separate examples (of the kind employed in most proverbs) into a single plot with a (presumably) common protagonist; three successive episodes; a build-up in scale from the first ('milk, [one person's] stomach pain') to the second ('words, [social conflicts], beating); a suspense (= narrative shift) in the first until after the second; a reversal-revelation type of denouement. Instead of generating this structural wealth from a deep design (DD), which should have appeared much earlier, the derivation "smuggles" the merging of the two subplots into the structure (in formula (16)) by means of an innocent COMBINATION, ostensibly aiming at economy. This is a typical instance of the "how-did-it-turn-out-so-well" inadequacy, discussed in the Postscript to Chap. 4.

21. Cf. the genre of *saddex* 'a three' (i.e., a triplet of maxims; see Moreno 1955) and that of poetic three-liners (see Andrezejewski and Lewis 1964: 134–45).

22. One might even speculate that $o + i \cong e$ is yet another echo of the 'summarizing' pattern.

23. Shifting within a sentence from one type of indefinite pronoun to another (which can appear in any order) is entirely normal in Somali (Abraham 1964: 158).

24. Note how the word *feedhahaaga* 'ribs-thy' both parallels and contrasts with its alliterative counterparts in the preceding lines (*fiiqsi* and *fiiro*): it also begins with an *f-* plus a long (but different) vowel and would end in a short vowel but for the possessive suffix and the definite article.

25. Cf. a similar (if less drastic) INCREASE in directness and concreteness in the end of La Rochefoucauld's maxim N313 [1978a: 582]. Note that the INCREASE in our proverb is not merely quantitative ('coming closer to the reader'), but rather qualitative—an unexpected switch from the framed, inner story to the outer, framing one (cf. Chaps. 4 and 11 on the effect of 'transfer to the frame').

Chapter 6. Pun and Punishment: The Structure of a Bertrand
Russell Aphorism

1. I have not had direct access to Russell's original text. I quote from Flew
1975: 5.
2. Generally speaking, the discovery of the theme and of the entire thematic-expressive structure of a text can be thought of as a procedure of "subtracting" EDs from T—an explicit and virtually formalizable procedure, in-
verse to that of derivation; see [1975b: 26ff.] and Glossary.
3. In discussing my analysis of Russell's wordplay (at the University of
Essex, December 1979), an English linguist went so far as to suggest a
quasimorphological (conjugational) relation between the two words—on the
pattern of *fly-flew!*
4. The "Shylock complex," and more generally, the situation of 'taking
literally', is an instance of the transactional "game" *Now I've Got You, You Son of
a Bitch,* whose underlying motive is seeking "justification for jealous rage"
(Berne 1972: 74–76). In addition to the already indicated relevant features of
this complex, I will mention 'pitilessness to the point of selflessness' (the
miser-usurer prefers the flesh of his debtor to thrice the sum of the debt!), cf.,
"in poker games . . . a NIGYSOB player . . . is more interested in the fact
that [the partner] is completely at his mercy than he is in . . . money-making"
(Berne 1972: 74).
5. For this view of humor I refer to the psychoanalytic tradition that goes
back to Freud's classic work on jokes (1969); cf. also Koestler 1967.
6. To substantiate my view of Russell's 'aggression' (in text (1) and elsewhere), I have compiled a brief dossier which the reader will find in the
Appendix to this chapter.
7. Cf. an old Jewish woman's rejoinder to her smart-aleck schoolboy
grandson's attempt to justify his unwillingness to take castor oil by contending
that the ancient Greeks, who created a great civilization, were unfamiliar with
castor oil: "Noo, but they all died, didn't they?" This is a typical instance of
'passing off "mandatory" death for a specific punishment' laid bare. For more
prestigious sources, cf. Aristotle's specification (in chap. 14 of his *Poetics*) of
the precise circumstances under which death should occur in order to make
sure the feelings of pity and fear (and not, say, repulsion) are evoked; cf.
similar remarks in a recent study: "Not just any death is preferable as the
pivot of tragedy . . . etc." (Gasparov 1979: 130).
8. Some of the successive numbered formulas are given in the text and
some in the figures.
9. Instead of deriving 'hate' from the 'militant stance', it could be included
in the theme, moreso because 'hate' seems to be an invariant motif in Russell
(see Appendix).
10. The concepts of "figure," i.e., a cluster of EDs that serves to CONCRET-
IZE a theme (e.g., 'ridicule', 'ecstasy', 'apprehension'), and of "comic figure" in
particular (= a figure CONCRETIZING 'ridicule') have been introduced in

Notes

[1978a: 583–89]. The comic figures "Caricature," "Failure," and "Passing-off" have also been described there, with special reference to a La Rochefoucauld maxim.

11. "Caricature through *even*" is based on CONTRAST through unfavorable circumstances (abbr.—CONTR*even*). "Caricature through extremity" can be exemplified by the joke about a drunkard who asked for water only when a fire broke out; another variant: even when there was a fire he didn't ask for water. The two versions illustrate two different subtypes of the "Caricature": (*a*) 'X changes only in an extreme situation'; (*b*) 'X does not change even in an extreme situation'. "Caricature through long duration" exhibits similar subtypes.

Since "Caricature" shows a tendency toward maximum hyperbolization, 'extremity' is often CONCRETIZED as 'death', and 'duration', as 'lifetime'. Cf. the "Caricature through death" in Sheridan's *School for Scandal*, where Sir Peter Teasle says that his brother died exclusively for the pleasure of burdening him with his daughter's upbringing. An example of "Caricature through death" as applied to the theme 'stupidity, obstinacy' is provided by the scene from Molière's *Le mariage forcé*, where the philosopher Pancrace prefers to die rather than to admit that one should say *the form* (and not *the figure*) *of a hat*. An example of "Caricature through a lifetime" as applied to 'stupidity' is the witticism *Once a thought came to his mind, but on finding no one there it left*.

Since 'lifetime' and 'death' are semantically related, there exists a standard COMBINATION of the maximum degrees of the two "Caricatures." The meaning-preserving transformation 'during one's lifetime' → 'until one's death' provides the formula: 'X does not change during his lifetime and even (variant: changes only) at the moment of death'. Cf. the reaction of a contemporary wag to the death of the Grand Duke Sergej Aleksandrovič, killed by the bomb of the revolutionary terrorist Kaljaev: *Velikij knjaz' vpervye v žizni poraskinul mozgami* 'For the first time in his life something blew the Grand Duke's mind' (English equivalent suggested by Daniel Laferrière). Our witticism (1) is based on another subtype of the standard COMBINATION of the "Caricatures"—'X does not change even at the moment of death'.

12. Situations of this kind are based on a special variety of CONTR*even*. The common CONTR*even* can be exemplified by situations like *Fools will be fools; He who is born a fool is never cured;* etc., where what the fools wish is of no consequence (they may well wish to be cured—the point is 'incurability', not 'obstinacy').

13. SUDDEN TURN is a type of RECOIL that underlies dramatic turns in plots. For more detail see [1976a, 1981a], Glossary, and Chap. 1.

14. The function of the figure "Punishment through wish fulfillment" is to ridicule 'stupidity'. This figure belongs to a larger set of "Punishments" whose instructive character is expressed by a similarity between 'guilt' and 'retribution': "Punishment by eternalizing the culprit's habits" (cf. the Grasshopper, who, in La Fontaine's fable "La cigale et la fourmi," spent the summer singing and when she asked for bread, was sent away to dance);

"Punishment by eternalizing something connected with the guilt" (when Midas preferred Pan's playing to Apollo's, the latter retaliated by giving him ass's ears); etc. In connection with the "objective" variant of "Punishment" it should be noted that the correlation of 'vengefulness" with ethical censorship may assume a variety of forms (recall Shylock, on the one hand, and "Noo, but they all died" on the other). In a novel by Alexsandr Grin, *Alye parusa* ("The scarlet sails"), Longren avenges himself upon the usurer who had refused credit to his wife (as a result, she died of hunger) by refusing to help him out of the water when he is drowning.

15. That "Passing-off" is, so to speak, operative within other figures means that it actually precedes them in the derivation. I placed it, however, on the same hierarchical level with the rest, so as not to complicate the description.

16. In other words, the initial term of "Failure" (= of "Punishment") COMBINES with one of the two "Caricatures" whereas the final one, i.e., the "punishment" proper, COMBINES with the other. A similar symmetrical pattern underlies La Rochefoucauld's maxim no. 313 (see [1978a]).

Chapter 7. 'Window' in the Poetic World of Boris Pasternak

1. See Levin 1966: 200–201; note that in Mandelstam's "Stone" the word "window" occupies the thirty-second place (ibid.).

2. Here are some examples from the novel (Pasternak 1958). "Son and father-in-law went through Mikulitsyn's dark study. It had an enormous window the length of the wall, overlooking the ravine. Earlier, while it was still light, the doctor had noticed the view from it over the gully and the plain beyond. . . . At the window stood a draftsman's table which also took up the width of the wall. . . . Now, as they went through, Yurii Andreievich once more thought with envy of the window with its vast view, the size and position of the table, and the spaciousness of the well-furnished room. . . . 'What a wonderful place you have! What a splendid study, it must be a perfect place to work in, a real inspiration'" (p. 275). "Once again, as so long before, Yurii Andreievich stood spellbound in the door of the study, so spacious and comfortable with its large, convenient table by the window" (p. 430). "The stillness that surrounded Yurii Andreievich breathed with happiness and life. The lamplight fell softly yellow on the white sheets of paper and gilded the surface of the ink inside the inkwell. Outside, the frosty winter night was pale blue. To see it better, Yurii Andreievich stepped into the next room, cold and dark, and looked out of the window. The light of the full moon on the snow-covered clearing was as viscid as white of egg or thick white paint. The splendor of the frosty night was inexpressible. His heart was at peace. He went back into the warm, well-lit room and began to write" (p. 436).

3. The content of this chapter should—ideally—comprise an entry for 'window' in an ideal poetic dictionary of Pasternak. How would such a dictionary, if compiled, compare with actually existing dictionaries of poets'

languages? Normally such dictionaries are compiled as frequency counts, thesauri, or concordances. All of these differ from linguistic dictionaries in that no semantic correlates are offered for the words in them (in the lexicography of natural languages these correlates take the form of either translations, as in bilingual dictionaries, or of definitions, as in unilingual explanatory dictionaries or dictionaries of slang or technical or foreign terms). The introduction of the concept of the poetic world permits a more or less rigorous answer to the question concerning what semantic correlates might be assigned to words of the poet's language. As I see it, the dictionary of a poet could be constructed as an interpretation of (all or the most significant of) his words and images in terms of the invariant motifs of his poetic world. The same words would obviously be defined differently for different poets, and these definitions would also be partly different from those that the words have in dictionaries of natural languages. The compilation of such poets' dictionaries is, in my view, one of the fundamental tasks of poetics. I am aware, of course, of the colossal scale of such a project, which presupposes that the dictionary compiler already has at his disposal a detailed description of the poet's poetic world. Hence work on such dictionaries should be seen not so much as a goal of research in poetics but rather as an appropriate method.

4. For a systematic presentation of my reading of Pasternak's PW see [1980e], cf. also [1980b, c, k, 1982a,g]. This reading owes much to Faryno 1970, Jakobson 1969/1935, Yu. Lotman 1978/1969, Nilsson 1978/1959, Plank 1966, 1972, Sinyavsky 1969/1965.

5. To make clear the difference between "pure" COMBINATION and COMBINATION into a construction let us take a closer look at one of the examples: *I treplet rečku vetkoj po ščeke* 'And [the wind] pats the river on the cheek with a twig.' Out of the three major varieties of contact—(a) metaphor 'the surface of the river = its cheek'; (b) the wind's 'touching' the surface with a twig; (c) the wind's 'lovingly contacting [patting]' the river's cheek—metaphor (a) is "purely" COMBINED with (b) but forms a construction with (c): no cheek—no patting. On the other hand, one can imagine plainer, but still perfectly poetical and Pasternakian versions, e.g.*"The wind touches the river's cheek with a twig" (the same "pure" COMBINATION of metaphor and 'touching', without the fusion of metaphor with 'loving contact'); *"The wind touches the river's surface with a twig" (only 'touching', without metaphor, which it does not depend on).

6. This typically Pasternakian emotion is captured by Anna Akhmatova in her poem "Boris Pasternak" (which pithily summarizes many of the features of his poetry): "Who lost his way a couple of paces from home, / Where the snow comes up to one's waist and one is done for" (Davie and Livingstone 1969: 152–53).

7. In the Afterword to *Safe Conduct*, written in the form of a letter to Pasternak's favorite poet, Rilke, he repeats the same construction, which consists of an everyday dining table, a landscape outside the window, and contact

with something sublime and grandiose which comes in from somewhere far away or from the sky: "Since the morning an unlaid table had been standing in the hall; I was sitting at it and pensively picking up fried potatoes from the frying pan, and, hesitating as it fell and seeming to be doubtful about something, outside the window the snow was coming down. . . . At that moment there was a ring at the street doorbell, I opened it and was handed a letter from abroad. . . . I suddenly stumbled on the . . . postscript which said that somehow or other you know of me. I moved back from the table and got up. This was the second shock of the day. I walked over to the window and burst into tears. I would not have been more surprised if someone had told me that they were reading me in heaven" (Pasternak n.d.). Note, in addition to various 'contacts', the varieties of 'magnificence': 'shock', 'tears'; the entire fragment looks like a plain prose rendering of a Pasternak poem.

8. Cf. in *Doctor Zhivago:* "They loved each other, not driven by necessity, by the "blaze of passion" often falsely ascribed to love. They loved each other because everything around them willed it, the trees and the clouds and the sky over their heads and the earth under their feet. Perhaps their surrounding world, the strangers they met in the street, the wide expanses they saw on their walks, the rooms in which they lived or met, took more delight in their love than they themselves did. Ah, that was just what had united them and had made them so akin! Never, never, even in their moments of richest and wildest happiness, were they unaware of a sublime joy in the total design of the universe, a feeling that they themselves were a part of that whole, an element in the beauty of the cosmos. This unity with the whole was the breath of life to them" (Pasternak 1958: 501).

9. The 'hole in a fence' clearly attracts Pasternak as a ready-made object which combines an 'aperture in the wall' (i.e., yet another variant of window, door, garden gate, and so on) with the motif, which is so crucial for him, of 'everyday, unpretentious, provincial life' (cf. his penchant for courtyards, backyards, "women in cheap workaday clothes," and so on). "Only the ordinary transformed by genius is wondrous" (Pasternak 1958: 285). The linking of the ordinary and the genius, the simple and the great, is one of the aspects of the contact between the insignificant "here and now" and the infinite "out there."

Chapter 8. Pushkin's Invariants

1. The first to do so was Geršenzon (1919, 1922, 1926), whose formulation of the problem seems strikingly explicit and modern even today (see Chap. 3, § 1, item 5), however mystic his tone. Several invariants were discovered by Blagoj (1931: 196–244). A structural approach to the problem was originated by Jakobson (1975) (see Chap. 3, § 1, item 3). My description follows in many respects these works and also: Bicilli 1926; Bočarov 1974; Yu. Lotman, 1977;

Xodasevič 1924, although not all cases of indebtedness or affinity are indicated in the references.

2. For a more leisurely presentation see [1976d, 1979g].

3. To be sure, this alternative reading is not ungrammatical.

4. Valuable observations about Pushkin's linguistic invariants are contained in Jakobson 1981, 1975, 1976. On the PE approach to the description of code-sphere motifs see [1980k, 1982a,c].

Chapter 9. Invariants and the Structure of a Text: Pushkin's "I loved you . . . "

1. To be sure, the present exposition does not measure up to this ideal. The artistic wealth of the poem and limitations of space rule out a full-fledged derivation that would account for both the poem's expressiveness (along the lines of Chaps. 5 and 6) and its "Pushkinianity" (in terms of Chaps. 3 and 8). As a compromise, I try to cover the most essential points of the structure and I do so, roughly, in the order a derivation would—proceeding in concentric circles (theme, deep design, deep structure, surface structure; cf. Chap. 6). Repetitions are, unfortunately, inevitable: even the most abstract levels of the structure have to be justified—for the reader's sake—by direct reference to their textual manifestations. For a minute analysis of the poem's every level see [1976d (2)].

2. On Pushkin's invariants see Chap. 8; in connection with theme (2) see especially § 5.

3. On this type of correlation between Θ*loc* and the author's invariant motifs see Chap. 3, end of § 5., and Chap. 10, § 2.1.5. The similarity between the local theme (1) and the typically Pushkinian M̃*inv* in (2) accounts not only for Pushkin's treatment of the theme but also for its very choice.

4. A convincing way to make sure there *is* an intensification is by switching around the stanzas. In this case it will result in a distinct "dying down" effect, which incidentally is not out of place in Pushkin's PW: switches between 'passion, movement, etc.' and 'impassivity, immobility, etc.' occur in either direction; see Chap. 8.

5. On the expressive potential of the "fragmentative" pattern 4 + (2 + 2), as well as of the "summative" (2 + 2) + 4 pattern, see Mazel' and Cukkerman 1967: 393–44. For cases of inexact matching (like 0.4 + [0.3 + 0.3]) see § 2.1, note 6 and also Chap. 5, § 6.

6. The pause which separates it is brought about by the syntax (end of clause), the caesura, and the stress on the second ictus causing the line "to disintegrate . . . into 2 foot and 3 foot iambs" (Taranovsky 1971: 421). The leitmotif thus isolated does not occupy exactly one-half of the line—the ratio is 4:6 feet. As a result, the ensuing rhythmic fragmentation is inexact, too: 0.4 + (0.3 + 0.3), rather than 0.5 + (0.25 + 0.25).

7. Cf. Chap. 11, § 2, especially §§ 2.2–2.4.

8. The "dampening" point of view of *byt' možet* "perhaps" is discussed in §
2.2; what is relevant right now is the way the parenthesis undermines the
intonational unity.

9. Parallel constituents make division more equal and thus more explicit;
in this poem this effect is saved for the corresponding line of stanza 2: . . .
bezmolvno, beznadežno.

10. I mean the 'breakthrough' achieved in line 7, see § 1.2.

11. This detached third-person view of the speaker's own suffering self is
none other than a typical linguistic manifestation of 'superior peace', cf.
formulas (3), (5), and (7), "prescribing" recourse to this motif, and its discussion in Chap. 3, (27)–(33), and Chap. 8, (42)–(43).

12. I.e., the '"I" who loved' and the '"I" who speaks about that love' are
two different subjects (see Todorov 1968: 121). The consistent development
of the "splitting" effect in stanza 1 helps bring out this expressive potential of
the past tense, and it is perceived, through the subsequent repetitions of the
leitmotif *Ja vas ljubil*, as an essential part of its meaning.

13. This 'superiority' reaches its peak in stanza 2, where "I" gives orders—
grammatically, at least—to all three participants in the love conflict and even
to God himself. The "three- (sometimes four-) level pattern," often with the
detached "I" located "in the neighborhood of God," is a recurrent subtype of
'superior peace', discussed in detail in [1979g; 1980d]; cf. some of the examples mentioned in note 11.

14. *Styk* and *kol'co* are terms used by Osip Brik and after him by Žirmunskij
(1975: 451).

15. This cumulative effect is reinforced by the artfully organized rhythmic
development from *bezmolvno* 'speechlessly' to *beznadežno* 'hopelessly': the ‿́‿
motif is "stretched out" into -‿́‿.

16. Thus, the climactic sixth line can be said to summarize the rhyme
vocalism of the poem (see (6)).

17. Indeed, if the seventh line had been attached syntactically to lines 5–6,
the effect would have been that of a 'bold breakthrough of passion' into the
second half of the stanza—consider the following alternative solution:

Ja vas ljubil bezmolvno, beznadežno,	I loved you speechlessly, hopelessly,
To robost'ju, to revnost'ju tomim,	Now by shyness, now by jealousy
Tak plamenno, tak iskrenno, tak	tormented,
nežno, . . .	So ardently, so sincerely, so
	tenderly, . . .

Or the effect might have been achieved, say, by switching the rhyme scheme
from *a b a b* to *a b b a* (something like *tomim—beznadežno—nežno—drugim*). This
would delay the appearance of the rhyme to line 5 until the eighth line and
thus clearly upset the inertia and the midstanza boundary.

18. Slonimskij (1959: 120ff.) was the first to draw attention to this ana-
coluthon. He believes that it expresses an 'outburst (*proryv*) of an altruistic
emotion'. In my opinion, on the contrary, it is the 'egotistic emotions' that

'show through' here, whereas the 'altruistic self-denial' plays the role of the 'restraining veil or shroud', expressed iconically by the oblique constructions.

19. In PE terms, such "poetic uniqueness" is accounted for by the simple fact that there is *strictly one* ready-made object capable of covering the given set of expressive functions, and hence only one—unique—artistic solution (cf. Chap. 6, beginning of § 5).

Chapter 10. Comparing Poetic Worlds

1. The following descriptions of PWs are used without further reference: Akhmatova—[1979a]; Cvetaeva—[1979b,c]; Fet—Buxštab 1970: 76–160; Mandel'štam—[1979i]; Okudžava—[1979e]; Ovid—[1962c, 1967c, 1980f]; Pasternak—[1978f, 1980e] and Chap. 7; Pushkin—[1979g] and Chap. 8.

2. On various correlations between Θloc and Θinv, in particular, on their neutralization, see [1976c: 39; 1977b: 91ff.] and Chap. 3, § 5.

3. Past 1 is *Iz suever'ya* ("Out of superstition"), Past 2, *Nikogo ne budet v dome* . . . ("There will be no one in the house . . ."); Ok1, *Mne nužno na kogonibud' molit'sja* . . . ("I must worship somebody . . ."); Ok 2, *T'moju zdes' vsë zanavešeno* . . . ("Everything here is curtained with darkness . . .").

4. To my knowledge, so far this has passed unnoticed by students of Russian poetry.

5. Pasternak, as a translator of Shakespeare and other Western poets, always insisted on the principle of free interpretation. He begins his poem portraying a fellow poet ("To Anna Akhmatova") with the following declaration: "It seems to me, that I will pick the words, / Similar to your primordiality. / But if I make a mistake,—I don't care two straws about it. / All the same I won't part with the mistake." (Akhmatova's portrayal of Pasternak's PW [see Chap. 3, § 1] is, on the contrary, very accurate.)

6. In part—because, as we recall from § 4, common details can also derive, in different authors, from different motifs and themes. In nonintertextual cases it is even theoretically possible that similar text elements will involve no common elements at the level of themes, i.e., that they can be fully accounted for by the respective different central themes. In intertexts, however, a common element is always provided by $\Theta spec$, which reflects the fact of one poet's commenting on another.

7. A linguistic analogy to different derivations of similar motifs is, of course, the derivation of homonymous sentences from different deep structures in generative grammar (the classic example is *They are flying planes*). In that case the intertextual replacement of derivations can be likened to the clash of two possible readings of a sentence in a pun.

8. In terms of the Class I–Class II dichotomy intertextual themes like (34), of course, come under the latter heading: they are "about literature" rather than "about life." They could, however, form a class by themselves, if a more detailed, trichotomous division were to be set up: Class I themes—"referen-

tial" messages about life; Class II themes—"code-oriented" messages about linguistic and literary competence and conventions; Class III themes—"inter-textual" messages about other texts (see [1982c,j]).

Chapter 11. How to Show Things with Words: On the Iconic Representation of Themes by Expression-Plane Means

1. In other words, we have to do here with what we call CONCR via EDs (in this case, via REPETITION), see Introduction, Glossary, and also [1974a: 29ff.; 1976b: 228ff.]; for the iconic correspondence between REPETITION and 'monotony' cf. note 13.

2. A more refined instance of a similar code sphere CONCR of 'only' can be observed in Afanasij Fet's lyric *Tol'ko v mire i est' čto tenistyj*. . . . ("In the entire world there is only the shadowy . . .") with its theme 'for the poet in the whole world there exists only his beloved'. In fact, four out of the eight lines almost *verbatim* repeat the first; there are only two different rhymes; the rhythmical, phonetic, etc., effects are deliberately monotonous; the space described is enclosed. (These considerations were prompted by M. L. Gasparov's oral discussion of the poem.) Cf. also Pasternak's poem *Nikogo ne budet v dome* . . . ("There'll be no one in the house . . .") in which a similar code-sphere CONCR of 'only' is evident in the lines: *Tol'ko kryši, sneg i, krome / Kryš i snega,—nikogo* 'Only the roofs, the snow and besides / The roofs and the snow no one'.

3. Note how this theme and a fairly moderate treatment of the form of limerick in (3) differ from the extremist theme and design of Ben Jonson's text (2): in (3) the form is preserved, in (2), destroyed.

4. Formula (4) consists exclusively of the elements expressed iconically (see items 1–7, preceding the formula) and arranged in an intuitively plausible way. In fact, this formula is not the theme, i.e., the most general thematic invariant, of text (3), but rather a paraphrase of its deep poetic structure.

5. I have in mind here the twofold orientation of poetic language toward both (*a*) destruction of the automatized conventional relation between the signifier and the signified (Shklovsky 1965; Jakobson 1973a: 208) and (*b*) restoration of similarity between the two, which compensates for the arbitrariness of the relation (Genette 1968: 150). For an interesting comparison of the two principles and the respective definitions of the poetic function see Smirnov 1977: 23–24.

6. The discussion in § 1.2 is partly prompted by Ètkind 1970: 177. Note the similarity of (8a) and (3), where the theme 'only' is expressed by filling three lines with repetitions of one and the same word (cf. note 2). Characteristically enough, rule (8b) is especially active in the last line of the stanza (*Ostanovil* 'Stopped' marks the final stop); correspondingly, in the third line (*Zagorodil* 'Blocked'), it is rule (8a) that comes to the fore. To hazard a tempting guess, I suggest that the very application of rule (8) to the *shorter lines in the stanza* also has a thematic function: 'blocking the gorge at its narrowest point (in a "tight

place between the cliffs") <u>CONCR</u> one word takes up an entire short line (there being longer lines in the stanza)'. This calligram stands out quite clearly on a printed page owing to the central position of the shorter lines, so that the stanza presents an iconic image of an archetypal gorge narrowing down toward its base.

7. Cf. Jakobson 1976, McCune 1977, and [1981b].

8. On such inexact summative patterns, cf. Chap. 5, § 6.

9. Incidentally, of all the eight hemistichs only one other exhibits the properties 1 and 2, namely *prazdnyj derža čerepok*, where, however, the overall thematic-expressive situation is altogether different.

10. Both the summative pattern and the effects of 'dynamization by stretching' and 'containment by shrinking' (which are mentioned in item 2) occur also in "I loved you once . . .", the former in line 6, the latter in lines 5 and 7; see Chap. 9.

11. Cf. the basically identical role played by phonetic similarity in Pasternak's lines from *Ballada* ("The ballad"), . . . *kak budto čto obrel, / Obryvy donizu obšarja* '. . . as if [he] had acquired something, / Having combed the cliffs down [to the bottom]', where "the transmission, along the fragment, of the cluster *ob-r* corresponds to the identity of the movement's subject, water" [1980e: 236]. One is further tempted to suggest that the absence of stress in the cluster *ur-n* in the word *uroniv*, as well as its discontinuity, function as an iconic CONCR of the 'disintegration of the broken urn'.

12. For more detail see [1974a: 32ff.]. Curiously enough, Pushkin's fairly precise translation (*Dobryj sovet* ["Good advice"], 2: 129; see Ètkind 1973: 207ff.) ignores the code-sphere construction under consideration: Parny's thirteen-line poem is translated by three quatrains and throughout the rhyming is *a b a b* instead of *a b b a*.

13. Themes other than 'postponing the end', too, can well be expressed by adding "extra" lines with the same rhyme, for instance, 'monotony, absence of change'. Cf. Zinaida Gippius's eighteen-line poem *Odnoobrazie* ("Monotony") (1895), which contains only two different rhymes arranged in the following way: *A A b A A b A A b A A A b A A A A b*. First, a rhyming pattern is established: to one masculine rhyme correspond two contiguous feminine rhymes (conveying 'monotony'); then an extra feminine rhyme and finally two extra feminine rhymes are added ('the monotony increases'). Furthermore, it is in these same "extra" lines that the 'monotony' is directly CONCRETIZED in the referential sphere as well: the twelfth line reads: *O, esli by xot' ten' dviženʹja* 'Oh, if there were at least a shadow of movement!'; the seventeenth reads: *I vse navek bez izmenenʹja* 'And everything forever without change'. A similar theme is expressed in much the same way in Pasternak's *Vysokaja bolezn'* ("The lofty malady"): there are several long sequences that contain only two or three different rhymes—a device laid bare by the poet (*Ešče nudnej čem rifmy èti . . .* 'More boring still than these rhymes . . .'). Note the natural affinity between sequences of identical rhymes expressing 'monotony' and code-sphere CONCR of 'only, nothing except' (cf. note 2).

14. The fact that the whole of the second line is occupied lends the 'continuation' a certain stability, cf. rule (8) and comment 3 on (3), which also involve the 'filling of a whole'; by way of contrast, cf. rule (26c).

15. *Zamestitel'nica* is aptly discussed by Ju. Lotman (1968); for my comments on his analysis and on the poem itself see [1978d: 420–21].

16. Cf. § 1.3 (comment 2). A COMB of 'relay' with 'reaching over a boundary' is also attested in the fragment mentioned in note 11, as well as in *Zamestitel'nica* (where the rhyme in -óčet is carried over from the first stanza into the second.

17. Rule (28) is a particular case of rule (21): the identity of an object is in both rules CONCRETIZED through the continuation of one and the same sentence, and in rule (28) it is additionally CONCRETIZED through phonetic similarity.

18. This expressive pattern is a particular case of VARIATION through all; see Glossary and [1977a: 139–43]; cf. also Chap. 5, note 9.

19. For a detailed analysis of the poem see [1979i]. As regards the 'transfer's' potential for expressing 'complete annihilation', it is a typical function of this construction in jokes. Cf.

Kosygin proposes to Brezhnev to permit Jews to emigrate. Brezhnev objects: "First we let the Jews go, then the Tatars will apply, after them others, and before long only the two of us will be left." Kosygin: "You speak for yourself. I won't be left here with you, I'll go too."

Especially remarkable is the way 'completeness' is stressed by the 'transfer'. The underlying rule 'all' $\xrightarrow{\text{CONCR}}$ 'even X' $\xrightarrow{\text{CONCR}}$ 'something taken for granted' $\xrightarrow{\text{CONCR}}$ 'part of the frame' is based on frame's being taken for granted (see (33a)) and on the expressive construction CONTRAST of the "even X" type [1976a: 40, 42]. The resulting code-sphere expression of the theme ('everything, even the frame') echoes its referential counterpart ('everybody, even the rulers').

Chapter 12. On the Preparation of the Final Rhyming Word: PRESAGE and RECOIL in Rhyming

1. "Dynamic" orientation toward a final result, a closure, is a constitutive feature of the material under discussion. This approach is alien to Russian academic tradition (cf. Žirmunskij 1975: 235–432), which sees such patterns as nondirected alliterations. The two exceptions I know are Štokmar (1958), who, however, assumes that the patterns he so thoroughly describes are the invention of Mayakovsky, and Saljamon (1971), who devotes himself exclusively to one type of phonetic foreshadowings. In Western poetics recent interest in closure produced such major contributions as Hymes 1960, with its concept of "statistically summative" words, Masson 1976, and Smith 1968

Notes

(especially pp. 158–71), to which my approach is very close. Some of the techniques discussed were consciously elaborated by early French poets and described in contemporary treatises on versification, see Elwert 1970.

2. Barbara Herrnstein Smith speaks of "something like mathematical ratios, where the reader can easily 'solve for x' . . ." (1968: 169).

3. A third dimension is often the grammatical one, cf. ex. (6), where *be* prepares the form (infinitive) of R2 = *hear and see*, or ex. (1), where *do* prepares the active voice of *woo*.

4. On the way enumerations and other constructions express themes like 'many, all', see [1977a] and Chaps. 4 and 5.

5. The PRESAGE in ex. (15) is no less strong for it, as *(ne) videt'* '(not) to see' / *nenavidet'* 'to hate' is as banal a rhyme in Russian poetry as *love/dove* in English or *amour/toujours* in French. This "vocabulary-of-rhymes" dimension in PRESAGES is one of the "codes" (in the sense of § 1.1) not considered here.

6. 'Paradox, antithesis' is not the only type of theme conveyed iconically by palindromes or milder inversions. Cf. the following

. . . *encore* (R1),	. . . *still,*
Détache ton amour des faux biens *que*	Detach your love from the false values
tu perds (Pre₁R2)	*you lose,*
Adore (Pre₂R2) ici l'écho *qu'adorait*	Adore here the echo *adored* by
(Pre₃R2) *Pythagore* (R2).	Pythagoras.

Here the inverted anagram of R2 = *Pythagore* in Pre₁R2 *que tu perds* (supported by *encore* and *qu'adorait*) is motivated by the 'echo' theme.

7. Themes coupled with stress shift are sometimes less paradoxical, cf.:

Si ponas Ypolitum *hodie* (PreR2) *Papie*	If you place Hippolytes *today* in *Pavia*
(R1)	He will not be an Hippolytes the next
Non erit Ypolitus in sequenti *die* (R2)	day.

Here the shift of stress to the "next" syllable (*hódie* / *sequenti díe*) seems to express iconically the 'transition to the *next* day'.

8. Under certain conditions close ties between R1 and PreR2 completely obliterate further links and expectations. Cf. M. L. Gasparov's observations (in a private letter to me, February 13, 1979): "A. Fet's poem

Zaigrali (A) na *rojali* (A)	They started *playing* the *piano*
I pod zvon cužix *napevov* (X)	And to the ringing of alien *tunes*
Zavertelis', *zapljasali* (A)	There started turning, *dancing*
Izumitel'nye *kukly* (X) . . .	Marvelous *dolls* . . .

has a refinedly unusual rhyme pattern: instead of *X A X A* it is rhymed *A X A X*, rhymes in *odd* lines only. I am sure that many readers failed to notice it was rhymed verse at all. The internal rhyme in the first line (. . . (A) . . .A/ . . . X/ . . . A/ . . . X), seems not to strengthen, but to further weaken the percep-

272

tion of the subsequent rhyme A, creating the impression that what matters here is the interplay of irregular alliterations, and even if they involve canonical positions, they do so accidentally."

9. On the role this motif plays in the structure of Archpoet's *Confession*, see [1980g].

10. Joseph Brodsky seems to play with this effect in the Sixth of his "Twenty sonnets to Mary Stuart," a pastiche that lays bare the structure of Pushkin's "Ja vas ljubil . . . ." The sequence of exaggerated allusions culminates in a spectacular trampling on a "wrong" rhyme:

sej žar v krovi, širokokostnyj *xrust* (R1),	this heat in the blood, the broad-boned
čtob plomby v pasti plavilis' ot žazdy	*crackle,*
kosnut'sja—"*bjust*" (AntiR2)	so that the fillings in my muzzle
začerkivaju—*ust* (R2)!	should smelt out of the thirst
	to touch your—"bust" I cross out—
	lips.

To be sure, AntiR2 = *bjust* 'bust' is not a lexical variant of R1 = *xrust* 'crackle' and thus the RECOIL pattern is not exactly the same as in Pushkin. Also, thematically the unacceptability of *bjust* and the resulting sublimation is much cruder: not 'another instead of me', but 'lips instead of breasts'. Yet, this crudeness is in harmony with Brodsky's principle of laying the device bare. As a result, the pattern realized in Pushkin by a subtle interplay of rhyme PRESAGES and frustrations is spelled out by Brodsky, who speaks of crossing out one rhyme in favor of another.

Glossary

A. Author.

AntiX. The first term of the RECOIL sequence (i.e., the PreX of RECOIL).

AUGM. See *AUGMENTATION*.

AUGMENTATION: AUGM. Substitution for X of its "big" variant X!, exceeding X in some respect (size, intensity, etc.): $X \xrightarrow{\text{AUGM}} X1$; e.g., 'love' $\xrightarrow{\text{AUGM}}$ 'love at first sight'.

central invariant theme (of $\bar{T}$): $\Theta inv(\bar{T})$: Θinv. The theme of the set $\bar{T}$ of an author's texts.

Class I theme. A theme which is a message about the referential sphere.

Class II theme. A theme which is a message about the code sphere.

code sphere. That sphere of literary discourse and, accordingly, of the model's "dictionary" which (as opposed to the referential sphere) comprises their "internal" code—natural language with its rules and components and literature with its conventions, genres, devices, etc.

COMB. See *COMBINATION*.

COMBINATION: COMB. Substitution for entities X, Y, . . . of one entity which is a CONCRETIZATION of all of them: $X, Y \xrightarrow{\text{COMB}} Z$; e.g., 'to touch', 'to cause pain' $\xrightarrow{\text{COMB}}$ 'to wound'.

common invariant motif (of $\bar{T}1$, $\bar{T}2$ or of A1, A2): $Minv,com(\bar{T}1,\bar{T}2)$: $Minv,com(A1,A2)$: $Minv,com$. A motif which is invariant both in the set of texts $\bar{T}1$ by A1 and in the set of texts $\bar{T}2$ by A2.

common theme: $\Theta com(T1,T2)$. The common thematic entity of texts T1 and T2.

CONCD. See *CONCORD*.

CONCORD: CONCD. Substitution for X, Y, . . . of the same number of entities all of which have characteristic P. Subtypes: 1. *CONCORD proper* of X with a Y which already contains P by CONCR of X with P as accession, Y remaining unchanged: $X, YP \xrightarrow{\text{CONCD}} XP, YP$; e.g., 'touch', 'love' $\xrightarrow{\text{CONCD}}$ 'embrace', 'love' (P = 'affection'). 2. *mutual CONCORD* by CONCR of X and Y with the same new P as accession: X, Y $\xrightarrow{\text{CONCD}}$ XP, YP, e.g. 'to love', 'to hate' $\xrightarrow{\text{CONCD}}$ 'to embrace', 'to wound' (P = 'touch').

CONCR. See *CONCRETIZATION*.

CONCRETIZATION: CONCR. Substitution for entity X of a more concrete entity X1 which contains all the properties of X and some accession P; i.e., a transition from a general case to a particular one: X $\xrightarrow{\text{CONCR}}$ XP; e.g., 'touch' $\xrightarrow{\text{CONCR}}$ 'embrace'

CONCRETIZATION via ED(s). 1. CONCR of a thematic entity X into an ED that brings about a pattern iconically expressing X; e.g., 'monotony' $\xrightarrow{\text{CONCR}}$ REPETITION. 2. CONCR of one ED into another, which implements the effect of the first; e.g., CONCORD $\xrightarrow{\text{CONCR}}$ REDUCTION, i.e., CONCORD of X and Y by removal of their differing components.

CONTR. See *CONTRAST*.

CONTRAST: CONTR. Substitution for X of the pair X and its opposite: X $\xrightarrow{\text{CONTR}}$ X, AntiX, e.g., 'love' $\xrightarrow{\text{CONTR}}$ 'love', 'hate'.

CONTRAST through *even:* CONTR*even*. CONTRAST through unfavorable circumstances, i.e. CONTRAST where AntiX is an obstacle to the existence of X, e.g., 'love' $\xrightarrow{\text{CONTR}\,even}$ 'love in spite of mortal danger'.

CONTRAST with identity: CONTR*id*. *CONTRAST AUGMENTED* by CONCORD of its terms, e.g., 'embrace', $\xrightarrow{\text{CONTR}id}$ 'embrace', 'wound'.

contrastive VARIATION: VAR*contr*. VARIATION into a contrasting pair: X $\xrightarrow{\text{VAR}contr}$ X1, AntiX1; e.g., 'to touch' $\xrightarrow{\text{VAR}contr}$ 'to embrace', 'to wound'.

CONTR*even*. See *CONTRAST through even*.

CONTR*id*. See *CONTRAST with identity*.

DD. See *deep design*.

deep design (of T): DD. The next stage of derivation after Θ(T): the most abstract formulation of the structure of text T; unlike Θ(T), it is already an expressive structure; DD is shared by a large set of (potential or real) texts synthematic to T.

deep structure (of T): DS. An abstract formulation of the structure of text T shared by a subset of synthematic texts to T which is narrower than that covered by DD.

derivation (of T). Description of the expressive structure of text T in the form of a hierarchy of ED-transformations, with its theme Θ(T) as input and T as output; comprises ideally four main stages (= approximations of T): theme, deep design, deep structure, surface structure.

"dictionary of reality": DR. The "lexicon" component of the model (as opposed and complementary to the "grammar" component, EDs), which is supposed to model the writers' and readers' shared knowledge of and experience with "life" and "letters" that makes possible their literary intercourse; DR consists of the referential and code spheres; its format is determined by elementary EDs: it contains all the specific CONCRs, AUGMs, CONTRs, and some other ED-rules for each thematic entity listed in it; DR is an ideal point of reference and exists only in the form of separate ad hoc fragments.

DIV. See *DIVISION*.

DIVISION: DIV. Substitution for X of its parts: X $\xrightarrow{\text{DIV}}$ X1, X2, . . .: 'lovers' embrace' $\xrightarrow{\text{DIV}}$ 'glances meet', 'lips kiss', 'his arms encircle her', 'her arms encircle him'.

DR. See *"dictionary of reality."*

DS. See *deep structure*.

ED(s). See *expressive device(s)*.

expressive devices: EDs. The ten elementary theme-preserving transformations which form the "grammar" of the model (as opposed to its "lexicon", DR), accounting for the expressiveness of literary texts: CONCR, REP, AUGM, DIV, VAR, CONTR, CONCD, COMB, PREP, RED. They combine into complex EDs and figures, can be predisposed by thematic entities (see *CONCRETIZATION via ED*), and form derivations.

expressiveness. "Pure" expressive power, as opposed to content, information, message (Tolstoy's "contagiousness").

figure. A complex combination of EDs predisposed by one of literature's typical thematic entities ('ridicule', 'ecstasy', etc.)

INCR. See *INCREASE*.

INCREASE: INCR. PRESAGE by REPETITION with AUGMENTATION; e.g., 'to touch'—'to hit'—'to wound'—'to kill'.

integral theme: Θint. The theme of the text that includes both its local and invariant themes.

invariant (of X, Y, . . .). A construct obtained by subtracting EDs from entities X, Y, . . .; usually CONCR or VAR are subtracted, so that invariant = common denominator.

invariant motif (in $\bar{T}$ by A): $Minv(\bar{T})$: $Minv(A)$: $Minv$. An invariant thematic entity that is part of author A's PW; i.e., part of the invariant derivation of A's texts $\bar{T}$.

invariant theme: Θinv. 1. $\Theta inv(\bar{T})$: $\Theta inv(A)$. Central invariant theme or one of the most abstract invariant motifs in author A's texts $\bar{T}$. 2. $\Theta inv(T)$. The invariant component of the text T's theme Θ, derivable from $\Theta inv(\bar{T})$.

local theme (of T): $\Theta loc(T)$. The particular component of text T, as distinct from its invariant theme $\Theta inv(T)$.

M. See *motif*.

$\bar{M}$. Motifs.

$Minv$: $Minv(\bar{T})$: $Minv(A)$. See *invariant motif*.

$Minv,com$. See *common invariant motif*.

motif: M. A recognizable—recurrent, invariant, cross-literary or "ready-made"—thematic entity.

poetic world (of A): PW(A): PW. The system of author A's invariant motifs; the invariant derivation of everything invariant in A's texts, $\bar{T}$(A).

PREP: See *PREPARATION*.

PREPARATION: PREP. Substitution for X of a sequence of its "inadequate" versions: X $\xrightarrow{\text{PREP}}$ PreX1–PreX2–. . . X. There are three types of PREP according to the types of PreX's 'inadequacy'": PRESENTATION, PRESAGE, RECOIL.

PreR. The first term of a PRESAGE of a rhyming word (a PreX to R1 or R2).

PRESAGE: PRESG. PREPARATION by foreshadowing PreX-es which are "incomplete" X-es (i.e., PreX-es proper): X $\xrightarrow{\text{PRESG}}$ PreX1–PreX2– . . . X; e.g., 'embrace' $\xrightarrow{\text{PRESG}}$ 'mere touch'—'embrace'.

PRESENTATION: PREST. PREPARATION by a "zero" PreX, i.e., by a perceivable absence of X: X $\xrightarrow{\text{PREST}}$ O–X; e.g., 'embrace' $\xrightarrow{\text{PREST}}$ 'no touch'—'embrace'.

PRESG. See PRESAGE.

PREST. See *PRESENTATION*.

PreX. 1. The first, "inadequate" term of the PREPARATION sequence. 2. "PreX proper": the first term of the PRESAGE sequence.

PW:PW(A). See *poetic world*.

R1, R2. The first and second terms of a rhyming pair.

reading. The pair "expression plane, one possible content plane" of a literary work or set of works.

"ready-made" object (for functions X, Y, . . .). A motif, usually quite concrete, that covers all the functions X, Y, . . . specified by a given derivation and is part of the given "dictionary" (of the poet, the genre, the culture, etc.).

REC. See *RECOIL*.

REC-MOV. See *RECOIL MOVEMENT*.

RECOIL: REC. PREPARATION by PreX which is AntiX: X $\xrightarrow{\text{REC}}$ AntiX–X; e.g., 'to embrace' $\xrightarrow{\text{REC}}$ 'to wound'—'to embrace'.

RECOIL MOVEMENT: REC-MOV. RECOIL PREPARED by another RECOIL, e.g., 'to kill' $\xrightarrow{\text{REC-MOV}}$ 'to wound—to embrace—to kill'.

RED. See *REDUCTION*.

REDUCTION: RED. Substitution for XP of its part X sufficient for the reconstruction of XP (by the reader): XP $\xrightarrow{\text{RED}}$ X; e.g., 'loving embrace' $\xrightarrow{\text{RED}}$ 'embrace'.

referential sphere. That sphere of literary discourse and, accordingly, of the model's "dictionary," which (as opposed to code sphere) comprises their "external" referents, i.e., the world of nature, life, ideas, etc.

relations (of causality, contrast, domination, [literal] equivalence, realization, retrospective recognition, etc.). Relations obtaining between thematic entities at certain stages of derivation (and in the text) and created by corresponding EDs; e.g., CONTR creates relations of contrast and domination; CONCD creates equivalence; and so on.

REP. See *REPETITION*.

REPETITION: REP. Substitution for X of a series of similar entities: X $\xrightarrow{\text{REP}}$ X, X₁, X₂, . . . ; e.g., 'an attempt' $\xrightarrow{\text{REP}}$ 1st attempt, 2d attempt, . . .'.

specific theme (of T): Θ*spec*(T). The particular component of text T's theme, as distinct from its common components (Θ*com*; Θ*loc,com*).

SS. See *surface structure*.

S-TURN. See *SUDDEN TURN*.

subtheme. Part of a theme.

"subtraction" (of EDs). Reverse operation of derivation, i.e., of the application of EDs.

SUDDEN TURN: S-TURN. RECOIL or RECOIL MOVEMENT COMBINED into a causal sequence, e.g., 'infliction of a wound leads to pity and embrace which strangles to death'.

surface structure (of T): SS. The most concrete stage of derivation of text T; the last of the sequence of constructs approximating the structure of T, which covers a narrow set of texts that are synthematic to T and closely similar to it in structure.

synthematic (to T). Text(s) or thematic entities whose theme is the same as Θ(T).

T. see *text*.

T(A). Text by author A.

text: T. 1. The expression plane of a literary work. 2. A reading of a literary work.

T̄(A): T̄. A (complete) set of texts by author A.

Θ. See *theme*.

Θ*com*. See *common theme*.

Θ*int*. See *integral theme*.

Θ*inv*. See *invariant theme*.

Θ*loc*. See *local theme*.

Θ*loc,com*. Common local theme.

Θ*spec*. See *specific theme*.

thematic entity. Any input or output of an ED, i.e., a theme or a result of its ED-transformations.

theme: Θ. 1. Θ(T) or Θ(T̄): Θ. The overall invariant of T or T̄: the top thematic entity of the derivation of T or T̄. 2. The input thematic entity of one or several EDs: the theme (in sense 1) of a part of a derivation.

VAR: See *VARIATION*.

VAR*contr*. See *contrastive VARIATION*.

VARIATION: VAR. Substitution for X of its clearly different CONCRETIZATIONS: X $\xrightarrow{\text{VAR}}$ X₁, X₂, . . . ; e.g., 'to touch' $\xrightarrow{\text{VAR}}$ 'to embrace', 'to wipe', 'to catch', ...

VARIATION through all: VAR*tot*. *VAR* through a set X_1, X_2, . . . which covers (exhausts or represents) the entire range of possibilities, e.g., 'place' $\underrightarrow{\text{VAR}tot}$ 'land', 'sea', 'air'.

VAR*tot*. See *VARIATION through all*.

Bibliography

1962

a. Žolkovskij, A. K., and Ju. K. Ščeglov. O vozmožnostjax postroenija strukturnoj poètiki [On the possibilities of setting up structural poetics]. In *Simpozium po strukturnomu izučeniju znakovyx sistem: Tezisy dokladov*, 138–41. Moscow: Institut Slavjanovedenija AN SSSR. Italian version in *Questo e Altro*, 1964, 6–7 (abstract of 1967a).

b. Ščeglov, Ju. K. K postroeniju strukturnoj modeli novell o Šerloke Xolmse. [Toward a structural model of Sherlock Holmes stories.] In *Simpozium po strukturnomu izučeniju znakovyx sistem: Tezisy dokladov*, 153–55 (abstract of 1973b). Moscow: Institut Slavjanovedenija AN SSSR.

c. Ščeglov, Ju. K. Nekotorye čerty struktury *Metamorfoz* Ovidija [Some features of the structure of Ovid's *Metamorphoses*]. In *Strukturno-tipologičeskie issledovanija*, edited by T. Mološnaja, 155–66. Moscow: Institut Slavjanovendenija AN SSSR.

d. Žolkovskij, A. K. Ob usilenii [On amplification]. In *Strukturno-tipologičeskie issledovanija*, edited by T. Mološnaja, 161–71. Moscow: Institut Slavjanovedenija AN SSSR. Italian version in *I sistemi di segni e lo strutturalismo sovietico*, edited by R. Faccani and U. Eco, Milan: Bompiani, 1969.

1967

a. Žolkovskij, A. K., and Ju. K. Ščeglov. Iz predystorii sovetskix rabot po strukturnoj poètike [From the prehistory of Soviet research in structural poetics]. In *Trudy po znakovym sistemam* (Tartu) 3: 367–77.

b. Žolkovskij, A. K. Deus ex machina. In Trudy po znakovym sistemam (Tarty) 3, 146–55, and in *Sign, Language, Culture*, edited by A. J. Greimas et al., 539–47. The Hague: Mouton. Italian version in *I sistemi di segni e lo*

strutturalismo sovietico, edited by R. Faccani and U. Eco, Milan: Bompiani, 1969.
c. Ščeglov, Ju. K. K nekotorym tekstam Ovidija [On some of Ovid's texts]. In *Trudy po znakovym sistemam* (Tartu) 3: 172–79.
d. Žolkovskij, A. K., and Ju. K. Ščeglov. Strukturnaja poètika—poroždajuščaja poètika [Structural poetics is generative poetics]. *Voprosy literatury* 11, no. 1: 74–89; German version in *Literaturwissenschaft und Linguistik,* edited by J. Ihwe, Frankfurt am Main: Athenäum Fischer, 1972; English version in *Soviet Semiotics,* edited by D. Lucid, Baltimore: Johns Hopkins University Press, 1978; Polish version in *Pamętnik Literacki* 60 (1969), no. 1.

1970

a. Žolkovskij, A. K. Poroždajuščaja poètika v rabotax S. M. Ejzenštejna [A generative poetics in the works of S. M. Eisenstein]. In *Sign, Language, Culture,* edited by A. J. Greimas et al. 451–68. The Hague: Mouton. Italian version in *Cinema e Film* 1 (1967), no 3; French version in *Ça (Cinema)* 2 (1975), no. 7/8; Spanish version in *Semiologia del Teatro,* edited by J. M. D. Borque and L. G. Lorenzo, Barcelona: Planeta; Polish version in *Kino* (Warsaw) 11 (1976), no. 12 (132); English version in *Russian Poetics in Translation* 8: 40–67.
b. Ščeglov, Ju. K. "Matrona iz Èfesa" [The Ephesus Widow"]. In *Sign, Language, Culture,* edited by A. J. Greimas et al., 591–600.
c. Žolkovskij, A. K. Somalijskij rasskaz *Ispytanie proricatelja:* Opyt poroždajuščego opisanija [The Somali story *A Soothsayer's Trial:* An attempt at generative description]. In *Narody Azii i Afriki* 1970, 1; Spanish version in *Prohemio* 1 (1970), no. 3; French version in *Analyse et validation dans l'étude des données textuelles,* edited by M. Borillo and J. Virbel, Paris: CNRS, 1977.

1971

Žolkovskij, A. K., and Ju. K. Ščeglov. K opisaniju smysla svjaznogo teksta (na materiale xudožestvennyx tekstov) [Describing the meaning of a coherent (literary) text]. Predvaritel'nye publikacii Problemnoj Gruppy po Èksperimental'noj i Prikladnoj Lingvistike, Moscow: IRJa AN SSSR, vyp. 22, 54 pp.; Spanish version in *Prohemio* 3 (1972), no. 2; English version in 1975b.

1972

Žolkovskij, A. K., and Ju. K. Ščeglov. K opisaniju smysla svjaznogo teksta II. Tema i priëmy vyrazitel'nosti. Primer vyvoda teksta iz temy [Describing

Bibliography

... II. Theme and expressive devices. An example of theme-text derivation]. Predvaritel'nye publikacii Problemnoj Gruppy po Èksperimental'noj i Prikladnoj Lingvistike, Moscow: IRJa AN SSSR, vyp. 33, 77 pp.

1973

a. Žolkovskij, A. K., and Ju. K. Ščeglov. K opisaniju ... III. Priëmy vyrazitel'nosti, č. 1 [Describing ... III. Expressive devices, pt. 1]. Predvaritel'nye publikacii Problemnoj Gruppy po Èxperimental'noj i Prikladnoj Lingvistike, Moscow: IRJa AN SSSR, vyp. 39, 87 pp.
b. Ščeglov, Ju. K. K opisaniju struktury detektivnoj novelly. Une déscription de la structure du roman policier [in Russian]. In *Recherches sur les systèmes signifiants*, edited by J. Rey-Debove, 343–72, The Hague: Mouton.

1974

a. Žolkovskij, A. K., and Ju. K. Ščeglov. K opisaniju ... IV. Priëmy vyrazitel'nosti, č. 2 [Describing ... IV. Expressive Devices, pt. 2]. Predvaritel'nye publikacii Problemnoj Gruppy po Èksperimental'noj i Prikladnoj Lingvistike, Moscow: IRJa AN SSSR, vyp. 49, 90 pp.
b. Žolkovskij, A. K. K opisaniju svjazi meždu glubinnymi i poverxnostnymi urovnjami xudožestvennogo teksta [Describing the links between the deep and the surface level of a literary text]. In *Materialy Vsesojuznogo Simpoziuma po Vtoričnym Modelirujuščim Sistemam* (Tartu) 1 (5): 161–67.
c. Žolkovskij, A. K. K opisaniju ... V [Describing ... V. (1. The poetic world of an author and some problems of literary translation. 2. The place of 'window' in Pasternak's poetic world [abstract of 1978f]. 3. Invariant motifs and the text structure)]. Predvaritel'nye publikacii Problemnoj Gruppy po Èxperimental'noj i Prikladnoj Lingvistike, Moscow: IRJa AN SSSR, vyp. 61, 77 pp.

1975

a. Žolkovskij, A. K., and Ju. K. Ščeglov. K ponjatijam "tema" i "poètičeskij mir" [Toward the concepts of "theme" and "poetic world"]. In *Trudy po znakovym sistemam* (Tartu) 7: 143–67 (revised version of 1971). English version in 1975b. Italian version in *La semiotica nei paesi slavi*, edited by Carlo Prevignano, 392–425, Milan: Feltrinelli, 1979. Japanese version in *Bungaku*, 47 (1979), nos. 5–6. Swedish version in *Textkoherens: An Anthology*, edited by J. de Kaminsky and G. Lavén, Uppsala: Uppsala University (*Uppsala Slavic Papers*, 2 [1981]).

b. Shcheglov, Yu. K., and A. K. Zholkovskii. Generating the literary text. In *Russian Poetics in Translation* 1, 77 pp. (revised English versions of 1971 and 1973b).

c. Ščeglov, Ju. K. Semiotičeskij analiz odnogo tipa jumora [A semiotic analysis of one type of humor]. *Semiotika i informatika* 6: 185–198.

1976

a. Žolkovskij, A. K., and Ju. K. Ščeglov. *Matematika i iskusstvo (poètika vyraziteľnosti)* [Mathematics and art (poetics of expressiveness)]. Moscow: Znanie, 64 pp.

b. Ščeglov, Ju. K., and A. K. Žolkovskij. Poetics as a theory of expressiveness: Towards a "Theme-Expressiveness Devices-Text" model of literary structure. *Poetics* 5: 207–46; Russian version in *Voprosy kibernetiki* 17. Short English version in *Degrés* 8 (1980), no. 22, 11–15.

c. Žolkovskij, A. K. K opisaniju odnogo tipa semiotičeskix sistem (poetičeskij mir kak sistema invariantov) [Describing one type of semiotic system: Poetic world as a system of invariants]. *Semiotika i informatika* 7: 27–61 (revised version of 1974c [1]).

d. Žolkovskij, A. K. *K opisaniju* . . . *VI*, čč. 1–3 [Describing . . . VI, pts. 1–3 (1. Some of the invariants of Pushkin's poetic world. 2. Analysis of *Ja vas ljubil* . . .)]. Predvariteľnye publikacii Problemnoj Gruppy po Èksperimentaľnoj i Prikladnoj Lingvistike, Moscow: IRJa AN SSSR, vyp. 76–78, 48 pp., 48 pp., and 29 pp.

e. Žolkovskij, A. K. Zametki o tekste, podtekste i citacii u Pasternaka [Notes on text, subtext, and quoting in Pasternak]. In *Boris Pasternak: Essays*, edited by N. Å. Nilsson, 67–84, Stockholm: Almqvist & Wicksell.

1977

a. Žolkovskij, A. K., and Ju. K. Ščeglov. K opisaniju priëma vyraziteľnosti VAR'IROVANIE [Describing the expressive device of VARIATION]. *Semiotika i informatika* 9: 106–50.

b. Žolkovskij, A. K. On three analogies between linguistics and poetics (semantic invariance, obligatoriness of grammatical meanings, competence *vs.* performance). *Poetics* 6: 77–106. Russian version in *Semiotika i informatika* 10.

c. Žolkovskij, A. K. Razbor stixotvorenija Pushkina *Ja vas ljubil* . . . [Analysis of Pushkin's poem *Ja vas ljubil* . . .]. *Izvestija AN SSSR, SLJa*, 36 (3): 252–63. An expanded Russian version is in *Russian Literature* 7: 1–25 (both are short versions of 1976d).

d. Ščeglov, Ju. K. K opisaniju . . . VII, čč. 1, 2 [Describing . . . VII, pts. 1, 2

Bibliography

(1. The structural invariants of Molière's comedies. 2. The structure of *Mr. de Pourceaugnac*)]. Predvaritel'nye publikacii Problemnoj Gruppy po Èxperimental'noj i Prikladnoj Lingvistike, Moscow: IRJa AN SSSR, vyp. 101–2, 43 pp., 51 pp.

1978

a. Shcheglov, Yu. K., and A. K. Zholkovskij. The poetic structure of a maxim by La Rochefoucauld. An Essay in *Theme* ↔ *Text* Poetics. *PTL (Poetics and Theory of Literature)* 3: 549–92. Russian version in *Paremiologičeskij sbornik*, edited by G. L. Permjakov, Moscow: Nauka, 1978 (revised versions of 1972).

b. Žolkovskij, Aleksandr K., and Jurij K. Ščeglov. Sovremennaja lingvistika i metodologija izučenija literaturnogo proizvedenija [Modern linguistics and the methodology of the study of literary works]. In *Tekst. Język. Poetyka*, edited by M.-R. Mayenowa, Warsaw: 217–39, Ossolineum. Japanese version in *The Journal of Human Sciences* (St. Andrew's University, Sakai): 18 (1982), no. 1.

c. Žolkovskij, A. K., and Ju. K. Ščeglov. K opisaniju . . . VIII. *Vojna i Mir* dlja detskogo čtenija: Invariantnaja tematiko-vyrazitel'naja struktura detskix rasskazov L. N. Tolstogo, čč. 1–2 [Describing . . . VIII. *War and Peace* for children's reading: The invariant thematic-expressive structure of L. N. Tolstoy's children's stories, pts. 1–3]. Predvaritel'nye publikacii Problemnoj Gruppy po Èxperimental'noj i Prikladnoj Lingvistike, Moscow: IRJa AN SSSR, vyp. 104–6, 49 pp., 47 pp., and 42 pp.

d. Žolkovskij, A. K. How to show things with words (ob ikoničeskoj realizacii tem sredstvami plana vyraženija [on the iconic representation of themes by expression plane means]). *Wiener Slawistischer Almanach* 2: 5–24. English version in *Poetics* 8 (1979): 405–30.

e. Zholkovsky, A. K. The literary text—thematic and expressive structure: An analysis of Pushkin's poem "Ya vas lyubil . . . ." *New Literary History* 9: 264–78 (revised English version of 1976d).

f. Zholkovsky, A. K. The window in the poetic world of Boris Pasternak. *New Literary History* 9: 279–314; Russian version in *Russian Literature* 7 (1). Hungarian version in *Helikon* (Budapest), 13 (1977), no. 1.

g. Žolkovskij, A. K. At the intersection of linguistics, paremiology and poetics: On the artistic structure of proverbs. *Poetics* 7: 309–32; Russian version in *Paremiologičeskij sbornik*, edited by G. L. Permjakov, Moscow: Nauka, 1978.

1979

a. Ščeglov, Jurij K. Čerty poètičeskogo mira Axmatovoj [Traits of Akhmatova's poetic world]. *Wiener Slawistischer Almanach* 3: 27–56.

b. El'nickaja, Svetlana I. O nekotoryx čertax poètičeskogo mira M. Cvetaevoj [On some features of M. Cvetaeva's poetic world]. *Wiener Slawistischer Almanach* 3: 57–73.

c. El'nickaja, Svetlana I. O nekotoryx . . . [2]. *Wiener Slawistischer Almanach* 4: 19–40.

d. Žolkovskij, A. K. O podgotovke rifmy: PREDVESTIJA i OTKAZY v rifmovke [On the preparation of rhymes: PRESAGES and RECOILS in rhyming]. *Wiener Slawistischer Almanach* 4: 125–51.

e. Žolkovskij, A. K. Raj, zamaskirovannyj pod dvor: zametki o poètičeskom mire Bulata Okudžavy [Paradise disguised as a courtyard: Notes on the poetic world of Bulat Okudžava]. *Neue Russische Literatur* 1: 101–20 (Russian version), 281–306 (German version).

f. Ščeglov, Ju. K. The poetics of Russian epigram. *Neue Russische Literatur* 1: 121–42 (Russian version), 307–33 (German version).

g. Žolkovskij, A. K. Materialy k opisaniju poètičeskogo mira Pushkina [Materials toward a description of Pushkin's poetic world]. In *Russian Romanticism* edited by N. Å. Nilsson, 45–93, Stockholm: Almqvist & Wicksell (revised version of 1976d (1). Short Russian version in *Trudy po znakovym sistemam* (Tartu), 11: 3–25. Revised English version of 1976d in *Russian Poetics in Translation* 8: 62–107.

h. Shcheglov, Yu. K. The poetics of Molière's comedies. *Russian Poetics in Translation* 6: 1–83 (revised English version of 1977d).

i. Žolkovskij, A. K. Invarianty i struktura teksta [Invariant motifs and text structure]. II. Mandel'štam: "Ja p'ju za voennye astry . . .," *Slavica Hierosolymitana* 4: 159–84.

j. Ščeglov, Ju. K., and A. K. Žolkovskij. Ex ungue leonem: The invariant structure of Leo Tolstoy's children's stories. *Poetics* 8: 431–34 (authors' statement of 1978c). Short English version in *VS (Versus)* 24: 3–36. Russian version in 1982f.

k. Ščeglov, Ju. K., and A. K. Žolkovskij. The "Eclipsing" construction and its place in the structure of L. Tolstoy's children's stories. *Russian Literature* 7: 121–59. Russian version in 1980j.

1980

a. Zholkovsky, A. K. Pun and punishment: Struktura odnoj "ubijstvennoj" ostroty Bertrana Rassela, in 1980j, 47–60.

b. Zholkovsky, A. K. Comparing poetic worlds. *Diacritics* 10, no. 4 (winter 1980): 60–74. Russian version in 1982f.

c. Žolkovskij, A. K. Tema i variacii: k sopostavitel'nomu opisaniju PM Pasternaka i Okudžavy [A theme and variations: Toward a contrastive description of Pasternak's and Okudžava's poetic worlds]. In 1980j, 61–86.

d. Žolkovskij, A. K. 'Prevosxoditel'nyj pokoj': ob odnom invariantnom motive Pushkina ['Superior peace': On one of Pushkin's invariant motifs]. In 1980j, 87–114.

Bibliography

e. Žolkovskij, A. K. Invarianty i struktura poètičeskogo teksta. Pasternak [Invariant motifs and the structure of the poetic text. Pasternak]. In 1980j, 205–44.

f. Ščeglov, Ju. K. Struktura *Metamorfoz* Ovidija [The Structure of Ovid's *Metamorphoses*] (manuscript).

g. Žolkovskij, A. K., and Ju. K. Ščeglov. Ispoved' Arxipoèta Kël'nskogo: glubinnaja i poverxnostnaja struktury na službe ambivalentnoj temy [The Archpoet of Cologne's "Mock penitent": The deep and the surface structure at the service of an ambivalent theme]. In 1980j, 145–204. English version in *Working Papers and Pre-Publications of Centro Internazionale di Semiotica e di Linguistica*, nos. 103–105. Urbino: Università di Urbino, 1981.

h. Žolkovskij, A. K. Materialy k opisaniju poetičeskogo mira Bulata Okudžavy [Materials toward a description of Bulat Okudžava's poetic world] (revised and expanded version of 1979e; manuscript).

i. Žolkovskij, A. K., and Ju. K. Ščeglov. O prieme vyraziteľnosti PREDVESTIE [On the expressive device of PRESAGE]. In 1980j, 13–46.

j. Žolkovskij, A. K., and Ju. K. Ščeglov. Poètika vyraziteľnosti. Sbornik statej [Expressive poetics: A collection of papers]. *Wiener Slawistischer Almanach* (special vol. 2).

k. Žolkovskij, A. K. "Obstojateľstva velikolepija": ob odnoj pasternakovskoj časti reči ["Circumstances of magnificence": On one Pasternakian part of speech]. In *Voz'mi Na Radost'. To Honour Jeanne van der Eng*, edited by B. J. Amsenga et al. Amsterdam: Slavic Seminar, 157–68.

1981

a. Žolkovskij, A. K., and Ju. K. Ščeglov. O priëme vyraziteľnosti OTKAZ [On the expressive device of RECOIL]. *Slavica Hierosolymitana* 5–6: 109–36.

b. Žolkovskij, A. K. Zametki o "Carskoseľskoj statue" [Notes on "A Statue in Carskoje Selo"]. *Russian Language Journal* 35, no. 120: 127–50 (Special Pushkin issue, edited by S. Senderovich).

c. Ščeglov, Ju. Mir Mixaila Zoščenko [The world of Mixail Zoščenko]. *Wiener Slawistischer Almanach* 7: 109–54.

d. Ščeglov, Ju. K. Tema, tekst, poètičeskij mir ("Sur une barricade" Viktora Gjugo) [Theme, text, poetic world (V. Hugo's "Sur une barricade")]. *Neue Russische Literatur* 2–3: 257–80.

1982

a. Zholkovsky, A. K. 'Distributive contact': A syntactic invariant in Pasternak. *Wiener Slawistischer Almanach* 9: 119–49.

b. Ščeglov, Ju. K. Krylataja strofa Denisa Davydova [A provocative stanza of Denis Davydov's]. *Neue Russische Literatur* (forthcoming).
c. Zholkovsky, A. K. Poèzija i grammatika pasternakovskogo "Vetra." *Russian Literature* (forthcoming).
d. Ščeglov, Ju. K. Iz nabljudenij nad poètikoj Axmatovoj (Razbor stixotvorenija "Serdce b'ëtsja rovno, merno . . . ") [From observations on the poetics of Akhmatova (An analysis of the poem "The heart is beating evenly, measuredly . . . ")]. In 1982f, 49–90.
e. Žolkovskij, A. K. Poètika vyrazitel'nosti (= porozdajuščaja poètika = model' "Tema ↔ Tekst"): k istorii termina i koncepcii [Poetics of expressiveness (= generative poetics = the "Theme ↔ Text" model): Towards the history of the term and framework]. In 1982f, 1–18.
f. Ščeglov, Ju. K., and A. K. Žolkovskij. Stat'i po poètike vyrazitel'nosti [Papers in a Poetics of Expressiveness]. *Russian Literature* (special issue), 11(1).
g. Zholkovsky, A. The 'sinister' in the poetic world of Pasternak. In *Myth in Literature. A Symposium,* edited by A. Kodžak and K. Pomorska (forthcoming).
h. Shcheglov, Yury and Alexander Zholkovsky. *Poetics of Expressiveness: A Theory and Applications.* Amsterdam: John Benjamins (forthcoming).
i. Zholkovsky, A. K. *Themes and Texts: Toward a Poetics of Expressiveness* (the present volume).
j. Zholkovsky, A. K. Poems. In *A Handbook of Discourse Analysis,* edited by Teun A. van Dijk. London: Academic Press (forthcoming).
k. Zholkovsky, A. K. 19 oktjabrja 1982 g. [October 19, 1982], or The semiotics of a Soviet cookie wrapper. *Wiener Slawistischer Almanach* (special Mel'čuk issue, forthcoming).
l. Zholkovsky, A. K. Poetry of grammar, poetic worlds, and grammatical motifs. In *The Proceedings of the 7th Annual Meeting of the Semiotic Society of America.* Bloomington: Indiana University Press (forthcoming).

Works Cited

Abraham, Ray Clive. 1964. *Somali-English Dictionary*. London: University of London Press.

Akhmatova, Anna. 1977. *O Pushkine: Stat'i i zametki*. Leningrad: Sovetskij Pisatel'.

Andrzejewski, B. W., and I. M. Lewis. 1964. *Somali Poetry: An Introduction*. Oxford: Clarendon Press.

Aristotle. 1961. *Aristotle's Poetics*. Translated by S. H. Butcher. New York: Hill & Wang.

Bergson, H. 1956. Laughter. In *Comedy, Laughter*, edited by Sypher Wylie. Garden City: Doubleday.

Berne, Eric. 1972. *Games People Play: The Psychology of Human Relationships*. London: Penguin.

Bicilli, P. 1926. *Ètjudy o russkoj poèzii*. Prague: Plamja.

Blagoj, D. D. 1931. *Sociologija tvorčestva Pushkina*. Moscow: Mir.

Bočarov, S. G. 1974. *Poètika Pushkina*. Moscow: Nauka.

Brooks, Cleanth. 1975. *The Well Wrought Urn*. New York: Harcourt Brace Jovanovich.

Burke, Kenneth. 1957. *The Philosophy of Literary Form*. New York: Random House (Vintage Books).

Buxštab, Boris. 1970. *Russkie poèty*. Leningrad: Xudožestvennaja literatura.

Čudakov, A. P. 1972. *Poètika Čexova*. Moscow: Nauka.

Čukovskaja, L. K. 1976. *Zapiski ob Anne Axmatovoj*. Vol. 1. Paris: YMCA.

Davie, Donald, and Angela Livingstone, eds. 1969. *Pasternak: Modern Judgments*. Nashville: Aurora Publishers.

Eisenstein, Sergej. 1964–70. *Izbrannye proizvedenija v šesti tomax*. Vols. 2–5. Moscow: Iskusstvo.

———. 1968. *Film Essays, with a Lecture*. Edited by Jay Leyda. London: Dobson.

———. 1975a. *Film Form*. Edited and translated by Jay Leyda. New York: Harcourt Brace Jovanovich.

_____. 1975b. *The Film Sense*. Edited and translated by Jay Leyda. New York: Harcourt Brace Jovanovich.

Elwert, W. Theodor. 1970. *Französische Metrik*. Munich: Max Hüber.

Empson, William. 1965/1935 *Seven Types of Ambiguity*. New York: New Directions.

Erlich, Victor, ed. 1978. *Pasternak: A Collection of Critical Essays*. Englewood Cliffs: Prentice-Hall.

Ètkind, E. G. 1970. *Razgovor o stixax*. Moscow: Detskaja literatura.

_____. 1973. *Russkie poèty-perevodčiki ot Trediakovskogo do Pushkina*. Leningrad: Nauka.

Faryno, Jerzy. 1970. Wybrane zagadnienia poetyki Borisa Pasternaka. *Slavia Orientalis* 19 (3): 271–89.

Flew, Anthony. 1975. *Thinking about Thinking*. Glasgow: Collins.

Freud, Sigmund. 1961. *The Interpretation of Dreams*. Translated by J. Strachey. New York: Science Edition.

_____. 1969. *Jokes and Their Relation to the Unconscious*. Translated by J. Strachey. New York: Norton.

Galaal, Muuse, and B. W. Andrzejewski. 1956. *Hikmad Soomaali*. London: Oxford University Press.

Gasparov, M. L. 1979. Sjužetosloženie grečeskoj tragedii. In *Novoe v sovremennoj klassičeskoj filologii*, edited by S. S. Averincev, 126–66. Moscow: Nauka.

Genette, G. 1968. Langage poétique, poétique du langage. *Information sur les sciences sociales* 7 (2): 141–62.

Geršenzon, M. O. 1919. *Mudrost' Pushkina*. Moscow: Knigoizdatel'stvo pisatelei.

_____. 1922. *Gol'fstrem*. Moscow: Šipovnik.

_____. 1926. *Stat'i o Pushkine*. Moscow: GAXN.

Godzich, Wlad. 1978. The construction of meaning. *New Literary History* 9 (2): 389–97.

Greimas, A. J. 1970. *Du sens: Essais sémiotiques*. Paris: Seuil.

Hauff, Wilhelm. 1858. *Arabian Days' Entertainment*. Translated by Herbert Pelham Curtis. Boston: Phillips, Sampson & Co.

Hiż, Henryk. 1964. *The Role of Paraphrase in Grammar*. Transformations and Discourse Analysis Papers, 53. University of Pennsylvania, Department of Linguistics.

Hook, Sidney. 1976. Bertrand Russell the Man. *Commentary* 62 (July): 52–54.

Hymes, Dell H. 1960. Phonological aspects of style: some English sonnets. In *Style in Language*, edited by Thomas A. Sebeok, 109–31. Cambridge: MIT Press.

Jakobson, Roman. 1981/1961. Poèzija grammatiki i grammatika poèzii. In *Roman Jakobson. Selected Writings*, vol. 3, pp. 63–97. The Hague: Mouton.

_____. 1969/1935. The prose of the poet Pasternak. In *Pasternak: Modern Judgements*, edited by Donald Davie and Angela Livingstone, 135–51. Nashville: Aurora Publishers.

Works Cited

――――. 1971. On linguistic aspects of translation. In *Roman Jakobson: Selected Writings*, vol. 2, pp. 260–66. The Hague: Mouton.

――――. 1973a. 'Qu'est-ce que la poésie?' In *Roman Jakobson: Questions de Poétique*, 113–26. Paris: Seuil.

――――. 1973b. Structures linguistiques subliminales en poésie. In *Roman Jakobson: Questions de Poétique*, 280–92. Paris: Seuil.

――――. 1975. The statue in Pushkin's poetic mythology. In *Pushkin and His Sculptural Myth*, translated and edited by John Burbank, 1–44. The Hague: Mouton.

――――. 1976. Stixi Pushkina o deve-statue, vakxanke i smirennice. In *Alexander Puskin: A Symposium on the 175th Anniversary of his Birth*, edited by A. Kodjak and Kiril Taranovsky, 3–27. New York: New York University Press.

Kayden, Eugene M., trans. 1959. *Poems, by Boris Pasternak*. Ann Arbor: University of Michigan Press.

Kenin, Richard, and Justin Wintle, eds. 1978. *The Dictionary of Biographical Quotation*. New York: Knopf.

Koestler, Arthur. 1967. *The Act of Creation*. London: Pan.

Lawrence, D. H. 1955. *The Complete Short Stories of D. H. Lawrence*. Vol. 3. Melbourne: William Heinemann.

Levin, Ju. I. 1966. O nekotoryx čertax plana soderžanija v poetičeskix tekstax. In *Strukturnaja tipologija jazykov*, edited by V. V. Ivanov, 199–215. Moscow: AN SSSR.

Lévi-Strauss, Claude. 1960. L'analyse morphologique des contes russes. *International Journal of Slavic Linguistics and Poetics* 3 (1960): 122–49.

――――. 1963. *Structural Anthropology*, translated by Claire Jakobson and Brooke Grundfest Schoepf. New York: Basic Books.

Lomonosov, M. V. 1952/1748. Kratkoe rukovodstvo k krasnorečiju. In M. V. Lomonosov. *Polnoe sobranie sočinenij*. vol. 7, pp. 89–378. Moscow: AN SSSR.

London, Jack. 1960. *Stories*. New York: Platt & Munk.

Lotman, Ju. M. 1968. Analiz dvux stixotvorenij. In *Tezisy letnej školy po vtoričnym modelirujuščim sistemam, Kjaèriku, 10–20 Maja 1968*. 191–224. (Tartu).

Lotman, Yu. 1977. *The Structure of the Artistic Text*. Translated by R. Vroon. Ann Arbor: University of Michigan, Department of Slavic Languages and Literatures.

――――. 1978/1969. Language and reality in the early Pasternak. In *Pasternak: A Collection of Critical Essays*, edited by Victor Erlich, 1–20. Englewood Cliffs: Prentice-Hall.

McCune, Keith. 1977. Two Constructive Principles in Pushkin's Elegiac Distichs. Ph.D. dissertation, University of Virginia.

Mandelstam, Nadezhda. 1970. *Hope against Hope: A Memoir*. New York: Atheneum.

Mandel'štam, Osip. 1967. *Sobranie sočinenij*. 3 vols. Edited by G. P. Struve and B. A. Filippov. Washington, D.C.: Inter-language Literary Associates.

Masson, David I. 1976. *Poetic Sound-Patterning Reconsidered.* Proceedings of the Leeds Philosophical and Literary Society, Literary and Historical Section, vol. 16, no. 5. Leeds: W. S. Maney & Son.

Mazel', L. A. 1965. O sisteme muzykal'nyx sredstv i nekotoryx principax xudožestvennogo vozdejstvija muzyki. In *Intonacija i muzykal'nyj obraz*, edited by B. M. Jarustovskij. Moscow: Muzyka.

———. 1966. Èstetika i analiz. *Sovetskaja muzyka* 12: 20–30.

———. 1976. O dvux tipax tvorčeskogo zamysla. *Sovetskaja muzyka* 5: 18–32.

———. 1978. *Voprosy analiza muzyki: Opyt sbliženija teoretičeskogo muzykoznanija i èstetiki.* Moscow: Sovetskij kompozitor.

Mazel', L. A., and V. A. Cukkerman. 1967. *Analiz muzykal'nyx proizvedenij.* Moscow: Muzyka.

Mel'čuk, I. A. 1974. *Opyt teorii lingvističeskix modelej "Smysl–Tekst."* Moscow: Nauka.

———. 1981. Meaning–text models: A recent trend in Soviet Linguistics. *Annual Review of Anthropology* 10: 27–62.

Mel'čuk, I. A. and A. K. Žolkovskij. 1970. Towards a functioning 'Meaning–Text' model of language. *Linguistics*, 57: 11–47.

Minsky, M. 1975. A framework for representing knowledge. In *The Psychology of Computer Vision*, edited by P. H. Winston, 211–77. New York: McGraw-Hill.

Moreno, Martino Mario. 1955. *Il Somalo della Somalia.* Rome: Istituto Poligrafico dello Stato.

Nilsson, Nils Åke. 1978/1959. Life as ecstasy and sacrifice: Two poems by Boris Pasternak. In *Pasternak: A Collection of Critical Essays*, edited by Victor Erlich, 51–67. Englewood Cliffs: Prentice-Hall.

Nizhny, Vladimir. 1979. *Lessons with Eisenstein.* Translated and edited by Ivor Montagu and Jay Leyda. New York: Da Capo.

Olesha, Yury. 1979. *No Day without a Line.* Translated by Judson Rosengrant. Ann Arbor: Ardis.

Ovsjaniko-Kulikovskij, D. N. 1923. *Teorija poèzii i prozy.* Moscow: Gosizdat.

Padučeva, E. V. 1977. O semantičeskix svjazjax meždu basnej i ee moral'ju. *Trudy po znakovym sisteman* (Tartu) 9: 27–59.

Pasternak, Boris. 1958. *Doctor Zhivago.* Translated by Max Hayward and Manya Harari. New York: Pantheon.

———. 1959a. *The Poetry of Boris Pasternak 1917–1959.* Selected, edited, and translated by George Reavey. New York: Putnam.

———. 1959b. Translating Shakespeare. Translated by Manya Harari. In *I Remember*, by Boris Pasternak, translated and edited by David Magarshack, 123–50. New York: Pantheon.

———. 1960. Three letters. *Encounter* 15 (August), 3–6.

———. 1965. *Stixotvorenija i poèmy.* Moscow: Sovetskij Pisatel'.

———. 1969. *The Blind Beauty: A Play.* Translated by Max Hayward and Manya Harari. New York: Harcourt Brace & World.

————. n.d. Afterword to *Safe Conduct*. The Boris Pasternak Archive, in care of Evgenij and Elena Pasternak.

Permjakov, G. L. 1968. *Izbrannye poslovicy i pogovorki narodov Vostoka*. Moscow: Nauka.

————. 1979a. *Poslovicy i pogovorki narodov Vostoka*. Moscow: Nauka.

————. 1979b. *From the Proverb to the Tale*. Moscow: Progress.

Plank, Dale L. 1966. *Pasternak's Lyric: A Study of Sound and Imagery*. The Hague: Mouton.

————. 1972. Readings of "My Sister Life," *Russian Literature Triquarterly* 2: 323–27.

Poe, Edgar Allan. 1965/1846. The philosophy of composition. In *Literary Criticism of Edgar Allan Poe*, edited by Robert L. Hough, 20–32. Lincoln: University of Nebraska Press.

Pritchard, J. B., ed. 1969. *Ancient Near Eastern Texts Relating to the Old Testament*. Princeton: Princeton University Press.

Propp, Vladimir. 1958. *Morphology of the Folktale*. Bloomington: Indiana Research Center in Anthropology.

Pushkin, A. S. 1937–49. *Polnoe sobranie sočinenij*. 16 vols. Moscow: AN SSSR.

Riffaterre, Michael. 1978. *Semiotics of Poetry*. Bloomington: Indiana University Press.

Russell, Bertrand. 1950. *Unpopular Essays*. London: Allen & Unwin.

————. 1965. *History of Western Philosophy*. Bury St. Edwards, Suffolk: Allen & Unwin.

Saljamon, L. S. 1971. Èlementy fiziologii i xudožestvennoe vosprijatie. In *Xudožestvennoe vosprijatie*, edited by B. S. Mejlax, vol. 1, pp. 98–112. Leningrad: Nauka.

Ščerba, L. V. 1957/1923. Opyty lingvističeskogo tolkovanija stixotvorenij I. "Vospominanie" Pushkina. In *Izbrannye raboty po russkomu jazyku*, by L. Ščerba, 26–44. Moscow: Učpedgiz.

Schank, R. C., and R. P. Abelson. 1977. *Scripts, Plans, Goals and Understanding*. Hillsdale, N.J.: Erlbaum.

Seldes, George, comp. 1966. *The Great Quotations*. New York: Stuart.

Shaw, J. Thomas. 1967. *The Transliteration of Modern Russian for English Language Publications*. Madison: University of Wisconsin Press.

Shklovsky, Viktor. 1929. *O teorii prozy*. Moscow: Federacija.

————. 1965. Art as technique. In *Russian Formalist Criticism*, edited by L. T. Lemon and M. J. Reis, 3–24. Lincoln: University of Nebraska Press.

————. 1969. "Poèzija grammatiki i grammatika poèzii," *Inostrannaja literatura* 6: 218–24.

————. 1973. The connection between devices of *syuzhet* construction and general stylistic devices. In *Russian Formalism. A Collection of Articles and Texts in Translation*, edited by Stephen Bann and John E. Bowlt, 48–72. Edinburgh: Scottish Academic Press.

Sinyavsky, Andrei. 1969/1965. Boris Pasternak. In *Pasternak: Modern Judge-*

ments, edited by Donald Davie and Angela Livingstone, 154–219. Nashville: Aurora Publishers.

Slonimskij, A. 1959. *Masterstvo Pushkina.* Moscow: GIXL.

Smirnov, I. P. 1977. *Xudožestvennyj smysl i èvoljucija poètičeskix sistem.* Moscow: Nauka.

Smith, Barbara Herrnstein. 1968. *Poetic Closure: A Study of How Poems End.* Chicago: University of Chicago Press.

Spurgeon, Caroline. 1935. *Shakespeare's Imagery and What It Tells Us.* New York: Macmillan.

Štokmar, M. P. 1958. *Rifma Majakovskogo.* Moscow: Sovetskij Pisatel'.

Švedova, N. Ju., ed. 1970. *Grammatika sovremennogo russkogo literaturnogo jazyka.* Moscow: Nauka.

Swift, Jonathan. 1940. *Gulliver's Travels.* New York: Dutton (Everyman's Library).

Taranovsky, Kiril. 1971. O ritmičeskoj strukture russkix dvusložnyx razmerov. In *Poètika i stilistika russkoj literatury,* edited by M. P. Alekseev, 420–29. Leningrad: Nauka.

———. 1976. *Essays on Mandel'štam.* Cambridge: Harvard University Press.

Todorov, Tzvetan. 1968. Poétique. In O. Ducrot et al., *Qu'est ce que le Structuralisme?* 97–166. Paris: Seuil.

Tolstoy, L. N. 1929. *What Is Art? and Essays on Art.* Translated by A. Maude. London: Oxford University Press.

———. 1978. *Tolstoy's Letters.* Vol. 1: *1828–1879.* Selected, edited, and translated by R. F. Christian. New York: Scribner's.

Tynyanov, Yury. 1963. *Problema stixotvornogo jazyka.* The Hague: Mouton.

———. 1978. Words and things in Pasternak. In *Pasternak: A Collection of Critical Essays,* edited by Victor Erlich, 32–38. Englewood Cliffs: Prentice-Hall.

Vygotsky, L. 1971. *The Psychology of Art.* Cambridge: MIT Press.

Xodasevič, Vl. 1924. *Poètičeskoe xozjajstvo Pushkina.* Leningrad. Mysl'.

Zavarin, Valentina, and Mary Coote. 1979. *Theory of the Formulaic Text.* Working Papers and Pre-Publications of Centro Internazionale di Semiotica e di Linguistica, no. 88–89. Urbino: Universita di Urbino.

Žirmunskij, V. M. 1975. *Teorija stixa.* Leningrad: Sovetskij Pisatel'.

Žukov, A. A., and E. S. Kotljar, eds. 1976. *Skazki Afriki.* Moscow: Nauka.

Index

"composite quotation," 65
composition. *See* deep design; deep structure
"compression"/"expansion," 78, 108, 120–26, 260
Conan Doyle, Arthur, 29, 58–59, 76, 98, 203–4
CONCORD, 25, 44–47, 68, 88–89, 95, 98, 100–101, 103–10, 218, 255, 260
CONCRETIZATION, 25, 30, 43–45, 47, 90–94, 100, 105, 106, 118–19, 127, 161, 171, 217–19, 259; via EDs, 87–91, 98, 103–4, 107–8, 259, 269. *See also* iconicity; thematic entity
constructs, 23, 47, 68, 76, 101, 175–77, 252, 258–59. *See also* description (strategy of)
"contagiousness." *See* expressiveness
'continuation', 187, 191, 223–25, 227–28, 230–32, 271. *See also* 'death'
CONTRAST, 40–43, 46, 47, 70, 90–91, 95–97, 100–102, 105, 107–8, 116, 118–19, 152, 177–78, 183–84, 247, 249, 252–53, 259–60, 262
convention, 20, 26, 28–29, 55–57, 59, 60, 218–20, 233, 257, 269
convincing expression, 41, 45, 53, 57, 61–62, 86, 88, 103, 107. *See also* expressiveness; functions; ready-made object
co-occurrence (shift of), 81, 141, 203
correspondence (theme-text). *See* derivation
counterpoint. *See* COMBINATION: of opposites
creative process. *See* competence
criticism. *See* poetics
Cvetaeva, Marina, 206, 268

'death', 113–31, 156–57, 167–69, 213, 225–27, 233–34, 261–62. *See also* 'continuation'
deconstruction. *See* poetics
deep design, 29, 87–90, 118–20, 181–82, 260
deep elements. *See* constructs
deep structure, 29, 91–94, 118, 120–26, 182–85, 269
denouement. *See* closure
derivation, 19–20, 24, 26–31, 35–52, 81, 86–131, 258–263, 266; invariant, 76–77; order of, 24, 28, 48–50, 97, 263; as slow motion approximation,

26, 47–48, 86, 100–101, 103–8, 118, 120, 126; "smuggling in," 26, 97–98, 260; as "translation," 27, 80–82, 130, 180–85, 195, 206–9, 214, 266–67. *See also* hierarchy
description (strategy of), 7–10, 13, 19–31, 46, 48–50, 67–68, 76–77, 86, 92, 97–102, 109, 111–12, 117, 175–77, 180, 196, 206, 236, 256–59, 264, 266. *See also* competence; constructs; experimental texts; poetics; "subtraction" (of EDs)
"dictionary of reality," 14, 26, 30–31, 40–45, 48–50, 62, 137, 152, 236, 263–64. *See also* rhyme: vocabulary of
DIVISION, 25, 43, 103, 105

'ecstasy', 38, 42–43, 47–48, 87, 255, 261
Eisenstein, Sergej, 7–8, 13, 22–23, 29, 35, 86–88, 255–56; Dessalines episode, 36–52, 54–55, 61; *Ivan the Terrible*, 57. *See also* Leyda, Jay; Montagu, Ivor; Nizhny, Vladimir
Eliot, T. S., 44
Empson, William, 22
Ètkind, Efim, 269–70
"expansion." *See* "compression"/"expansion"
experimental texts, 44, 98, 118, 126, 203, 258, 266, 267
explication. *See* formulation
explicitness. *See* formulation
expressive device(s), 9, 14, 19, 24–28, 30, 40–50, 102, 180, 236; *entries for individual EDs*
expressiveness, 19, 21–23, 25, 49, 61, 100–102, 108, 124, 176–77, 182, 219–20, 257. *See also* convincing expression; ready-made object

"Failure of pretensions." *See* figures
false turn. *See* RECOIL; SUDDEN TURN
Fet, Afanasij, 205, 268–69, 272
figures, 105–6, 112–13, 116, 120–29, 258–63. *See also* comism; 'ecstasy'
film directing. *See* Eisenstein, Sergej: Dessalines episode
Flaubert, Gustave, 64
foreshadowing. *see* PRESAGE
formalization. *See* formulation
formulation, 8–10, 20–31, 36, 48, 63, 65, 76, 86–87, 195. *See also* competence; description (strategy of); theme

Library of Congress Cataloging in Publication Data

Zholkovsky, Alexander, 1937–
  Themes and texts.

  Bibliography: p.
  Includes index.
   1. Literature.   2. Poetics.   I. Parthé, Kathleen.   II. Title.
PN45.Z43413 1983   808'.00141   83-45152
ISBN 0-8014-1505-5

Themes and Texts